Making Research R

Making Research Relevant is the ideal core textbook for master's-level introduction to research methods courses in mental health. Accessible and user friendly, it is designed to help trainees and practitioners understand, connect, and apply research to clinical practice and day-to-day work with students and clients. The text covers foundational concepts like research ethics and how to best consume research, as well as 11 applied, evaluative, and outcome-based research methods. Easy-to-read chapters are infused with case examples from diverse settings and paired with brief video lectures, which provide vignettes to guide application and visual components that demonstrate how research methods can benefit mental health practitioners in real-world scenarios.

Carrie A. Wachter Morris, PhD, is an associate professor of counselor education at the University of North Carolina at Greensboro and past president of the Association of Assessment and Research in Counseling.

Kelly L. Wester, PhD, is a professor of counselor education at the University of North Carolina at Greensboro. She has taught graduate courses in research and provided workshops on research methodology.

Making Research Relevant

Applied Research Designs for
the Mental Health Practitioner

Edited by
Carrie A. Wachter Morris
Kelly L. Wester

Routledge
Taylor & Francis Group

NEW YORK AND LONDON

First published 2018
by Routledge
711 Third Avenue, New York, NY 10017

and by Routledge
2 Park Square, Milton Park, Abingdon, Oxon, OX14 4RN

Routledge is an imprint of the Taylor & Francis Group, an informa business

Library of Congress Cataloging-in-Publication Data
Names: Wachter Morris, Carrie A., editor. | Wester, Kelly L., editor.
Title: Making research relevant : applied research designs for the
    mental health practitioner / edited by Carrie A. Wachter Morris,
    Kelly L. Wester.
Description: New York, NY : Routledge, 2018. | Includes
    bibliographical references.
Identifiers: LCCN 2018001742| ISBN 9781138632110 (hardcover :
    alk. paper) | ISBN 9781138632141 (pbk. : alk. paper) | ISBN
    9781315179353 (e-book)
Subjects: | MESH: Mental Health | Research Design
Classification: LCC RC467.8 | NLM WM 20 | DDC
    616.890072—dc23
LC record available at https://lccn.loc.gov/2018001742

ISBN: 978-1-138-63211-0 (hbk)
ISBN: 978-1-138-63214-1 (pbk)
ISBN: 978-1-315-17935-3 (ebk)

Typeset in Goudy
by Apex CoVantage, LLC

Visit the companion website: www.routledge.com/cw/wachter-morris

Contents

Figures

Tables

Textboxes

About the Contributors

Amy Allison received her master's in rehabilitation counseling and certificate of graduate studies in psychiatric rehabilitation from the University of South Carolina School of Medicine and received the Distinguished Rehabilitation Counseling Student Award for the 2015–2016 year. Amy currently works as a mental health specialist.

Jordan L. Austin is currently a doctoral student at the University of North Carolina at Greensboro, where she also graduated with her master's in clinical mental health counseling. She has practiced locally in the Greensboro area within couples and addictions counseling and is interested in promoting practitioners' consumption of research to better inform their clinical practice.

Casey A. Barrio Minton, PhD, NCC, is a professor of counselor education at the University of Tennessee, Knoxville. She served as president (2013–2014) and secretary (2010–2012) for the Association for Assessment and Research in Counseling (AARC). Casey has more than two dozen journal articles in professional counseling venues, four books, and nearly as many chapters and works. She presents regularly at local, state, and national conferences and serves the profession through her editorship of the *Journal for Counselor Leadership and Advocacy* and her presence on editorial boards including *Counselor Education & Supervision*.

Dr. Kathleen Brown-Rice is currently an associate professor of counselor education and chair of the Division of Counseling and Psychology in Education at the University of South Dakota. Her clinical work focuses on adolescents and adults with comorbid substance and trauma concerns. Dr. Rice's research efforts are on developing and enhancing ethical and competent services to clients and concentrate on three main areas: (a) professional counselor supervision and training, (b) Native American mental health with an emphasis on the implications of historical trauma, and (c) risky substance use. She incorporates neural imaging and genotyping in her research to further understand emotional regulation, resiliency, and intergenerational transmission of mental health and substance use disorders.

Karisse A. Callender is an assistant professor in the Department of Counselor Education and Counseling Psychology at Marquette University. Dr. Callender is a licensed professional counselor and substance abuse counselor who has worked in both outpatient and residential settings. Her areas of interest include single-case research designs, clinical supervision, well-being, addiction, and trauma.

Yuliya Cannon received a PhD in counselor education and supervision at the University of Texas at San Antonio. Dr. Cannon's commitment to gender equality and professional advocacy informs her research agenda. Specifically, her research interests include topics such as gender issues, research mentoring, and counselor development. In 2016, she received a Research Grant Award from the Association for Counselor Education and Supervision (ACES) to support her dissertation, a grounded theory study that examined the research mentoring experiences of female doctoral students. Through her clinical work with diverse populations, she developed a specialty working with developmental trauma. Dr. Cannon is currently working as an adjunct professor at the University of Texas at San Antonio.

Heidi Carlone, PhD, is the Hooks Distinguished Professor of STEM Education at the University of North Carolina at Greensboro in the Department of Teacher Education and Higher Education. She is a teacher educator and educational researcher who teaches, among other things, qualitative research methods. Her current scholarship leverages insights from research and practice. For example, insights from studying the culture of STEM learning settings allowed her to codevelop design principles for equitable science and engineering instruction, which then led to a collective redesign and further study of the revised learning goals and activities. Carlone publishes and presents her work in national and international venues and has earned nearly $5 million in funding from local and national foundations for her community-based scholarship.

Holly Downs is a senior research and evaluation faculty member at the Center for Creative Leadership (CCL) and is the principal investigator for CCL's Virtual Leadership Research Project. Her research and evaluation work emphasizes investigating programs delivered in traditional, hybrid, and digital learning environments to myriad audiences. She holds a PhD in educational psychology from the University of Illinois at Urbana-Champaign.

Laura M. Gonzalez has a PhD in counselor education from North Carolina State University and is currently a faculty member in the higher education program at the University of North Carolina at Greensboro. Her research agenda focuses on educational access for youth from Latino immigrant families, including outreach to inform and empower the parents regarding higher education in the United States.

Amanda Giordano, PhD, LPC, NCC, is an assistant professor at the University of North Texas. Giordano specializes in addictions counseling and religious/spiritual issues in counseling. She serves on the editorial board for *Counseling & Values* and the *Journal of Addiction & Offender Counseling*.

Ye He is an associate professor in the Teacher Education and Higher Education Department at the University of North Carolina at Greensboro. She works with both preservice and inservice teachers in the Teaching-English-to-speakers-of-other-languages (TESOL) field and teaches a doctoral-level course on mixed-methods research. Her research focuses on the promotion of strength-based, community-engaged culturally responsive practices in education.

Emily M. Janke, PhD, is an associate professor in the Peace and Conflict Studies department and the founding Director of the Institute for Community and Economic Engagement at the University of North Carolina at Greensboro. Emily's teaching and scholarship explore multiple aspects of community engagement, including community–university relationships and partnerships, institutional culture and change strategies, and the role of reciprocity, communication, and tension in win–win negotiations and collaborative relationships.

Dr. Maribeth F. Jorgensen is in her sixth year as an assistant professor of counselor education and currently works at the University of South Dakota. Her primary research focus is on understanding and facilitating the development of researcher identity in counseling students and licensed professional counselors. She has a passion to integrate research in all her professional roles with the hopes of teaching others that conducting and consuming research can be fun and empowering! Dr. Jorgensen has worked as a licensed professional counselor for eleven years and specializes in working with athletes and individuals experiencing grief and loss.

A. Stephen Lenz, PhD, LPC, is an associate professor of Counselor Education at Texas A&M University–Corpus Christi, past president of the Association for Assessment and Research in Counseling, and editor of *Counseling Outcome Research and Evaluation*. As a practitioner, Dr. Lenz has worked with children, adolescents, adults, and families as an LPC in community-based, university, and private-practice counseling settings. His research interests include community-based program evaluation, counseling outcome research, development/translation of psychological assessments, and meta-analysis.

W. Bradley McKibben, PhD, NCC, ACS, is an assistant professor in the Department of Counseling at Nova Southeastern University. His research interests include professional counselor development and relational/cultural issues in clinical supervision. He incorporates a variety of quantitative and qualitative methods, including survey design, into his supervision research efforts.

Heather Mayton is a doctoral student in her final year in the Counseling and Educational Development Department at the University of North Carolina at Greensboro. She received an MS degree in clinical mental health counseling from the University of North Carolina at Greensboro in 2012. Her areas of research interest include authenticity in counselors, grief counseling, and grief/loss by suicide.

Dee C. Ray, PhD, LPC-S, NCC, RPT-S, is Distinguished Teaching Professor in the Counseling Program and director of the Center for Play Therapy at the University of North Texas. Dr. Ray has published more than 100 articles, chapters, and books in the field of play therapy, specializing in research specifically examining the process and effects of child-centered play therapy. Dr. Ray is author of *A Therapist's Guide to Development: The Extraordinarily Normal Years*, *Advanced Play Therapy: Essential Conditions, Knowledge, and Skills for Child Practice*, and *Child Centered Play Therapy Treatment Manual* and is the coauthor of *Group Play Therapy* and *Child Centered Play Therapy Research*.

Heather Trepal earned her PhD in counseling and human development services from Kent State University. She is a professor and coordinator of the Clinical Mental Health Counseling Program in the Department of Counseling at the University of Texas at San Antonio. Dr. Trepal is a Licensed Professional Counselor and board-approved supervisor (Texas) with more than 17 years of experience in clinical mental health counseling settings. Her primary areas of research and clinical interests include self-harm (NSSI, eating disorders, and body image), gender issues and relational approaches to counseling, qualitative research methods, and counselor preparation and supervision.

Lindsey K. Umstead, MS, LPCA, NCC, is a doctoral student in counseling and counselor education at the University of North Carolina at Greensboro. Lindsey received her master's degree in counseling with a specialty in college counseling and student development from the University of North Carolina at Greensboro. Lindsey's research primary interests include research training in master's counselor education programs and research use and engagement among master's counseling practitioners.

Shreya Vaishnav is a doctoral student in the Department of Counseling and Educational Development at the University of North Carolina in Greensboro. Shreya grew up in Mumbai, India, and migrated with her family to the United States about 6 years ago. Her clinical and research interests focus on reducing mental health disparities among immigrants, especially refugees.

Dr. Amy Vetter is an associate professor in English education in the School of Education at the University of North Carolina Greensboro, where she teaches undergraduate courses in teaching practices and curriculum of English and literacy in the content area and graduate courses in youth literacies, teacher research, and qualitative research design. Her areas of research interest are literacy and identity, positioning theory, discourse analysis, and teacher research.

Carrie A. Wachter Morris, PhD, NCC, ACS, is an associate professor in the Department of Counseling and Educational Development at the University of North Carolina at Greensboro, where she coordinates the School Counseling master's track. She has authored or coauthored more than 25 national peer-reviewed journal articles, 20 chapters and other works, and two other books. She teaches coursework in pedagogy, advanced counseling theories, and evaluation in school counseling.

Michael Walsh is an assistant professor of neuropsychiatry and behavioral science in the University of South Carolina's Rehabilitation Counseling program. In addition to his work as a Counselor Educator, Mike is active in the field, maintaining a small private practice as well as providing research, consulting, and training to various mental health and vocational rehabilitation agencies.

Kelly L. Wester is a professor in the Department of Counseling and Educational Development at the University of North Carolina at Greensboro, where she teaches graduate courses in counseling theories, research, and supervises clinical work. She is also a coauthor of *Non-Suicidal Self-Injury: Wellness Perspectives on Behaviors, Symptoms, and Diagnosis.*

1 Introduction

*Carrie A. Wachter Morris, Kelly L. Wester,
Shreya Vaishnav, & Jordan L. Austin*

Research. It is a word that practitioners know, but it may be loaded with a variety of meanings. Some may agree that it is necessary and required, thus engaging in it in their daily practice. Others may view research as a swear word, something that is done begrudgingly when it is **required**. Still others may even see it as something to be avoided at all costs. Yet regardless of what your perspective is on research, all practitioners need to understand how to consume, apply, and conduct research. You might find yourself asking, "Why?" That is a great question, and we have a lot of different answers to it, many of which we will explain in this text.

You'll notice that throughout this chapter—and indeed, throughout the book—we use the word "practitioner" to describe an individual who might work with clients or students in a variety of mental health and educational settings. This is done purposefully, as a variety of individuals can learn from the research generated not only within their own field but also from sister professions with a similar goal of helping people. Thus, we hope that whatever your primary professional identity, whether it be that of counselor, school counselor, social worker, school social worker, marriage and family therapist, college counselor, student affairs specialist, psychologist, human development specialist, teacher, or one of the myriad practitioners that we have not directly named, that you can see yourself and your work represented within this text when we say "practitioner." Working together, we can increase what we all know about how to help our clients and students be successful. Before we dive into research, we want you to take a moment and think about the work that you do or the work that you hope to do in the future.

Picture yourself practicing—working with your clients or students. How do you want to impact them? How would you know whether you're effective as you help them navigate the challenges that they face? A practitioner's role is ultimately to help people find what they need to better function in their daily lives. This may be by helping them reduce psychological symptoms and maladaptive behaviors, by working with them to increase overall wellness, or by teaching them ways to cultivate healthier relationships. In working with others—whether you work with them in outpatient mental health, inpatient behavioral health, a K–12 school, a college or university, an integrated care setting, a private practice, or something else altogether—the fundamental outcome you are probably hoping for is to be effective in meeting your and your clients' or students' goals. This will mean that you want to be able to tell that what you are doing is, in fact, working.

And while your work with clients or students may be the primary reason that you want to be effective, it will not be the only reason. For example, in your work as a practitioner, you will often be working *for* somebody else. We know that some of you may be your own boss in a private practice or an agency that you own (which we will get to shortly), but many others of you will have bosses including principals, superintendents, directors, senior clinicians, department chairs, supervisors, or any number of other possible titles or roles. Ultimately, as your boss, *they* want to know that what you are doing is working. Otherwise, they may choose to replace you with another practitioner, or if budgets decrease, they may need to lay off individuals from their current jobs. If that is the case, more than likely they are going to select the individuals in their organization that are either (a) not necessary or (b) not able to show that they are effective at what they do. For example, we have seen school counselors save positions that were scheduled to be cut in lean financial times because they were able to demonstrate to their superintendents and school boards what they did in their schools makes a difference through not just anecdotal evidence but effectiveness data. When we are effective, we are more likely to be retained, receive pay increases or bonuses, and be promoted within an organization.

But, for argument's sake, let's say that you are your own boss. Though this may be true, your salary or payment may still come from third-party payers including insurance companies, grants, Medicare or Medicaid, or other outside payment agencies. More frequently, these agencies and organizations are asking for evidence that they are providing payment to practitioners who are effective. For some, this may mean that practitioners are solely utilizing empirically based treatments, such as cognitive behavior therapy. But other organizations and, we suspect, most third-party payers and insurance companies in the future will require data and evidence that what are you doing is working—not only to allow you to have additional sessions with clients but also to pay you for individual sessions. As a society, we have moved toward outcome-based evidence—and it may not be too far in the future that practitioners will have to provide evidence of their effectiveness in their day-to-day work with individuals.

Finally, and perhaps the most important of these factors to consider, is the client or the student—the consumer for whom you are providing a service. This may be in any setting and in any format (e.g., individual therapy, group therapy, family therapy, psychoeducation, classroom guidance, integrated medical care, assessments, consultation, and more). Ultimately, *they* want to know that what you are doing is working. They want to know that you are helping them reach their goals as you work with them. You owe it to them to be able to demonstrate, concretely, that you are an effective practitioner. First, let's take a simple example of what we mean. You have a mother who is bringing her adolescent child to you in an outpatient office setting. This child has been experiencing high levels of anxiety, to the point that she doesn't even want to leave the house. In what has taken at least an hour if not more, this mother has been able to get her teenage daughter to come and see you in your office. No small feat to say the least. Each time you get this youth to come and see you will continue to be a huge effort to this mom, which she is willing to do—as long as what you are doing is working. She will be able to know what you do is working because she will see it: she will see the symptoms decrease, she will notice her daughter's anxiety lessen and the ability for her to go to school or come to your office become easier week by week. While we can "see" symptomology decrease anecdotally, we also need to explore it empirically . . . through data . . . to show in numbers or subjective statements that what we are doing is working. More than likely in this particular case, this adolescent's anxiety, given how extreme it may currently be in this first visit, is not going to decrease in one week, nor probably within a month or two. So how do you help the mom (and the adolescent) know that what you are doing is working and that working to alleviate this high level of anxiety will take some time? You provide hard evidence of symptoms decreasing among previous clients. You provide data from research.

As another example, the population of many countries, including the United States, is becoming more racially and ethnically diverse (Zhou, 2003), and by 2020, it is projected that a majority of children attending schools will be children of color. Until recently, many of the interventions and theories guiding our work as practitioners have been focused on a Eurocentric view of clients and students. As the clients with whom we are working become more diverse, research is needed to ensure that ALL of our clients' needs are being met, particularly if their cultural identities have not traditionally been represented by clinical research. One of the best ways to generate this research is for practitioners to engage in research in their own settings and to share their results.

All of these individuals and organizations—your client or student, your boss, your employer, the place from where you are receiving your income, and you—all want to know that what you are doing is effective and working. This is where research comes into play. This is what research *does* for you and for the helping professions. It is how we know which treatments and interventions are most effective.

Are you convinced that research is vital to your clinical practice? Not yet? Okay, let's consider a more practical example. Picture yourself in your ideal position. Where are you? What are you doing? Now imagine you meet a client (or student or patient) for the first time. When this individual presents to you for treatment, what will you typically do? Usually, regardless of setting, we start by collecting information. In some settings, this may be through a formal, structured intake interview, while in others it may be a series of brief questions to help you understand why that particular person has sought your services.

Some practitioners have information in a file prior to the first meeting, while others may not. Regardless, your goal in this first meeting is typically to gather information about your client.

As you can see in Figure 1.1, the scientific method connects well to clinical practice—regardless of setting. In this example of meeting a client and collecting some information, you are asking questions to determine the problem and then searching for an explanation to the problem through the questions you may ask this client.

After you have gathered some initial information, you will likely construct an idea of what you believe may be the client's presenting issue. For example, is the client having difficulties or presenting with symptoms due to depression, anxiety, relationship conflict, or substance use? Might this student have family difficulties in their home or not have a good way of coping to manage their emotions or other problems? Typically, once you gather information from a client or student, you develop an idea of what you believe may be the underlying reason for the problem. This idea is what you would base your intervention or treatment on with this particular client—with the ultimate goal of helping that client reach a desired outcome.

Figure 1.1 Scientific Method Aligned With Clinical Practice

Once you create an idea (or, in research language, a hypothesis), you continue to collect more information from the individual both before and while you implement the treatment intervention. This information helps you to test this idea or theory that you have. If your theory or hypothesis about the client is supported, you move forward with treatment implementation. But if it was inaccurate based on the additional information you gather, you then move back to creating a new hypothesis about the underlying reasons that are driving the presenting concerns of this client.

Daily Knowledge

As we just discussed, you are already employing the scientific method in your day-to-day work with clients and students. You are, essentially, already conducting informal research. You know that there are a number of ways that research benefits those involved in your daily practice—your clients, yourself and your colleagues as practitioners, insurance companies, directors, and larger organizations. If we truly want to broaden our lens, the world has benefited from science and research. Aspects of science and research play out in your daily practice, regardless of whether you are engaging in more formal research. But let's take this one step further and explore how research has impacted the daily knowledge you have and some everyday activities you engage in through your clinical practice.

Consider that most practitioners are very aware of the importance of the therapeutic relationship. This information was provided to us empirically through research via multiple studies (Frank and Frank, 1993; Lambert & Ogles, 2014; Wampold et al., 1997; Wampold, 2007). These researchers explored factors that led to client change and then came up with common factors models. In these models, Lambert, Wampold, and colleagues found that the therapeutic relationship is one of the most important factors in whether a client experienced change. Not only that, but they found that this relationship was also intertwined with theoretical orientation, client expectancies, and client external resources.

We also know about the dodo bird effect (Luborsky, Singer, & Luborsky, 1975; Rosenzweig, 1936), which means that over time and multiple clinical trials, no one treatment is better than another in the long run. Yet this same research has shown us that counseling and psychological treatment is better than nothing (Luborsky et al., 1975; Rosenzweig, 1936). These are just a couple of ways that research has influenced what you already know and how we conceptualize our work with clients.

Practitioner-Scientist

While we have spent some time focusing on *why* research is important to practitioners and how research has influenced practice, we haven't mentioned much about how practice influences science. Honestly, without practice, there really is not much use for mental health research. It is the practitioners who often influence researchers in terms of what questions need to be answered. As a practitioner, you more than likely have questions when a new student or patient walks into your office or presents with symptoms or behaviors with which you are less familiar. You may consider, "What do I need to know to better understand what is going on for Gina?" or "How might I best help Samuel?" These questions and considerations may be related to diagnoses or treatments. For example, they may be about whether an intervention should be in a particular format or for a particular duration. Having these questions as a practitioner often helps lead researchers to answer these questions. Altering your programs or treatment methods with clients can create new questions. As a prime example, consider Marsha Linehan's dialectical behavior therapy (DBT; Linehan, 1993). She created this theory and method of treatment due to her own experiences both as a client and, later, as a mental health professional. Once she created these treatments, researchers and clinicians alike immediately started to ask questions about the effectiveness of them, leading into decades of research among various client populations in various settings to determine if DBT worked, who it worked for, and what parts of it work in which ways. And this is just one larger example of how practice influences research.

In talking about science and practice, we tend to discuss these as separate entities. Do you engage in practice, or do you engage in research? Are you a researcher? Are you a practitioner? As we noted in Figure 1.1, you technically engage in the scientific method daily with each person to whom you provide a service. Yet we don't typically think of that as "research." Even when mentioning identity development, historically we have discussed the identity development of counselors or mental health practitioners separately from researcher identity development (e.g., Auxier, Hughes, & Kline, 2003). Very few have mentioned that these two identities (e.g., practitioner identity and researcher identity) can, in fact, be integrated. Talking about how these two identities can grow and develop together, having bidirectional influence, is important (Spengler & Lee, 2017). For example, Jorgensen and Duncan (2015) asked master's-level counselors about their researcher identity. What they found was that researcher identity emerges and develops along with counselor identity to some extent—that students reported developing their researcher identities through faculty modeling, external facilitators (such as on-site supervisors of their clinical work), from internal facilitators (e.g., self-motivation, time management, research self-efficacy, thinking styles, curiosity), and through conceptual learning about research. What is really important, though, is that they did so when their counselor identity felt slightly more solid. The two interrelate. Spengler and Lee (2017) take this a little further to mention how when a mental health professional has a practitioner identity that is combined with a researcher identity, they ultimately practice differently. Being trained in research can influence mental health professionals in a way that they can approach their practice differently in terms of how they were able to see change, work with clients, and engage in treatment. Therefore, integrating both a practitioner and a researcher lens may be helpful in your practice, leading to bridging the scientist and practitioner gap rather than seeing research and practice as separate behaviors.

So, what does being a practitioner-scientist actually mean? Does this mean that you have to collect data in your mental health practice? Well, we certainly hope you do, but it doesn't have to equate data collection or formal research (but we want to mention one more time . . . we hope that you do collect data to determine your own effectiveness). Ultimately, we see being a practitioner-scientist as multilayered and containing three major tasks: consumption of research, application of research, and engagement in research (or conducting research).

Consume, Apply, Conduct

In asking counselors if they engaged in these research behaviors, Wester and colleagues (2006) discovered that unfortunately, a large number of counselors self-reported they did not. As can be seen from Figure 1.2, a maximum of 68% of counselors indicated they consumed professional empirical literature to inform their practice, with only 45% relying on what research may suggest when they are actually stuck with a client. This leaves 32% of counselors indicating that they do not consume empirical research. This means that 32% of counselors are stating that they do not use what we *know* to be evidence based, because they are not reading up-to-date literature on what we know to be effective in work with clients. This is scary. Would you want to go to those mental health providers?

Of those counselors that consumed research (again, remembering that this is of the 68% of counselors who consume research), 53% to 76% reported that they apply what they have consumed. Fifty-three percent indicate they based their interventions on what they consumed, 59% reported they recalled what they read while they were with their clients, and 76% indicated they would apply the information learned with clients in their clinical practice. This is good news—the majority of counselors who consumed research applied it. But again, 32% of counselors did not consume research at all (thus they had nothing to apply), and of those that consumed research, ultimately 24% are not applying in practice what they are consuming. What is the reason counselors did not consume research or apply what they did consume? That is less clear. It could be that they believed it was not relevant to their practice. Or maybe it was difficult to consume or apply (as academic researchers do not typically write in language that is easy to immediately apply).

As expected, fewer counselors indicated that they actively engaged in research or conducted research to determine if they were effective with their own clients. When asked, mental health providers typically overestimate their effectiveness with clients (Spengler & Lee, 2017); thus asking clients about outcomes is really important. But only 38% to 56% indicated they conducted research on their own practice. Thirty eight percent reported collecting data

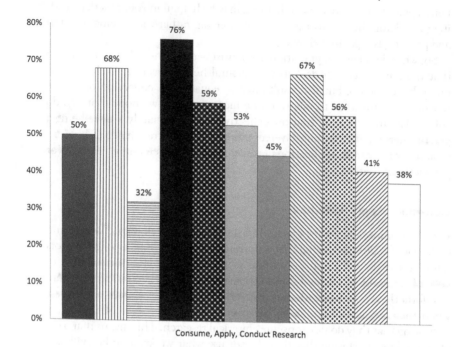

Consume, Apply, Conduct Research

■ Consume Literature to Support What I Do

☐ Consume Literature to Find New Empirically Supported Treatment

☐ Conduct Searches to Find Empirically Supported Treatment

■ Apply Info Learned from Consumption

◪ Recall Research When With Client

☐ Base Interventions on Empirically Supported Info

■ Search for Empirical Treatment When Feel Stuck

☒ Use Professional Literature as a Guide

☒ Evaluate My Own Effectiveness

☒ Collect Data in My Practice on Client Change

☐ Collect Data Clt Sessions to Determine if Interventions/Techs Are Working

Figure 1.2 Percentage of Counselors Who Consume, Apply, and Conduct Research in Their Clinical Practice

Credit line: (Wester et al., 2006)

on client sessions to determine effectiveness of interventions (this is a really low number, by the way!), while 41% said they collected some form of data to determine their own effectiveness, and 56% indicated they evaluated their own effectiveness (with less clarity on how they evaluated this). So approximately one-third to one-half of counselors in the study conducted by Mobley and colleagues reported that they evaluate, in some format, whether they are effective. How do you think that would make their stakeholders feel? Are these practitioners that you would want to see if you knew they never collected information to determine if what they did worked? Are they practitioners that you would refer your loved ones to for services?

As you can see, the rate of research consumption is the highest, followed by a slightly lower rate of application of research knowledge, with an even lower prevalence of conducting research on one's practice. But ultimately, engaging in at least one of these research practices would lead to being a practitioner-scientist, with higher levels of practitioner-scientist proficiency being demonstrated by engaging in all three forms of research in your practice.

Role of Evidence-Based Practice

In thinking about the role of research in clinical practice, it is difficult not to talk about evidence-based practice (EBP). Take a moment to consider what you believe evidence-based practice is before you continue to read.

Did you take a moment, or did you just read on? If you did not take a moment, seriously, pause to reflect on what you think of when you think about evidence-based practice. What do you consider to be the definition of evidence-based practice? Is it therapeutic interventions that are empirically supported by research? Is it specifically randomized clinical trials? Or is it generally empirically supported research? Is it somewhere in between those?

When someone who has not read much about evidence-based practice or seen a definition of evidence-based practice, they often believe that it equates solely to research-supported treatments or even something as extreme as only the most manualized treatments. This is what the name sounds like, right? Wrong. That is only one component of evidence-based practice. In reality, evidence-based practice is the integration of three things:

1. treatments and interventions that are supported empirically by the best available research
2. clinical expertise
3. client characteristics, culture, and preference (American Psychological Association [APA], 2006).

Similarly, as noted by APA (2006), this definition of evidence-based practice is similar to that created by the Institute of Medicine (2001), which suggests that evidence-based practice is the integration of the best research evidence combined with clinical expertise along with patient values.

Let's take a moment to consider this. If, as a practitioner, you based your interventions, classroom guidance, psychoeducation, or any other form of treatment solely on research, you lose the uniqueness and needs of each individual client who is sitting in your office. Additionally, you would fail to take into consideration client factors, resources, and even their expectancy (or desire) to change—all of which are part of the common factors model (Lambert & Ogles, 2014; Wampold et al., 1997). So more than likely, if you implement solely what researchers have found to be effective, even if you diagnose the symptoms correctly with your clinical expertise, the client may not change or reach their desired goal. At this point, you have taken the client voice out of the process. That is not an effective way of establishing a therapeutic relationship (which, again, has been found to be one of the most important factors in the room!).

Now, let's say you do take client values, culture, and context into consideration. You inquire if they would like to engage in a 16-week, empirically supported, dialectical behavior therapy treatment (Linehan, 1993). The client agrees that she is willing to engage in all components of this 16-week DBT treatment and believes this would be helpful. You selected this treatment because you have deemed that the client is at risk of suicidal behavior and is depressed for a variety of reasons including ineffective relationships and lack of distress tolerance. At this point, you have incorporated both what researchers have supported (i.e., DBT 16-week program) along with client values and preferences. However, if you misdiagnosed the client or your hypothesis about the underlying reasons for that diagnosis was incorrect, there is also the potential that the treatment will not work. For example, what if this client was depressed and suicidal because she watched her mother die by suicide a month ago and is traumatized and grieving? Or what if the client is constantly under the influence of a substance, but you are unaware of it or have neglected to assess for substance use or abuse? A lack of clinical expertise or the wrong diagnosis could lead to ineffective treatment. It is the integration of all three components, therefore, that is truly evidence-based practice (Figure 1.3). So let's think through each of these pieces, what they look like in practice, and why they are important.

Let's start with empirically supported treatments. These are the interventions and approaches that have been studied in ways that meet baseline requirements for rigor and shown a statistically significant degree of demonstrated positive outcomes for clients. So how do you find these treatments? A number of resources are available for free—either through technology,

Figure 1.3 Evidence-Based Practice

through local libraries, or through clinically affiliated organizations that may serve as information hubs. For example, online, a quick internet search may lead to sites like Google Scholar (https://scholar.google.com), NC Docks (https://libres.uncg.edu/ir/uncg/), or Open Education Resource Commons (www.oercommons.org/) that provide free access to a variety of academic and nonacademic resources that individuals may access. As open education resources are growing, some journals have been created that are truly open access and accessible to anyone who can hop online for a few minutes. An up-to-date list of open-access journals is currently available through the Directory of Open Access Journals, found at https://doaj.org/. Social media may also provide access to research, as individuals and groups use them as vehicles to distribute useful clinical research. Two examples are Mental Health Research, a United States–based Facebook page, and The Mental Elf, a United Kingdom–based Facebook page. Both disseminate research on a variety of mental health–related topics of interest to practitioners.

Next Steps: Learning to Conduct Research

It is important to be able to locate studies relevant to the work that we do as practitioners through accessing research literature. Most of the research on empirically supported treatments that we rely on comes from randomized clinical trials. These studies typically emerge from the medical profession, but we can also get important information about empirically supported treatments from well-designed studies with a variety of methodologies that we will present in this book. Quantitative designs, in particular, are particularly well suited to generating the type of research that will empirically support treatments, but qualitative methods can also give powerful insight into the ways that different interventions may be impacting our clients and students.

Doing a literature search is one way of learning about empirically supported treatments. Another way is to do research at your own clinical practice to contribute to the literature base. So, not only is research helpful for you (and all the other people who want to hear about how wonderfully effective you are), but it is also going to help other practitioners out there who are looking for ways to be as effective as you are!

Because of this, you will also need to understand how to read and critique literature. This includes all parts of an article, including methods and results. Chapter 2 gives an overview of how to best consume and understand literature so that you can truly integrate what you learn into your own clinical practice. After reading these first two chapters, we hope that you start thinking about how *you* can start to develop your own identity as a researcher. Chapter 3 talks about how to conduct research ethically and responsibly—something that is foundational to conducting research that increases what we know and also honors the trust that our clients have in us and also our ethical standard to do no harm. Chapter 4 introduces you to how to start thinking about conducting research, by digging into the details of survey design.

These first chapters form a foundation to then build your knowledge of a variety of different research methods and how they might naturally be suited to your work as a practitioner-scientist. While these are only a sampling of a number of research methods out there, these have been carefully selected to represent not only the methods that might be the most easily suited to your work as a practitioner but also a number of different philosophies of research. From the in-depth qualitative exploration of a single client, group, or practice given by a case study (Chapter 5) to the more controlled implementation of a single treatment of the single-case research design (Chapter 6), we hope to help you think through how even small numbers of clients can give you valuable information and insight when researched properly. From there, we start to look at larger groups of clients and how different client factors relate to each other in correlational and causal-comparative (Chapter 7) and quasi-experimental (Chapter 8) designs. We then go to the tried-and-true gold standard of randomized control trials, or RCT (Chapter 9). After discussing the highly controlled RCT method, we then shift gears to explore more client-driven qualitative methods like phenomenology (Chapter 10) and photovoice (Chapter 11). Bridging the qualitative and quantitative realms is mixed methods (Chapter 12), which allows practitioners to explore not only the numbers behind different behaviors but also the nuances specific to individual clients. Every practitioner needs a baseline knowledge of program evaluation (Chapter 13) to take a critical look at their own practice or curriculum. We then close with the newer action- and social justice–oriented advocacy-based research (Chapter 14).

Each chapter will walk you through not only the basics of the research method but also how it might be directly applied to specific questions or settings to help you picture how you might be able to tailor the approach for your own practitioner-scientist needs. Further, each chapter is paired with a brief narrated PowerPoint that will give highlights of the method and, often, an additional example from a different setting. We highly recommend taking advantage of both the text and the videos, as well as the reflection questions at the end of each chapter, to help guide your thinking about each method and your own development as a practitioner-scientist.

Questions for Further Review and Application

1. Do you believe that researcher identity and practitioner identity develop simultaneously or separately? Should they be integrated? Why or why not?

2. What do you think is needed at the practitioner level to feel confident in consuming, applying, and conducting research? Is something similar needed for all three or something different in terms of training and experience?

3. What is evidence-based practice? How will you know you are engaging in evidence-based practice in your own practice?

References

Auxier, C. R., Hughes, F. R., & Kline, W. B. (2003). Identity development in counselors-in-training. *Counselor Education and Supervision, 43*(1), 25–38.

Force, A. T. (2006). APA presidential task force on evidence based practice. *American Psychologist, 61*, 271–285.

Frank, J. D., & Frank, J. B. (1993). *Persuasion and healing: A comparative study of psychotherapy* (3rd ed.). Baltimore, MD: Johns Hopkins University Press.

Institute of Medicine. (2001). *Crossing the quality chasm: A new health system for the 21st century*. Washington, DC: National Academies Press.

Jorgensen, M. F., & Duncan, K. (2015a). A grounded theory of masters-level counselor research identity. *Counselor Education and Supervision, 54*, 17–31. doi:10.100 2/j.1556–6978.2015.00067

Lambert, M. J., & Ogles, B. M. (2014). Common factors: Post hoc explanation or empirically based therapy approach. *Psychotherapy, 51*, 500–504. Retrieved from http://dx.doi.org/10.1037/a0036580

Linehan, M. (1993). *Cognitive-behavioral treatment of borderline personality disorder*. New York, NY: Guilford press.

Luborsky, L., Singer, B., & Luborsky, L. (1975). Comparative studies of psychotherapies: Is it true that everyone has won and all must have prizes? *Archives of General Psychiatry, 32*(8), 995–1008.

Rosenzweig, S. (1936). Some implicit common factors in diverse methods of psychotherapy. *American Journal of Orthopsychiatry, 6*(3), 412.

Spengler, P. M., & Lee, N. A. (2017). A funny thing happened when my scientist self and my practitioner self became an integrated scientist-practitioner: A tale of two couple therapists transformed. *Counselling Psychology Quarterly*, 1–19.

Wampold, B. E. (2007). Psychotherapy: The humanistic (and effective) treatment. *American Psychologist, 62*, 857–873.

Wampold, B. E., Mondin, G. W., Moody, M., Stich, F., Benson, K., & Ahn, H. (1997). A meta-analysis of outcome studies comparing bona fide psychotherapies: Empirically, "all must have prizes". *Psychological Bulletin, 122*, 203–215.

Wester, K. L., Mobley, K., & Faulkner, A. (2006, September). *Evidence-based practices: Building a bridge between researchers and practitioners*. Orlando, Florida: Southern Association for Counselor Education and Supervision.

Zhou, M. (2003). Urban education: Challenges in educating culturally diverse children. *Teachers College Record, 105*, 208–225.

2 Understanding Existing Literature

Amanda Giordano

Your newest client's case is unique. Although you have worked with this presenting concern before, there are novel variables to consider, including the client's distinctive cultural identity and a co-occurring disorder. You wonder how others have worked with similar clients and whether those clinical efforts were effective. What approaches have others employed with members of this cultural group, and what were the outcomes? Has anyone ever addressed these presenting concerns simultaneously? If so, how? Thankfully, you can find many of these answers by exploring existing literature in counseling and related fields.

Importance of Understanding Existing Trends in the Literature

The introduction to Section C of the 2014 American Counseling Association (ACA) *Code of Ethics* states, "Counselors have a responsibility to the public to engage in counseling practices that are based on rigorous research methodologies." Additionally, the American Psychological Association's (APA, 2010b) *Ethical Principles of Psychologist and Code of Conduct* posits, "Psychologists' work is based upon established scientific and professional knowledge of the discipline" (2.04). Further, the National Association of Social Workers' *Code of Ethics* (2008) asserts, "Social workers should critically examine and keep current with emerging knowledge relevant to social work and fully use evaluation and research evidence in their professional practice" (5.02.c). These ethical codes are designed to protect our clients and ensure we provide them with the highest standard of care. Therefore, it makes sense that clinicians of all fields are obligated to utilize counseling techniques and foster clinical environments that are supported by sound research studies. Consider the harm that could come to clients if we operated on instinct alone and failed to consult existing literature to identify empirically supported clinical approaches. Thankfully, we have access to hundreds of years of research and relevant literature upon which to ground clinical practice.

In 1995, a division of the APA (Division 12) created a task force (Promotion and Dissemination of Psychological Procedures) to empirically validate clinical techniques (La Roche & Christopher, 2009). The goal of the task force was to identify counseling approaches that were supported by rigorous research, particularly studies utilizing randomized controlled trials. The efforts of the Division 12 task force are relevant to you because they contributed to a growing emphasis on identifying and incorporating empirically supported treatment (EST) into clinical practice. Now you can utilize strategies that have demonstrated effectiveness, and thus you will be better equipped to provide appropriate care to your clients and strong rationales to managed care organizations as to why your work is necessary (Sue & Sue, 2008). In addition to examining counseling techniques and approaches, APA Divisions 12 and 29 created a second task force to identify aspects of the counseling relationship supported by empirical research (Norcross & Wampold, 2011). This Evidence-Based Therapy Relationships Task Force determined that the therapeutic relationship contributed at least as much to the success of counseling as specific interventions and treatment methods (Norcross & Wampold, 2011). Thus, we now have evidentiary support for the fact that the strength of the relationships we build with our clients matters!

Despite the plethora of research available to clinicians, a gap exists between those generating research findings and the practitioners who would benefit most from the information. Indeed, Murray (2009) wrote, "For decades, however, the counseling profession has demonstrated a chasm between the knowledge developed by researchers and the practices used by clinicians" (p. 108). This research–practice gap can impede the progress, efficacy, and accountability of helping professions. What does this mean for you? One of your clinical responsibilities is to keep up with relevant research and apply it to your practice. To make reading research worth your time, researchers are charged with conducting studies that are relevant and meaningful to clinicians. Specifically, Wester (2011) stated that counseling research must have social validity or the potential to make a significant contribution to clinical practice, the counseling profession, or society at large. So those conducting research should be aware of the needs of clinicians and develop studies to address them. The next step is for practitioners like you to consume the research and let it influence your practice. Indeed, Balkin and Sheperis (2011) noted, "counselors must now be competent consumers of research conducted in the counseling profession and be able to make decisions about the applicability of research results" (p. 268). If researchers prioritize social validity and clinicians prioritize consuming the literature, the research–practice gap is likely to shrink.

Empirical Versus Nonempirical Literature

Sifting through existing literature can be a daunting task. There are many resources available such as peer-reviewed articles, book chapters, dissertations and theses, commentaries, magazine articles, and websites. How do you find credible, relevant sources? How do you differentiate between the many types of literature? What sources are the best match for your needs? To answer these questions, it is important to distinguish between empirical and nonempirical literature.

Empirical Literature

The word *empirical* simply means "originating in or based on observation or experience" (*Merriam-Webster's Collegiate Dictionary*, 2004, p. 408). Thus, empirical research seeks to verify or negate a specific question by collecting and analyzing data. You will notice that empirical research papers have a standard format including an introduction, a methods section, a results section, and a discussion of the implications (APA, 2010a). These articles present findings from original quantitative or qualitative investigations with the aim of contributing to the literature on a particular topic. Within the quantitative realm, researchers may conduct experiments, disseminate descriptive surveys, or utilize single-subject designs ($N = 1$), each of which you will be introduced to throughout the chapters in this book. Qualitative researchers, on the other hand, may conduct interviews or focus groups or engage in observations of members of a specific population in order to ascertain thick descriptions of a phenomenon. Both quantitative and qualitative studies seek to objectively examine constructs by employing standardized research techniques and analyzing the resulting data.

Nonempirical Literature

Conversely, rather than detailing a quantitative or qualitative study, nonempirical research consists of literature reviews, practice pieces, and conceptual works (APA, 2010a; Watts, 2011). When exploring a new topic, you may find a literature review particularly helpful, as it synthesizes all of the relevant literature and seminal works related to the subject. Baker (2016) noted that literature reviews should be free of bias, with clear inclusion criteria for the articles studied. Further, Pautasso (2013) purported that a quality literature review should be a focused summary of recent papers and original works pertaining to a designated topic. Literature reviews can provide a succinct overview of a construct so you can become familiar with the status of the topic in the field.

While literature reviews summarize many papers related to a given construct, practice pieces and conceptual works present new, original applications of a theory, technique, or clinical approach. For example, practice pieces describe the implementation of clinical interventions with new populations or provide specific details regarding the use of a novel counseling practice (Guiffrida, Schwitzer, & Choate, 2006). These papers often include a hypothetical case example or specific instructions describing how to alter a clinical technique for a specific purpose, such as a paper explaining how to apply acceptance and commitment therapy (ACT) to those with binge eating disorder (BED). You may find these "how-to" practice articles extremely relevant and applicable to your clinical work. Practice articles fall under the umbrella term *conceptual articles*, which Watts (2011) defined as papers that apply theoretical perspectives to particular clinical concerns, describe the use of a clinical procedure or intervention, discuss controversial or provocative issues in the counseling field, or respond to previously published works. Thus, broadly speaking, conceptual articles describe original, well-supported perspectives on current issues, clinical practices, or previous publications. Indeed, Balkin (2009) wrote that conceptual articles should be more than a synthesis of existing literature but instead offer innovative ways of applying theory or implementing clinical techniques.

Therefore, depending on your specific clinical needs, both empirical and nonempirical papers can be valuable resources. For example, suppose you just completed a training in motivational interviewing (MI) and want to know whether the approach is effective with adolescents. Empirical research studies reporting outcomes of MI interventions with adolescent clients may be most helpful in this situation. Once you know that MI is effective with adolescents, however, you may want to read a case example of how another clinician has used the approach. At this point, a conceptual piece detailing how to apply MI to an adolescent client may be most useful.

How to Access Existing Literature

Now that you are familiar with the different types of literature, how do you go about accessing these resources? In this technological age of smartphones, iPads, laptops, and abundant Wi-Fi access, retrieving literature has never been easier. For those affiliated with a university, the school's library system is an excellent and cost-effective resource. There are numerous electronic research databases that affiliates of universities can access for free. For those who are not connected to a university, these databases are still very useful, yet you must purchase the articles for a small fee (usually less than $20). Following are descriptions of several research databases that may be of interest to you:

- **Academic Search Complete** (www.ebscohost.com/academic/academic-search-complete): This multidisciplinary database contains articles from topics including anthropology, psychology, women's studies, and multicultural studies.
- **ERIC** (Education Resource Information Center; https://eric.ed.gov/): This extensive database provides resources relevant to education from a variety of disciplines. The database is sponsored by the Institute of Education Sciences.
- **PsycINFO** (www.apa.org/psycinfo): This vast database is sponsored by APA and contains articles from a variety of fields including behavioral science, mental health, and sociology.
- **SocINDEX** (www.ebscohost.com/academic/socindex-with-full-text): This focused database showcases articles relevant to sociology including topics such as criminology, gender studies, and substance use.

- **MEDLINE** (https://health.ebsco.com/products/medline-with-full-text): This comprehensive database is sponsored by the National Library of Medicine and contains resources relevant to nursing, health care, and medicine.
- **Google Scholar** (https://scholar.google.com): This search engine is dedicated to directing interested readers to a wide array of scholarly journal articles, books, theses, and dissertations.

While many journals require a subscription or small fee to access articles, some journals offer open access, meaning that readers do not have to pay to access content. The Directory of Open Access Journals (DOAJ; https://doaj.org) is a good place to begin your search for free, peer-reviewed papers. Finally, another way to obtain research is through membership in a clinical association, which often comes with access to the organization's journal. For example, members of the Association for Spiritual, Ethical, and Religious Values in Counseling (ASERVIC) receive electronic access to the division's journal, *Counseling & Values*.

When utilizing research databases, it is important to consider your search terms and the many ways in which authors can describe any one topic. For example, if you are interested in finding scholarly articles related to substance abuse, you could search using the terms *substance use, substance misuse, alcohol abuse, drug use, substance use disorder*, or *addiction*. Thus, if you vary your keywords, your searches will yield a greater breadth of papers. One way to help ensure you are not missing any important articles is to find a relevant paper and review the author's reference list. Rather than reinventing the wheel, you can begin your investigation on the subject by reading articles that another researcher deemed pertinent and helpful. Finally, another way you can access existing literature is to contact prominent researchers on the topic of interest (they will be flattered!) and request recommendations of essential books and articles. The extensiveness of counseling literature is a double-edged sword: on the one hand, we have research on almost every topic imaginable, but on the other hand, it can be difficult to know where to begin. Contacting a current expert in the field could be an efficient way to find a starting place for your investigation.

Consuming and Critiquing Empirical Research

So you know how to access the literature, but that is only the first step. Indeed, Reynolds (2000) offers five steps for applying existing research to clinical practice: (a) identify the specific clinical questions you would like to answer, (b) find existing research to address the question, (c) evaluate the quality of the research you found, (d) apply results of the research to your client, and (e) evaluate the outcomes. In this next section, we will focus on the third step of this process: how to evaluate the quality of research you find. To help us do this, we will be examining a recent publication written by myself and a colleague, which explored cybersex addiction among college students (Giordano & Cashwell, 2017).

Evaluating Introductions

The purpose of the introduction is to present a case as to why the current study is needed. The authors of the article should summarize important existing literature and identify unanswered questions, areas of disagreement, or the need for replication. There should be a logical flow in the presentation of supporting research leading to the purpose statement, or identified need for the study. Just because a topic has not been studied before does not mean it should be. For example, there may not be any research on the correlation between nail polish color and symptoms of depression, but that does not mean the research is needed! Thus, the introduction should present a compelling argument as to why the topic deserves to be investigated, describe the social validity of the research project, and explain how the study fits within the broader scope of literature. By the time you finish reading the introduction, you should think, "of course we need this study!"

Additionally, the introduction should be free of bias. Researchers should describe supporting evidence, contradictory findings, and areas of disagreement and provide multiple perspectives on the topic. The presentation of material should be objective, and authors should refrain from trying to influence readers by presenting only one side of an issue. For example, in a research paper describing the need for a new treatment protocol for childhood trauma, the authors should speak to the strengths and limitations of treatment approaches that already exist. Further, all major constructs in the research study should be discussed in the introduction with support from previous literature. Incomplete introductions may fail to describe a study variable, inadequately explain associations between primary constructs, or neglect to reference a theoretical orientation. You should be able to recognize these limitations and evaluate the extent to which the researchers investigated the phenomenon in question prior to beginning their study. Finally, as a critical consumer of research, you also must be able to evaluate the appropriateness of the resources cited in the introduction. Strong, quality articles utilize original rather than secondary sources, cite peer-reviewed articles rather than books or websites, and include the most recent references (Lambie, Sias, Davis, Lawson, & Akos, 2008). By the end of the introduction, you should have a solid understanding of why the research article was written and the need for the study.

Let's consider the article that my colleague and I wrote about collegiate cybersex addiction. In the introduction of the article, we clearly explained the need for this particular study at this particular time. Specifically, we noted the social validity of the study. What this means is we stated the prevalence of cybersex addiction among the general population, the negative consequences of cybersex addiction, reasons why cybersex may be more prevalent among college students, gender considerations in the use of the internet for sexual activity, and the lack of prior research examining cybersex among college students. Given these realities, we claimed that this study was needed to better inform clinical practice, particularly among college counselors. We then identified the two research questions guiding our work: "What is the prevalence of cybersex addiction among college students?" and "Do significant differences exist between men and women on cybersex addiction?" to better inform clinical practice among college counselors (Giordano & Cashwell, 2017). Our goal was to have readers fully convinced by the end of our introduction that this study was needed and meaningful.

Evaluating Methods Sections

The methods section is something that most individuals who do not identify as researchers typically skim through or skip over altogether. This usually occurs because methods (along with results) sections are not as easily understood, yet it is one of the most important sections of an article to determine if the findings of the study are actually applicable to your clinical practice, specific clients in your practice, or students in your school. Therefore, becoming a critical consumer of empirical research means that you must evaluate the quality of the methods section. The methods detail the type of study design (e.g., experimental, phenomenological, descriptive, or correlational, which you will read about later in this book) and how the researchers conducted the study, including things like sampling procedures and instrumentation.

Sampling Procedures

Empirical researchers should describe how they selected the participants in their study. Accessibility, funding resources, and required sample size all influence the choice of sampling procedures. For example, in quantitative research, the type of statistical analysis and number of variables dictate the minimum number of participants needed in the study. Multiple-regression analysis, bivariate correlations, and analysis of variance (ANOVA) could have up to 100 or more participants depending on the specific elements of the research project. Qualitative research, however, typically requires much fewer participants because the goal is to *understand* a phenomenon. Therefore, qualitative studies may have 8 to 50 participants depending on which qualitative tradition the researchers are using (Hays & Singh, 2011).

Probability sampling is the most rigorous form of obtaining participants and involves randomly selecting a sample from a population in such a way that each member of the population has an equal chance of being included in the study (Creswell, 2014; Sink & Mvududu, 2010). For example, if you wanted to study the prevalence of bullying in the middle school where you work, probability sampling would require that you list the names of all students enrolled in the school and randomly select a certain number to include in your study. There are many reasons why random sampling is not possible, however; thus researchers may use nonprobability sampling methods. Nonprobability sampling includes the solicitation of volunteers and utilization of the participants that researchers have access to (such as convenience sampling). For example, if you are interested in studying nonsuicidal self-injury among women, you may elicit volunteers from among the female clients seeking services at your practice to assess for self-injury. Although this does not represent the entire population of female clients, it is a realistic, cost-effective, and achievable way to obtain participants (Sink & Mvududu, 2010).

Consider again the study of cybersex among college students that we were talking about earlier. To employ probability sampling, we would have acquired the names of all undergraduate students from the registrar's office at my university, randomly selected several hundred, and called or emailed each one with an invitation to participate in the study. Although preferred, this would be logistically difficult and time consuming. Therefore, we utilized convenience sampling methods by emailing course instructors and asking if we could come to their classes to administer our survey to all consenting students in attendance. Although this form of sampling made the most sense for us, we still identified it as a limitation in our study, as we could not guarantee our sample was a true representation of all college students at the university.

So what does all of this sampling method information mean for you? When consuming literature, you should take the sampling method into account and evaluate whether the research will meet your clinical needs. For example, if the researchers used probability sampling to obtain results from a national sample of the United States, the findings may not be applicable to the Native American clients at your clinic in a small rural town in New Mexico. Conversely, if researchers used convenience sampling to assess clinical outcomes at a trauma center on a college campus, the results may not apply to your setting that serves largely older adult clients. Considering sampling procedures ensures that you are allowing the right type of research to influence your clinical work.

Another important sampling consideration is participants' demographics. What are the cultural identities of the participants included in the study? Can the results of this study generalize to other cultural groups? Before applying empirical research to your practice, you should consider the degree of similarity between the participants of the research study and your own clients. Was there evidential support that the technique or approach was effective for male clients? For clients who identify as bisexual? For clients with disabilities? For clients in poverty? For clients who identify as multiracial? According to the ACA *Code of Ethics* (2014), researchers should "describe the extent to which results are applicable for diverse populations" (G.4.a, p. 16). Therefore, you should know whether the results of the empirical study are likely to apply to your particular client population. If the sample used in the empirical research study is majority European American, you may need to adapt the intervention or approach to match the context of your clients from other cultural groups (Roysircar, 2009). In this way, you will offer culturally sensitive treatments.

Indeed, Nagayama Hall (2001) noted that it is inappropriate to extract ESTs with privileged populations and apply them to marginalized group members. Instead, you should provide culturally sensitive treatment by tailoring evidence-based practices to reflect the cultural context of each unique client (Nagayama Hall, 2001). So it is recommended that you always read the sampling section in an empirical article so you can see the relevance to your specific client or student population.

Returning to the study on cybersex, our convenience sampling procedures yielded a sample of 339 college students, of which the majority identified as female, White, and heterosexual. Although these demographics mirrored those among the students at the university, you would want to take caution when applying the results of our study to institutions with large numbers of students who identify in marginalized sexual orientation or racial groups, or for that matter even potentially to White male students, given the lower numbers of these individuals in the final sample.

Instrumentation

Another component of methods sections is a description of the instruments the researchers used to collect data. Typically, researchers consider a myriad of factors when determining instrumentation such as reliability, validity, cost, availability, number of items, and norming data. The authors should provide enough information so you can evaluate the quality and appropriateness of their measures. For example, researchers should report the reliability of the scores obtained for each scale. Reliability simply refers to the consistency of scores on a measure across time, conditions, and constructs (Creswell, 2014). If a measure has high reliability, it means that the scores from the instrument are relatively stable. For example, if an instrument claims to measure acculturative stress (AS), those with high levels of AS should score similarly on the instrument and those with low levels of AS also should score similarly (Heppner, Wampold, Owen, Wang, & Thomson, 2016). Additionally, reliable measures yield stable variable scores across situations, such that the individual with high AS will have high AS at the grocery store, at the gym, and on the school bus. Most often, reliability is reported in the form of Cronbach's alpha (ranging from 0 to 1), with higher alpha scores indicating greater levels of stability or reliability. Social science researchers tend to agree that Cronbach's alpha scores of .70 or higher indicate acceptable reliability. If reliability scores are lower than .70, you are unable to guarantee that your participants would report similar scores if they completed the measure at a different time or in different circumstances. This significantly limits the applicability of the research findings.

Let us return to the cybersex study. We utilized the Internet Scale of the Sexual Addiction Screening Test-Revised (SAST-R; Carnes, Green, & Carnes, 2010) to assess college student cybersex addiction. The scale had six items with "yes" or "no" answer choices. Our Cronbach's alpha level for the scores we obtained was .694, which is acceptable yet lower than we hoped. This reliability score indicates only modest stability among scores (i.e., college students with cybersex addiction scored similarly, and those without cybersex addiction scored similarly); therefore, we noted the low alpha level in the limitations section of the article.

With regard to validity, researchers should report evidence detailing the extent to which the measures they used actually assessed the constructs of interest. For example, does the measure claiming to assess AS actually assess AS, or something else like fear, depression, or neuroticism? This is important to you as a practitioner for several reasons. If there is no evidence of validity, you cannot guarantee that the findings of the research study actually reflect the variables you are most interested in. Consider a researcher who claims to have developed an effective treatment for obsessive-compulsive disorder (OCD), yet he offered no evidence of validity for his OCD measure. Although the participants' scores improved, was the researcher really measuring OCD? Perhaps his measure was really assessing generalized anxiety disorder or a social phobia. The lack of instrument validity makes it very difficult for you to know who would benefit from this newly developed treatment.

So when you are reading a methods section, what are you looking for to ensure that the researcher's measures are valid? Researchers can support the validity of their instrumentation by describing how the scores correlate with other instruments that assess the same construct (construct validity), how the items on the measure assess all aspects of the construct (content validity), or how the scores on the instrument accurately predict scores of related measures in the appropriate direction (predictive validity; Creswell, 2014). For example, the SAST-R demonstrated validity by accurately differentiating between men in inpatient treatment for sexual addiction and college males or male clergy without sexual addiction (predictive validity). Also, the items on the measure assessed four components of sex addiction confirmed by principle component analysis, namely, (a) preoccupation, (b) loss of control, (c) affect disturbance, and (d) relationship disturbance (content validity). Finally, to demonstrate construct validity, scores on the original SAST significantly correlated with the Boundary Violation Index; an assessment that measured attitudes and behaviors of sexual misconduct (Swiggart, Feurer, Samenow, Delmonico, & Spickard, 2008). With all these forms of validity, it is safe to assume that the SAST in fact measures sexual addiction.

Establishing the validity of a measure gives credence to the researchers' claims about the implications of the results. Despite the importance of this information, sadly, evidence of validity was found to be absent in more than half of the measures used in articles published in the counseling flagship journal, the *Journal of Counseling & Development* (JCD; Wester, Borders, Boul, & Horton, 2013). Therefore, when consuming existing literature, you must be wary of articles that do not provide support for the fact that their measures indeed assess the constructs under investigation.

Finally, along with reliability and validity, it is important for you to consider norming data when critiquing the instrumentation used in an empirical study.

Researchers develop assessment measures by testing them on a particular population called a *norming sample*. It is important for researchers to describe the development and norming data of the instruments utilized in their study, as well as the extent to which the measures are appropriate for the current sample. For example, was the instrument developed using White, middle-class college students? If so, to what extent is it appropriate to use with ethnically diverse low-income families? Cultural sensitivity in instrument selection is an important part of a research design because the meaning and experience of phenomena vary across cultural groups (Heppner et al., 2016). As you read empirical literature, consider whether the norming sample for the measures used in the study was appropriate for the researcher's participants. You can then take that one step further to consider whether the measure applies to your specific client population.

In the collegiate cybersex study, we utilized a subscale of the SAST-R, which Carnes and colleagues (2010) developed using samples of both male and female college students, clergy, and clients in treatment for sex addiction. The researchers found the measure to be reliable and valid across differing ages, occupations, and genders. In light of these findings, we were confident that we could utilize the SAST-R with both male and female college students. If Carnes et al. (2010) had developed the SAST-R using males only, we would have exercised caution employing the instrument with female college students. Investigating the development and norming process of the measure, however, gave us confidence to implement the SAST-R with multiple genders.

Examining Results

Although arguably the most meaningful, the results section of an empirical article can be the most intimidating. You may be experiencing anxiety symptoms just by thinking about the topic. But the results section can be your friend rather than your enemy. It is here that researchers detail the statistical analyses used to test the research questions and the results of those analyses. To critically consume existing counseling research, you must have a basic understanding of statistical methods and how to interpret outcomes. For example, one important consideration when critiquing a results section is whether the statistical analyses utilized in the study appropriately match the research question. You should be able to identify if the researchers used a group differences analysis when they were looking at variable relationships or vice versa. Once you determine that the researchers employed the appropriate analysis given the research question, you can then evaluate the statistical significance and effect size.

Statistical significance simply means that the researchers found an effect that did not happen by chance. That is an important first step to understanding the results of the study. However, statistical significance does not necessarily mean that the results are meaningful. Indeed, large sample sizes are likely to produce significant findings simply due to the volume of participants.

Table 2.1 Research Questions and Corresponding Analyses

Research Question	Statistical Analyses
Do relationships exist between variables?	Logistical regression, multiple regression, bivariate correlation
Do differences exist between groups?	*t*-test, analysis of variance (ANOVA), descriptive discriminant analysis (DDA), chi-square

Therefore, you must determine the *strength* of the observed significance, or the practical significance, by assessing the effect size. This value is what you may find most relevant to your clinical work, because it will help you determine which approach may be important to implement or not implement more than statistical significance will. The effect size reveals the magnitude of the effect that the researchers found. The units of measure for effect sizes are contingent upon the specific statistical analyses used, but small, medium, and large standardized benchmarks have been provided so we can interpret different units (Cohen, 1988).

Now the meaning of the effect size depends on the specifics of the research study. For example, if you are examining the outcomes of a new treatment for depression compared to treatment as usual (TAU), a large effect size indicates that not only was the treatment statistically significant, the magnitude of the effect of the new treatment was substantially better than TAU. You then can conclude that the researchers found a high degree of practical significance in their study. So do small effect sizes mean that the findings were not worthwhile? Not necessarily. Remember, the interpretation of effect sizes depends on the specific research questions being investigated. If a team of researchers was studying the effects of a new medication on curbing the cravings of adults addicted to heroin, even a small effect size would be important. Although the magnitude of the effect of the new medication was small, it still provided more relief to those addicted to heroin than a placebo did. Therefore, given the opioid epidemic in the United States, these would be meaningful results.

Evaluating Discussion Sections

The discussion section of an empirical article is where researchers interpret, evaluate, and make meaning of their research findings (Lambie et al., 2008). Here, you will find authors reiterating whether the results of their study supported or contradicted the proposed research questions. If the researchers found support for their hypotheses, they should elaborate as to what those findings mean for the field. If the researchers did not find support for their hypotheses, they should offer possible explanations for the unexpected findings. As a consumer of research, you should evaluate the extent to which the authors describe the implications of their findings. Do the researchers provide enough information in this section to answer your questions and help you contextualize the results? Do they provide practical implications for what their study means? Simply rewriting the results section without detailing how the findings fit within the broader scope of research does not meet the standard of social validity. On the other hand, overstating the findings and making generalizations beyond the scope of the study is misleading and potentially harmful to future clients. Consider a situation in which a researcher found that mindfulness-based cognitive behavioral therapy (MBCBT) had a statistically significant yet small effect on posttraumatic stress disorder (PTSD) symptoms among male combat veterans. Although the effect size was small and the study utilized only male veterans, this researcher claimed in his discussion section that all PTSD treatment centers should now begin using MBCBT. Do you see how misleading this would be? Researchers must find the delicate balance between describing the relevance of their results for clinicians while also staying within the bounds of their study.

Additionally, the discussion section should integrate the findings of the research study into previous literature. Did the researchers' findings confirm the results of previous studies? Did the results provide new information regarding a previously unexamined construct? How did this study advance the research in this area? What new questions are raised as a result of this study? A well-written discussion section should help you understand the constructs more fully, advise you as to how to use the findings in a practical way, and address the bigger picture.

Referring to the cybersex addiction study, we found that 10.3% of college students in our sample met criteria for cybersex addiction (indicating a problematic loss of control over online sexual activity). We found these results to be meaningful for several reasons: First, this percentage is larger than the prevalence rate of sexual addiction among the general adult population. Thus, there is reason to believe that the nature of college student development or characteristics of the collegiate setting increase the risk of cybersex addiction. Second, this substantial percentage of students with cybersex addiction has implications for clinical screening and training. Specifically, to what degree are college counselors assessing for problematic online sexual activity? Do they include items related to cybersex on their intake forms or mention it on their college counseling center website? Further, if compulsive cybersex is reported, to what extent do college counselors feel prepared to address the issue in counseling? What level of training have college counselors had pertaining to sex addiction, pornography addiction, and internet addiction? Third, our results were meaningful in that we found male college students were more likely to be addicted to cybersex than females were. How can we account for these gender differences? Is it merely biological, or are there societal norms that perpetuate addictive sexual behaviors among men? These considerations are presented in our discussion section, as we sought to apply our specific findings to the bigger picture of college student cybersex-related issues and describe practical implications for clinicians.

Finally, well-written discussion sections include a description of the study's limitations. Although no perfect study exists, you must review the limitations and determine whether they affect the practical significance of the findings. For example, a limitation may be the representativeness of the sample. Perhaps the researchers utilized convenience sampling methods and, as a result, 90% of the sample identified as female. How applicable are the findings to males? Are you able to generalize the findings across genders? Further, a potential limitation could be insufficient sample size. To what extent does this affect the accuracy of the statistical analyses? Is there a large enough sample to truly identify an effect where one exists? Moreover, perhaps scores on the study instruments yielded low Cronbach's alpha levels. Can readers rely on the interpretation of data derived from unreliable and inconsistent measures? It is important that you consider the impact of the limitations on the strength, rigor, and validity of the study.

As I mentioned earlier, my colleague and I noted several limitations in our study of collegiate cybersex addiction. Along with a lower-than-desired Cronbach's alpha level and a predominantly female, White, heterosexual sample, we also noted that the sample came from one large public university in the southwestern United States. Therefore, we are unable to conclude if the same levels of cybersex addiction would be found in a small, Catholic, private school in New England. The generalizability of the findings is an additional limitation. By listing these shortcomings, we hoped to be as transparent as possible so readers could come to their own conclusions about the trustworthiness and applicability of our results.

Table 2.2 Evaluating Existing Empirical Research

Manuscript Section	Evidence of a Strong Study
Introduction	• Summarize important existing literature (recent literature and seminal works) • Logical flow to purpose statement • Compelling need for the study ("of course this study is needed!") • Bias free (provide multiple perspectives and differing opinions)
Methods	• Appropriate sampling procedures (rationale for probability or nonprobability) • Participant demographics match population under study • Obtained required sample size • Reported evidence of instrument reliability (> .70) and validity (construct, content, or predictive) • Norming sample of instrument matched sampled in research study
Results	• Statistical analyses matched research questions • Reported statistical significance • Reported and interpreted effect size
Discussion	• Provided meaningful interpretation of results • Described practical implications of the findings • Stayed within the bounds of the study • Accurately described study limitations

Applying Existing Research to Practice

Now that you are familiar with how to access and critique existing research, the final step is to apply what you discover to your own clinical practice. Recall that Reynolds (2000) described the last two steps of the process of utilizing research as applying the findings to your clients and evaluating the outcomes. If the research article meets your standards of applicability (i.e., uses reliable and valid measures, matches your client's demographics, employs appropriate statistical analyses, yielded a desired effect size, detailed practical impacts, and identified limitations), you may choose to let the research influence your clinical work. Once implemented, you are obligated to then assess the outcome. Did the services you provided based on the research lead to the expected effects? If so, should you continue? If not, should you adjust? Client reports or standardized assessments can help you ascertain whether or not the research you implemented was effective for your unique client's case.

It is important to note that the integration of evidence-based practice should influence and not determine your clinical work. Indeed, research is supplemental to the clinical judgement of the counselor. Reynolds (2000) wrote, "clinicians should use their own clinical and professional experience in combination with the results of research based external evidence to make decisions about the care of their patients" (p. 258). Therefore, using both clinical judgement and evidence-based practice can help you provide the best care to your clients.

Ethical and effective client care should be your motivation to examine existing literature, because, let's face it, consuming research can be a daunting task. You will need to carve out sufficient time to identify, access, and read articles. You will need to think critically and evaluate whether the study meets your standards of applicability. Finally, after applying research to a particular client case, you must assess the outcomes to determine whether you should continue or adjust the services you provided. To facilitate the process and perhaps make it more enjoyable, consider forming a research group with other clinicians in your practice or local community. You can schedule regular times to meet and discuss current research, describe how you are applying results within your practice, and gain multiple perspectives regarding clinical outcomes.

Next Steps

This chapter provided an overview of accessing, critiquing, and applying existing literature in meaningful ways. There is much value and practicality in reviewing research in the counseling field. Perhaps you find yourself wrestling with an important question about the care of a client with a learning disability. Perhaps you are interested in starting a research project on client self-efficacy but do not know where to start. Perhaps you would like to begin a group counseling program in a school yet need to provide evidential support to the principal. Reviewing and evaluating existing literature can be a helpful strategy in each of these situations. As researchers continue to disseminate rigorous, relevant research and clinicians continue to consume and apply the research to their practice, the research–practice gap will diminish and the field of counseling will progress.

Resources for More Information

Peer-Reviewed Journal Articles

Balkin, R. S., & Sheperis, C. J. (2011). Evaluating and reporting statistical power in counseling research. *Journal of Counseling & Development, 89,* 268–272.

Cohen, J. (1992). A power primer. *Psychological Bulletin, 112,* 155–159. doi:10.1037/0033-2909.112.1.155

Lambie, G. W., Sias, S. M., Davis, L. M., Lawson, G., & Akos, P. (2008). A scholarly writing resource for counselor educators and their students. *Journal of Counseling & Development, 86,* 18–25.

Reynolds, S. (2000). Evidence based practice and psychotherapy research. *Journal of Mental Health. 9,* 257–266. doi:10.1080/713680248

Sink, C. A., & Mvududu, N. H. (2010). Statistical power, sampling, and effect sizes: Three keys to research relevancy. *Counseling outcome Research and Evaluation, 1,* 1–18. doi:10.1177/2150137810373613

Trusty, J., Thompson, B., & Petrocelli, J. V. (2004). Practical guide for reporting effect size in quantitative research in the Journal of Counseling & Development. *Journal of Counseling & Development, 82,* 107–110.

Books

Cohen, J. (1988). *Statistical power analysis for the behavioral sciences* (2nd ed.). New York, NY: Academic Press.

Creswell, J. W. (2014). *Research design: Qualitative, quantitative, and mixed methods approaches* (4th ed.). Thousand Oaks, CA: Sage Publications.

Field, A. (2013). *Discovering statistics using IBM SPSS statistics: And sex and drugs and rock 'n' roll* (4th ed.). Thousand Oaks, CA: Sage Publications.

Heppner, P. P., Wampold, B. E., Owen, J., Wang, K. T., & Thompson, M. N. (2016). *Research design in counseling* (4th ed.). Thousand Oaks, CA: Sage Publications.

Sue, D. W., & Sue, D. (2016). *Counseling the culturally diverse: Theory and practice* (7th ed.). Hoboken, NJ: John Wiley & Sons.

Questions for Further Review and Application

1. What clinical questions are you most interested in answering? What would be the best sources to consult when answering these questions?
2. Statistical significance is different than practical significance. How can you critique the practical significance of empirical research?
3. What are some characteristics of a sound, rigorous methods section? What errors may exist in the methodology of an empirical research study?

4. What is the difference between empirical and nonempirical literature? Provide examples of each type.
5. How would you describe a well-written, strong introduction section to an empirical research study? What would be the characteristics you would look for?
6. Are empirically supported treatments appropriate for all cultural groups? How do counselors ensure they are providing culturally sensitive treatments?

References

American Counseling Association. (2014). *ACA code of ethics.* Retrieved from www.counseling.org/knowledge-center/ethics

American Psychological Association. (2010a). *Publication manual of the American Psychological Association* (6th ed.). Washington, DC: Author.

American Psychological Association. (2010b). *Ethical principles of psychologists and code of conduct.* Retrieved from www.apa.org/ethics/code/principles.pdf

Baker, J. D. (2016). The purpose, process and methods of writing a literature review: Editorial. *Association of Operating Room Nurses: AORN Journal, 103,* 265–269. doi:10.1016/j.aorn.2016.01.016

Balkin, R. S. (2009). Publishing a conceptual manuscript: An editorial perspective. *Journal of Professional Counseling: Practice, Theory, & Research, 37,* 1–2.

Balkin, R. S., & Sheperis, C. J. (2011). Evaluating and reporting statistical power in counseling research. *Journal of Counseling & Development, 89,* 268–272.

Carnes, P., Green, B., & Carnes, S. (2010). The same yet different: Refocusing the Sexual Addiction Screening Test (SAST) to reflect orientation and gender. *Sexual Addiction & Compulsivity, 17,* 7–30. doi:10.1080/10720161003604084

Cohen, J. (1988). *Statistical power analysis for the behavioral sciences* (2nd ed.). New York, NY: Academic Press.

Creswell, J. W. (2014). *Research design: Qualitative, quantitative, and mixed methods approaches* (4th ed.). Thousand Oaks, CA: Sage Publications.

Giordano, A. L., & Cashwell, C. S. (2017). Cybersex addiction among college students: A prevalence study. *Sexual Addiction & Compulsivity, 24,* 47–57.

Guiffrida, D., Schwitzer, A. M., & Choate, L. H. (2006). Publishing in the journal of college counseling, part II: Comments on disseminating college counseling knowledge through professional issues and innovative practice articles. *Journal of College Counseling, 9,* 29–32.

Hays, D. G., & Singh, A. A. (2011). *Qualitative inquiry in clinical and educational settings.* New York, NY: Guilford Press.

Heppner, P. P., Wampold, B. E., Owen, J., Wang, K. T., & Thompson, M. N. (2016). *Research design in counseling* (4th ed.). Thousand Oaks, CA: Sage Publications.

La Roche, M. J., & Christopher, M. S. (2009). Changing paradigms from empirically supported treatment to evidence-based practice: A cultural perspective. *Professional Psychology: Research & Practice, 40,* 396–402. doi:10.1037/a0015240

Lambie, G. W., Sias, S. M., Davis, L. M., Lawson, G., & Akos, P. (2008). A scholarly writing resource for counselor educators and their students. *Journal of Counseling & Development, 86,* 18–25.

Merriam-Webster's Collegiate Dictionary (11th ed.). (2004). Springfield, MA: Merriam-Webster.

Murray, C. E. (2009). Diffusion of innovation theory: A bridge for the research-practice gap in counseling. *Journal of Counseling & Development, 87,* 108–116.

Nagayama Hall, G. C. (2001). Psychotherapy research with ethnic minorities: Empirical, ethnic, and conceptual issues. *Journal of Consulting and Clinical Psychology, 69,* 502–510. doi:10.1037//0022–006x.69.3.502

National Association of Social Workers. (2008). *Code of ethics.* Retrieved from www.socialworkers.org/pubs/code/code.asp

Norcross, J. C., & Wampold, B. E. (2011). Evidence-based therapy relationships: Research conclusions and clinical practices. *Psychotherapy, 48,* 98–102. doi:10.1037/a0022161

Pautasso, M. (2013). Ten simple rules for writing a literature review. *PLoS Computational Biology, 9,* 1–4. doi:10/1371/journal.pcbi.1003149

Reynolds, S. (2000). Evidence based practice and psychotherapy research. *Journal of Mental Health. 9,* 257–266. doi:10.1080/713680248

Roysircar, G. (2009). Evidence-based practice and its implications for culturally sensitive treatment. *Journal of Multicultural Counseling & Development, 32,* 66–83.

Sink, C. A., & Mvududu, N. H. (2010). Statistical power, sampling, and effect sizes: Three keys to research relevancy. *Counseling Outcome Research and Evaluation, 1,* 1–18. doi:10.1177/2150137810373613

Sue, D., & Sue, D. M. (2008). *Foundations of counseling and psychotherapy: Evidence-based practices for a diverse society.* Hoboken, NJ: John Wiley & Sons.

Swiggart, W., Feurer, I. D., Samenow, C., Delmonico, D. L., & Spickard, W. A. (2008). Sexual Boundary Violation Index: A validation study. *Sexual Addiction & Compulsivity, 15,* 176–190. doi:10.1080/10720160882055939

Trusty, J., Thompson, B., & Petrocelli, J. V. (2004). Practical guide for reporting effect size in quantitative research in the Journal of Counseling & Development. *Journal of Counseling & Development, 82,* 107–110.

Watts, R. E. (2011). Developing a conceptual article for publication in counseling journals. *Journal of Counseling & Development, 89,* 308–312.

Wester, K. L. (2011). Publishing ethical research: A step by step overview. *Journal of Counseling & Development, 89,* 301–307.

Wester, K. L., Borders, L. D., Boul, S., & Horton, E. (2013). Research quality: Critique of quantitative articles in the Journal of Counseling & Development. *Journal of Counseling & Development, 91,* 280–290.

3 Research Ethics in Practice

Kelly L. Wester, Carrie A. Wachter Morris,
Jordan L. Austin, & Shreya Vaishnav

We would guess that throughout your clinical training experiences, various aspects of ethics have been drilled into your head—doing no harm to the client, beneficence, engaging in effective practice, and even aspects about dual relationships and bartering with your client. However, did you know that almost all mental health professions have a code of ethics specific to research? You might have, but these are often discussed less frequently or skimmed over. Yet research influences our practice by informing us about what is considered to be evidence-based or empirically supported. Research helps to provide new, updated information in order to move each specific discipline forward, and, truthfully, research *should* influence your practice on a daily basis.

While we all know that ethical behavior is important, what exactly is research ethics? Research ethics is the "study or science of right and wrong—of what one ought to do when confronted with conflicting values or obligations" (Steneck, n.d., p. 240). It is deciding right versus wrong when it comes to engaging in any aspect of research at any level. As you read in Chapter 1, research can happen at multiple levels, including consuming existing research, applying what you have consumed, and engaging in or conducting research.

Practitioners should be competent, and thus ethical, in their research behaviors—with the minimal level of this being the ability to read and critique existing research (Wester & Borders, 2014). This is tied to staying up to date on the current practices, questions, interventions, and treatments you should be offering, as well as the knowledge that has been generated about various diagnoses, symptoms, and behaviors that impact human beings in terms of daily functioning. Consumption of research is important to be able to provide up-to-date, empirically supported, informative interventions to clients and students with whom you interact in your practice. Frankly, to not read and consume current research does your clients a disservice.

Another level of doing research as a practitioner is to *apply* what you are reading. In order to do this ethically, however, you need to know *how* to read and critique the current research you are consuming, as well as how to make ethical and practical decisions on how to apply it. Just because something is published doesn't mean that it is good, nor does it mean that it applies directly to your clients or students. The information on how to read and critique existing research is covered in Chapter 2, so we wouldn't recommend skipping that chapter!

At another level, research ethics also applies to *conducting* research—whether that be on a larger scale or within your own practice, even with one person. We are going to focus a little more on how research ethics applies to conducting research in this chapter, although ethics would apply to consumption, application, and engagement in research.

Okay, so let's jump off the soapbox temporarily about how ethical practitioners need to engage in research at the various levels (but don't worry, we will get back to that again!) and move into exactly what research ethics are when it comes to conducting research. We'll start with a case study that we will refer to throughout as we walk through various aspects of research ethics.

Zeke comes into your office. He reports being angry and frustrated, has yelled at others, punched walls, and ultimately been difficult to be around given his mood and behavior. When asking additional questions, you also find that he has had past suicidal ideation, but nothing current and no intentions to hurt or kill himself. You also find that others have been bullying him. Other students have been making repeated jabs at him personally in ways that have made him question his confidence and efficacy in his daily tasks and activities, as well as feeling less clear about his interpersonal relationships.

Most mental health practitioners have ethical codes that state, in working with Zeke, you need to ensure that you are effective and knowledgeable in what you are offering in terms of interventions and treatment. Mental health practitioner ethical codes include, but are not limited to, the American Counseling Association (ACA, 2014), American Psychological Association (APA, 2016), and the National Association of Social Workers (NASW, 2017). These are just some of the organizations that require you to abide by their ethical codes if you are a member. But other professional organizations, licensure boards, and divisions of larger organizations include their own ethical codes as well. Let's step back to the basic level of research—consumption. It is your ethical obligation to know how to provide Zeke services. That is, what is the most up-to-date knowledge that we have on bullying, anger, and potentially depression along with suicidal ideation? We know some of the outcomes and consequences of bullying based on the research, and we also know that while depression has specific symptoms noted in the *Diagnostic and Statistical Manual of Mental Disorders*, researchers have noted a connection between anger and depression (Busch, 2009). We also know various behavioral and cognitive behavioral treatments have been found to be effective in working with individuals who exhibit depression (e.g., Sturmey, 2009), as well as coping with the negative effects from being targeted with bullying behaviors (Association for Behavioral and Cognitive Therapies, 2017). However, the use of any of these treatments or interventions should depend on a critique of what you are reading. How would the treatment differ if your client was 5 years old versus 17 years old versus 39 years old? We would assume that treatment would be quite different, and the research would support that as well. Additionally, what is the setting that you are working in? Some settings allow for manualized, long-term treatment, while other settings do not (e.g., brief inpatient crisis treatment, school settings). So research *consumption* is where to begin when you consider what you are offering to clients or students as effective forms of treatment. Ethically, you would apply only what is most relevant.

Now let's get more into conducting research within your practice. In Zeke's case, maybe you have scoured the literature and not found something that really fits his presenting symptoms and concerns, or maybe you have applied the various treatments and interventions without success. Maybe, through your years of experience, you have begun to formulate a new form of treatment that you have engaged in, combining or integrating different techniques or theories you have learned along the way. You think (based on anecdotal information from previous clients) that this "new treatment" works. In all of these cases, it may be time to conduct your own research to truly determine what works based on data rather than anecdotal information or simply your perception.

As you will read throughout this text, research can look different in terms of the various methodologies and designs you can select. Selecting a research design that will actually answer your question is one ethical consideration (Wester, 2011). Every step of the research process, from idea inception through methodological design and implementation of procedures all the way into publication and disseminating your results, entails ethical decisions (Wester, 2011). Bersoff and Bersoff (2008) even suggested that ethical decision making is a methodological issue, as you need to make decisions related to procedures throughout the entire research process that will often have ethical considerations. Given all this, let's step back for a minute and talk about research integrity, which is an overarching umbrella for research ethics. From there, we will get into more detail about which ethical principles are important to follow when conducting research.

Research Integrity

You are a member of how many professional organizations? One? Three? More than three? Take a moment and consider. Now that you have a list in your mind, does each of these organizations have an ethical code? Do you know? If they do, are you aware of the ethical code of *each* organization and the indicated details around what you need to do when confronted with difficult situations in which right or wrong decisions could be made? In order to practice with integrity, you need to abide by all of the ethical codes of organizations that you are a paying member of, affiliated with, or employed by. Now take a moment and consider each of these organizations again—do their ethical codes include research ethics? In the same sense of using ethical codes within practice, knowledge of your organizations' research ethics is important in order to engage in research with integrity.

As stated, you need to abide by the ethical code of conduct for any professional organization of which you are a member. These codes likely include ethics governing both practice and research. Research integrity is defined as "a commitment to intellectual honesty and personal responsibility" (Institute of Medicine, 2002), in which you adhere to rules, regulations, guidelines, and commonly accepted professional codes or norms (Office of Research Integrity, 2003) of the organizations to which you belong and affiliate. Steneck (n.d.) specifically states this when talking about engaging in responsible conduct of research, or

> conducting research in ways that fulfill professional responsibilities of researchers, as defined by their professional organizations, the institutions for which they work, and, when relevant, the government and public.

We would make the argument that all research you would conduct is relevant to the public given that individuals within the public are the clients to whom you are providing services—whether they be in outpatient or inpatient, hospital, medical, or K–16 settings. Each individual you work with and their families could benefit or be harmed by the research you (or other mental health professionals) conduct.

When examining the various organizational ethical codes provided by ACA, APA, and NASW, they are more similar than they are different. Each one stresses the need to ensure participant safety, to allow for informed consent of participants to partake in research on their own volition, and to do no harm. Each also mentions aspects of publication, confidentiality, and ensuring engagement in responsible conduct of research. While each of these ethical codes goes beyond the basic principles required of conducting human-subject research, let's take a moment and focus on the minimal three principals that should always be considered when conducting research with humans: (1) respect for persons, (2) beneficence, and (3) justice. Each of these principles is inherent in the Belmont Report, which is considered one of the cornerstone documents of ethical procedures to assist in the protection of the rights of individuals participating in research.

Belmont Report

The Belmont Report was developed by the National Commission for the Protection of Human Subjects of Biomedical and Behavioral Research in 1979 due to multiple atrocities in how human beings were treated as research subjects. The Belmont Report provided federal regulations to protect the rights of individuals that were, unfortunately, not being protected by researchers. Take a moment and consider any research studies that you have been a human subject in—do you recall getting informed-consent documents telling you about the study and what would be required of you, along with any potential risks that could be a result of participating in the research study? Did you receive any incentives? Did you feel coerced to participate? Hopefully the answers to these questions reflect the pillars of ethical research of nonmaleficence, beneficence, and autonomy. Yes, you received an informed consent detailing what you were being asked to do, as well as the risks of participating, with an emphasis on your right to withdraw from the study at any time. Maybe you received incentives, but in the long run hopefully these incentives were not so bountiful that you felt coerced to participate in the research, even if you did not want to. These are all considerations that you need to think through when you are designing and engaging in research. Let's take a minute to walk through some pivotal moments in the history of research to determine *how* we even got to a place, decades ago, of needing regulations around engaging in research—and then we will talk through how these regulations impact you on a day-to-day or study-to-study level.

Historically, researchers executed studies involving human beings that led to suffering, pain, and death. In these studies, you will find that various components of beneficence, respect for persons, and justice are missing. In each of these studies, the behavior of the researchers and the subsequent consequences and harm that came to the participants is what led to the principles noted in the Belmont Report, and ultimately the protocols in which institutional review boards (IRBs) use to evaluate research today.

Nazi Medical War Crimes

The Nazi Medical War Crimes is one of the most infamous, horrendous research studies that is publicly known. In World War II, Nazi physicians performed medical experiments on thousands of prisoners in concentration camps. Their goal was to better understand how the human body reacts to various realities, such as viruses, extreme temperatures and conditions, and the injection or digestion of poisons, gasoline, and other contaminants. The results of these studies were suffering and death for the individuals who were participants. They were prisoners, and not one participant was provided with the ability to consent to participate in these studies. Rather, they were forced to participate. Ultimately, the Nazi physicians were tried for crimes against humanity; however, that did not undo the cruelty and deaths that had already been caused.

Tuskegee Syphilis Study

This study was one of the longest-running studies in the United States. The Tuskegee Syphilis Study was conducted for 40 years, spanning from 1932 to 1972. The goal of this study was to specifically explore the impact of syphilis on the human body. However, many horrific acts occurred within this study, including but not limited to lack of informed consent, deceiving participants about the nature of the study, not informing participants of risks of participation, and failing to disband the study once known risks emerged. Ultimately, the researchers of this study enrolled 600 Black males, 400 of whom were infected with the syphilis virus and 200 who were considered controls. None of these 600 males was provided with an informed consent about this study, and, actually, they were provided with misinformation that they were being provided with "free treatment." While they received what was perceived to be treatment, it had nothing to do with alleviating or curing the syphilis virus, and so this information was misleading to the participants. By 1936 and within 4 years of starting this study, it was clear from the data that the 400 males with syphilis had a greater number and severity of symptoms and complications compared to the males without syphilis—therefore, the researchers already knew risks existed without treatment. Even armed with this information, neither did they inform participants nor did they alter or implement treatment. Within 10 years of the start of the study, it was obvious that the death rate for participants with syphilis was at least double that of the controls, yet nothing was done at this point *and* the study continued until 1972—an additional 30 years. To make matters worse, penicillin was introduced in the 1940s, but researchers of the Tuskegee Syphilis Study did not inform participants or provide penicillin as a treatment option for them.

Willowbrook Study

In the 1950s and 1960s, a study was conducted in the Willowbrook state school. This school was originally developed for children who were "mentally defective." The goals of this study were to explore the effects of hepatitis on kids within a controlled environment. Parents who tried to enroll their children in the school were informed that the school had limited spaces available and that the only way to enroll a child in the school was to consent to allow the child to be injected with the hepatitis virus. Parents were provided no other information other than statements that assuaged any fears by stating that all children would end up with the virus anyway given the crowded and unclean nature of the school facilities. The information provided to parents could be incorrectly deemed "consent" in some ways, but it ultimately included misinformation and inaccurate details. Furthermore, it was coercive in nature, as the school did have vacancies but was only admitting children of parents who agreed to allow their children to be injected with hepatitis. Additionally, parents were not provided with information about the long-term chronic liver disease that would develop later in life due to the virus.

Jewish Chronic Disease Hospital Study

While the Tuskegee Syphilis Study was continuing, in 1963, researchers in the Jewish Chronic Disease Hospital in New York began a study to determine if the human body could reject cancer cells or if, due to other medical illnesses or ailments, fighting off cancer cells was improbable. The researchers, therefore, asked participants if they would like to engage in a treatment intervention without indicating what this treatment intervention was or the risks associated with it. Ultimately this "treatment intervention" was injecting live cancer cells into participants' bodies. There was no informed consent and no written documentation. Now it can be noted that written documentation for medical procedures was not common in this era. When confronted with cruelties performed on the patients, the researchers stood by their actions, indicating that they did not inform patients about the live cancer cells because they believed it would frighten patients. This behavior and belief maps onto what Bersoff and Bersoff (2008) suggested as a reason why ethical breaches in research occur—when researchers see human participants as a means to an end and no longer view them as individual people.

The accumulation of the horrors that each of these studies created led to the Belmont Report. The Belmont Report outlines the three ethical principles that all researchers should follow in the design and follow-through of their studies. These principles include respect for persons, beneficence, and justice for all participants. So what do these actually mean?

Respect for Persons

Respect for persons entails two components: (1) autonomy and (2) protections for vulnerable populations. Any individual who is being considered as a participant for a research study needs to be treated as an autonomous agent in their own right (National Institute of Health [NIH], 2002), meaning that they have the ability to make decisions for themselves and that their thoughts, opinions, and choices should never be ignored, obstructed, or disrespected by the researcher. Additionally, certain populations, such as prisoners, inpatient populations, children, the elderly, individuals with mental incapacities, and even pregnant women (due to their unborn children) are considered vulnerable populations. Thus, special caution must occur to make sure steps are taken within the consent process to respect the rights of these individuals who may not have as much freedom as other individuals to decline to participate in a research study.

How does this play out in research? First and foremost, the idea of autonomy and protections occurs within the informed consent. With the informed consent process, you are providing your clients, students, or research participants with enough information for them to make an informed decision about whether they would like to participate in this study. To make an informed decision, individuals need to know what they will be asked to do in the study (e.g., complete survey questionnaires about a particular topic, press buttons, engage in exercise, receive a clinical treatment, take medication), how long this process may take (e.g., 15 minutes, 1 hour a week for 12 weeks), and the risks of participation (e.g., emotional distress, pain, embarrassment, illness). Individuals should also be made aware of whether the information they provide will be confidential or even anonymous or whether the information can be known by people outside the study (e.g., in publications, presentations, other clinicians). Knowing this information allows for individuals to make an informed choice as to whether they believe that the risks of participating outweigh the benefits of participating.

Respect for persons also includes ensuring that participation in research is voluntary and that individuals can withdraw at any time. Additionally, it is important that no coercion is occurring—or unjust persuasion to participate in the study. Coercion is dependent on the situation, the population, and the context. For example, you can see how incarcerated individuals are a vulnerable population—do they have the ability to voluntarily make a decision to participate in the study, or are they forced to do so because the study is being implemented prison-wide? Context can lead to coercion, or lack of ability to decline participation in a study. Incentives can do the same thing. For example, let's suggest that we ask you to take part in a study, and we offer you $20. Would this entice you to participate? You may say "yes" . . . or maybe your response is "it depends." It may depend on whether we are asking you to answer a packet of questionnaires that may take you 30 minutes or if we instead indicated that we needed you to drive to a specific location 40 minutes away one time per week for 4 weeks. We may even ask you to ingest a pill. You can see how in one case an incentive may be enticing—although not enticing enough to be coercive—while in another scenario it may not be worth it at all. Take this same $20 incentive, and now imagine a family who is struggling to make ends meet or put food on the table for their children. This same $20 might become more coercive, as it meets a life need that isn't otherwise met. You can see how this family, as an example, might engage in more risk-taking behaviors in a study for the same $20 incentive. Studies have resulted in participant death due to the nature of the incentive or the perceived lack of choice (Wolf, 2009).

Let's apply this idea of respect for persons to Zeke, considering that you are wanting to collect data and study whether your "new treatment" is effective in decreasing symptoms of depression and anger. Zeke is a client with whom you would like to not only apply the treatment but also begin collecting information and data. In the case of research, you can actually apply the treatment or intervention and never collect data—and as long as you are abiding by your professional organizations' ethical codes of providing effective treatments and doing no harm to your client, you can continue to offer this treatment. Collecting data from Zeke, however, adds a new layer. You now need not only to ask him if he would like to participate in the treatment, but you also need to ask him if he is willing to participate in the research side of this by providing you with data (e.g., answering questionnaires, providing information through interviews in your sessions, allowing you to use your behavioral observations). So you need to provide Zeke with informed consent to participate in research that is separate from his consent to engage in treatment with you generally. He needs to know:

1. That this is a research study, which is separate from the actual treatment.
2. That his choice to provide you with data is voluntary, and that he would be able to receive the treatment even if he said "no."

3. What he would need to do (e.g., participate in treatment, answer questionnaires five times throughout treatment) if he decided to participate.
4. That he can withdraw from providing you with study data at any point in time without penalty (e.g., fees wouldn't go up, treatment would still be offered).
5. What the risks are to participate (e.g., would information be released, confidentiality questioned, would he not receive another form of treatment, would he experience emotional distress in answering questions).
6. What the benefits are to participate in the research (e.g., would he receive free treatment, would he gain anything—incentive not included).
7. Are there incentives to participate (e.g., typically defined as monetary or material in nature but could be other things as well)?

Once he has all of this information, Zeke can make an informed choice of whether to participate. This is all, of course, assuming that Zeke is considered an adult who can make decisions on his own, and he is not a member of what is considered to be a vulnerable population. If, for example, he is under the age of 18, he is considered to be a child; you not only have to gain parental consent with all of the information provided earlier, you still need to gain Zeke's assent as well—and talk to him using developmentally appropriate vocabulary. Additionally, if Zeke was residing within a prison, then you have different considerations to make sure he is not coerced into the study. Those might include that this study was not being inflicted on him as a prisoner because of "easy access" to him and that it was a study that truly needed a prison population to answer the question.

Beneficence

The ethical principle of beneficence refers to the responsibility that you have as a researcher to "do good." Essentially, is the result of your study going to enhance knowledge or add quality information to the topic or discipline area? We stated that, ethically, research should be enhancing and expanding our knowledge within our (or other) disciplines, and thus, each study should have an element of social validity. Rosenthal (2008) went further to state that doing research with no social validity and that doesn't lead to influential outcomes is ultimately unethical. What he means by this is that the risks and cost to participants in terms of their time, money, and energy expended to participate in this study outweigh the benefits (or lack thereof) to the knowledge gained. We would hope that if you are conducting research, you have an intention behind it—such as wanting to know if you are effective, desiring to gain understanding about the impact of a new treatment method or technique, or seeking to provide better comprehension about a particular symptom, behavior, or diagnosis.

Under the principle of beneficence, you need to consider all aspects of your study prior to even implementing it. This means considering each decision well in advance before asking your clients or students to participate. You have to consider and plan for all possible scenarios that might occur and the risks that individuals might experience. According to the American Counseling Association (2014), as a researcher, you are responsible for designing, planning, conducting, and reporting research.

Let's apply this to Zeke. The intervention and engagement in research needs to have minimal interference in Zeke's life and daily functioning, including in the treatment you are offering. While you believe you are offering an effective treatment to him, you have to acknowledge if there is (a) a better treatment out there for his diagnosis, symptoms, or behavior, or even for Zeke specifically, or (b) if you realize in the middle of treatment this is not working for Zeke, you need to abandon your research study with Zeke and offer him a treatment that might be more effective for him.

While beneficence may seem to be common sense, the difficulty with it is there is no "right way" to determine if the benefits outweigh the risks for each participant, as each person is different. Beneficence tends to be subjective to some extent. However, it should be noted that this judgment should not simply be made one time in the research process (e.g., beginning). Rather, this evaluation should be continual throughout the process, and it should be based on each individual. Some have even questioned whether those providing a service should be the evaluators of that service (Coyle & Olsen, 2005), suggesting that bias may be an inherent flaw in making beneficence judgment calls. Wanting the data to demonstrate a positive outcome could potentially lead to coercion or ignoring of negative outcomes. It is believed that you can conduct research on your own practice, but you need to be cautious or pull in a collaborator who does not have a conflict of interest in the study to help you see when you may be violating ethical boundaries.

Justice

The principle of justice deals with objectively evaluating fairness to participants of the research study. Justice lends itself to inquiring if the benefits outweigh the risks in the study. This does not just mean outweighing them generally but ultimately asking the question of "who bears the burden of risks and who receives the benefits?" Risks include threats to participant safety, interfering with day-to-day life, the methods used for sampling or selecting participants, and ensuring participants receive what they are promised (i.e., incentives, benefits of the study, interventions and treatments, outcomes). In this principle, if the participant experiences all of the risks and none of the benefits, then justice does not exist—even if the benefits would be expanding knowledge in the field. Not all participants may experience a benefit in the immediate future, but the risks should not drastically outweigh the benefits. An example may be that participating in a 30-minute survey about depression with no immediate benefits (e.g., no free intervention or training, no immediate outcome) may not have a large differential for someone to participate when comparing participant risks to benefits. The risks here are likely not high. However, in an extreme example, being injected with the hepatitis virus with no benefit does lack justice.

Other aspects of injustice that can result in a study would be to claim that participants would receive $5 upon completion, and somehow one participant does not receive this $5. In this case, injustice has occurred. Another aspect to consider is whether traveling to your office for 1 hour per week for 12 weeks is even feasible for a client, and, if not, then the client's life may be impacted by participating in the study. Finally, considering who to include in your study is important, as is how you ask the questions or collect information. For example, in the case example study exploring this new treatment, is there a reason why you may include Zeke in your study, but you may not include Lauren (an 18-year-old White female) or Micah (a 47-year-old Black male)? The National Institute of Health (2002) speaks to the selection of human subjects, stating that selection of research participants needs to be equitable. In conducting your study, you need to consider from whom you need information (e.g., age group, sex, gender) based on who the particular study is designed for with the knowledge that no population should be overburdened to participate in research without benefits, and no population should be excluded without good reason (NIH, 2002). Additionally, no person should be a research participant unwillingly, nor should individuals be selected solely due to convenience and access. Justice (though respect and beneficence can be argued here as well) also includes the types of questions and information you collect from individuals. Various organizations have developed competencies and standards of care when researching marginalized or vulnerable populations. One recent example of this is the Standards of Care for Research with Participants Who Identify as LGBTQ+ (Griffith et al., 2017), which was developed by individuals affiliated with the Association for Lesbian, Gay, Bisexual, and Transgender Issues in Counseling and the Association for Assessment and Research in Counseling.

Institutional Review Board

This is a lot of information to remember and balance when conducting research. That said, we cannot overstate the importance of thinking through all of these things from the beginning and considering them not only when you are developing your idea but also when you are designing it and carrying it out. The good news is that most researchers do not have to do this on their own. Checks and balances exist in most systems—at least when you are first designing and proposing your study. All institutions that have any federal funding typically have (or have access to) an institutional review board (IRB). An IRB is a group of individuals (typically around five or more) from various disciplines that assists with ensuring respect, beneficence, and justice of all human participants by examining and evaluating your study before you can conduct it (Leedy & Ormrod, 2005). Their task is to weigh the risks versus the benefits to determine how your client, student, or participant will be directly impacted. The IRB will examine the safeguards you have put into place regarding the risks that you have identified, and the board will determine if there are risks inherent in your study that you haven't identified. They will explore the way in which you are gaining informed consent to determine if this meets all respects for persons in terms of autonomy, along with taking into account any vulnerable populations, oversampling of populations, or inappropriate exclusion of other populations. But what happens if you are working with an agency that does not have federal funding or access to an immediate IRB? There are other ways to make sure you have oversight. For a fee, commercial IRBs do exist, or you can partner with another researcher who is at an institution with access to an existing IRB (Rice, 2008). Most all schools, universities, and hospitals have IRBs within their organization and would have easy access.

You may think that with the creation of the Belmont Report and the oversight of the IRB, research is free from misconduct. Or even if there is occasional misconduct, all research follows the guiding principles of respect, beneficence, and justice. Unfortunately, you would be incorrect in those assumptions. In a study exploring counseling professionals (including educators, students, and practitioners), 24% to 45% of participants self-reported the likelihood that they would deviate from the responsible conduct of research with specific behaviors (Wester et al., 2008). More specifically, 24% reported they would be likely to use deception to persuade individuals to participate in their study, while 4% reported they would be likely to report false data to gain grant funding. In another study (Wester et al., 2010), 7% of counseling practitioners reported they wouldn't get parental consent before approaching a vulnerable population of children to participate in a study, and 3% reported publishing before removing identifying information about participants. These irreparable actions violate client confidentiality and research participant rights.

In another recent study funded by the National Institutes of Health, researchers explored babies born prematurely at 24 to 27 weeks. At this preterm birth, babies are typically at risk for death or eye disease. This study was designed to divide babies into two groups: one group receiving higher amounts of oxygen and the second receiving lower amounts of oxygen. This study resulted in the death of 221 out of 1,163 babies across both groups (Macklin, 2015). While the study was not found to be unethical, the Office of Human Research Protections determined that the informed consent documents lacked information about the consequences of using varied levels of oxygen with this at-risk population, which resulted in the inability of the parents to make an informed choice.

Another recent case that resulted in legal allegations is the example of *Taus v. Loftus*. In this example, a researcher had produced—with client permission—video recordings of her as a child, again in her late teens, and finally as an adult. These videos revealed the process of repressed memory that can occur in the case of child sexual abuse. The video recordings had been used, with client permission, in educational training and had been written about professionally in peer-refereed articles, with the original authors removing all identifying information. However, another researcher (Loftus), who had a desire to combat the statements behind repressed memories from the initial author, hired a private detective to dig into and collect information about the client's personal life and history (Kluemper, 2014). While Loftus was not the clinician of the client, she was in the role of a researcher. Others have reflected on the role that Loftus had—given that she was not the client's clinician and thus was not bound by the same ethics of confidentiality of mental health practitioners (Koocher, 2014). What can be determined, though, is that Loftus did not abide by the basic principles of respect, beneficence, and justice. Ultimately, she never asked for permission to dig into the life of this client by utilizing a private detective and to then disclose personal and identify information in the public domain through presentations and publications. Additionally, the data was flawed, and only one side was provided without doing a thorough unbiased analysis (Koocher, 2014), thus inhibiting beneficence. Only harm came from the outcome of this research without a quality product.

Ultimately, the takeaway message we have for you is that research ethics must be considered from the start of your idea and should be considered throughout the entire research process. It should underscore the design of your study and procedural decisions, as well as the analyses and dissemination of your research findings. When you are both the mental health provider and researcher, an added layer is required to ensure that your client or student always receives adequate and ethical care; your research study does not supersede this care. This may look similar in some instances and different in others when it comes to qualitative and quantitative research designs, but ultimately, you should always consider the three overarching ethical principles of *respect for persons*, *beneficence*, and *justice*.

Resources for More Information

Peer-Reviewed Journal Articles

Wester, K. L. (2011). Publishing ethical research: A step-by-step overview. *Journal of Counseling and Development, 89*, 301–307.

Wester, K. L., & Borders, L. D. (2014). Research competencies in counseling: A Delphi study. *Journal of Counseling & Development, 92*, 447–458.

Books and Other Resources

*Your discipline's, organization's, or place of employment's ethical codes regarding research.

Ethics in Mental Health Research. (n.d.). *Ethics in mental health research.* Retrieved November 8, 2017, from http://emhr.net/

Office of Research Integrity. (2000). *Office of research integrity policies.* Retrieved November 9, 2017, from https://ori.hhs.gov/ori-policies

Wester, K. L. (2005). *Conducting research responsibly: Cases for counseling professionals. Handbook and DVD.* Greensboro, NC: NBCC.

Questions for Further Review and Application

1. What are the three main principles for ethically conducting research?
2. What is the committee that typically has oversight to assess the risk versus benefits to research participants?
3. What is the reason the Belmont Report was created?
4. When considering conducting research in your own practice, what are some of the questions you need to consider in order to make sure you are abiding by the three ethical principles?

References

American Counseling Association. (2014). *ACA code of ethics.* Alexandria, VA: Author.

American Psychological Association. (2016). Revision of ethical standard 3.04 of the Ethical Principles of Psychologists and Code of Conduct (2002, as amended 2010). *American Psychologist, 71,* 900.

Association for Behavioral and Cognitive Therapies. (2017). *Bullying.* Retrieved November 9, 2017, from www.abct.org/Information/?m=mInformation&fa=fs_BULLYING

Bersoff, D. M., & Bersoff, D. N. (2008). Ethical perspectives in clinical research. In D. N. Bersoff (Ed.), *Ethical conflicts in psychology* (pp. 387–389). Washington, DC: American Psychological Association.

Busch, F. N. (2009). Anger and depression. *Advanced in Psychiatric Treatment, 15,* 271–278.

Coyle, A., & Olsen, C. (2005). Research in therapeutic settings: Ethical considerations. In R. Tribe & J. Morrissey (Eds.), *Handbook of professional and ethical practice for psychologists, counsellors, and psychotherapists* (pp. 249–262). New York, NY: Brunner-Routledge.

Griffith, C., Akers, W., Dispenza, F., Luke, M., Farmer, L. B., Watson, J. C., Davis, R. J., & Goodrich, K. M. (2017). *Standards of care for research with participants who identify as LGBTQ+.* Retrieved November 14, 2017, from www.algbtic.org/standards-of-care.html

Institute of Medicine. (2002). *Integrity in scientific research: Creating an environment that promotes responsible conduct.* Washington, DC: National Academy of Sciences Press.

Kluemper, N. S. (2014). Published case reports: One woman's account of having her confidentiality violated. *Journal of Interpersonal Violence, 29,* 3232–3244.

Koocher, G. P. (2014). Research ethics and private harms. *Journal of Interpersonal Violence, 29,* 3267–3276.

Leedy, P. D., & Ormrod, J. E. (2005). *Practical research: Planning and designing.* Upper Saddle River, NJ: Pearson.

Macklin, R. (2015). Can one do good medical ethics without principles? *Journal of Medical Ethics: Journal of Institute of Medical Ethics, 41,* 75–78.

National Association of Social Workers. (2017). *Code of ethics of the National Association of Social Workers.* Washington, DC: Author.

National Commission for the Protection of Human Subjects of Biomedical and Behavioral Research. (1979). *The Belmont Report: Ethical principles and guidelines for the protection of human subjects of research.* Retrieved from http://ohsr.od.nih.gov/guidelines/belmont.html#gob3

National Institute of Health. (2002). *Responsible research: A systems approach to protecting research participants.* Washington DC: National Academies Press.

Rice, T. W. (2008). How to do human subjects research if you do not have an institutional review board. *Respiratory Care, 53,* 1362–1367.

Rosenthal, R. (2008). Science and ethics in conducting, analyzing, and reporting psychological research. In D. N. Bersoff (Ed.), *Ethical conflicts in psychology* (pp. 390–397). Washington, DC: American Psychological Association.

Steneck, N. H. (n.d.). *ORI introduction to the responsible conduct of research.* Office of Research Integrity. Retrieved November 9, 2017, from https://ori.hhs.gov/ori-introduction-responsible-conduct-research

Steneck, N. H. (2006). Fostering integrity in research: Definitions, current knowledge, and future directions. *Science and Engineering Ethics, 12,* 53–74.

Sturmey, P. (2009). Behavioral activation is an evidence-based treatment for depression. *Behavior Modification, 33,* 818–829.

Wester, K. L., Willse, J., & Davis, M. S. (2008). The Responsible Conduct of Research Measure: The initial development and pilot study. *Accountability in Research, 15,* 87–104.

Wester, K. L., Willse, J., & Davis, M. (2010). Psychological climate, stress, and research integrity among counselor educators. *Counselor Education and Supervision, 50,* 39–55.

Wolf, L. E. (2009). IRB policies regarding finder's fees and role conflicts in recruiting research participants. *Ethics and Human Research, 31,* 14–19.

4 Evaluating and Designing Surveys

W. Bradley McKibben

Throughout this book, you are exposed to a variety of methodologies that can be used to answer important research questions. Many of the methodologies discussed in this book, including quantitative and experimental designs, may utilize surveys as part of the study. Have you ever thought about where these surveys come from, how a survey is created, or whether a survey is actually a good one? There is an old saying that a worker is only as good as one's tools, and this holds true for survey-based research as well. The conclusions we draw from responses to a survey are only as good as the extent to which those responses are valid and reliable. The purpose of this chapter is to familiarize you with the process of designing a survey so that you have the tools to develop your own survey, should the need arise. You will learn how surveys are typically used in counseling research, what surveys are designed to do, and the steps you need to take in designing a survey. Because this chapter merely scratches the surface of survey design, the chapter will conclude with additional resources that can further guide you through the process.

Introduction to Survey Design

Surveys are a common tool that practitioners and other helping professionals use to gain information about human behavior, thoughts, emotions, personality traits, and more. Whereas researchers in natural sciences such as biology, chemistry, or physics can observe and study physical phenomena more directly, behavioral scientists such as counselors, social workers, or psychologists tend to study occurrences that are difficult to observe directly because they exist in the psychological realm rather than the physical world. For example, a chemist can study the molecular composition of cells through carefully organized experiments and observations. Because a cell is a physical object, the cell and its components can be studied directly. Now, consider the cognitive-behaviorally oriented practitioner who is interested in negative thought patterns. Many people likely would agree that such thought patterns exist, but they cannot be observed directly in the physical world. We cannot observe negative thought patterns in a vial or under a microscope.

A fundamental way that behavioral scientists come to understand psychological phenomena is by understanding how people express and experience them. By understanding people's experiences and expressions of psychological phenomena, we develop and test theories that describe and explain the human condition (e.g., behaviors, thoughts, emotions). There also might be differing definitions or theories of such phenomena, depending upon who you ask. These phenomena, often referred to as constructs, can be defined in ways that we can systematically study them.

Constructs, theories, and ideas about the human condition are often where surveys come into play. In the behavioral sciences, where counseling lies, the survey is one of our microscopes or vials, metaphorically speaking, to measure aspects of the human condition not directly observable by physical means. A survey allows us to gather information from people about their experiences, expressions of, reactions to, or opinions about a construct of interest. A construct is how we operationally define something we are interested in knowing more about and need to measure, such as negative self-talk, happiness, or depression. A well-designed survey allows a practitioner to get as close as possible to measuring the construct of interest in a valid and reliable way. And it is this point, the idea of measuring a construct as purely as possible, that drives the design of any new survey.

When to Design a Survey

A good litmus test of when it is time to design a survey is when you have a question you want to answer or a construct you are interested in, but you cannot find a way to measure it. Although innumerable surveys exist already, the human psyche, the human condition, society, and culture are infinitely complex and ever evolving. Further, as practitioners and other behavioral scientists continue to learn about people, the theories and conceptual frameworks that inform our understanding will be refined or debunked, and new ones will be developed. Thus, it is very possible that you will stumble upon a question or hypothesis about people through your work with clients that someone else has not developed a way to measure.

When you want or need to measure something and there is no (good) way to do it, then survey design may be appropriate. However, in order to design a survey, you need to know enough about your construct of interest to be able to operationalize it for measurement. That is, you need to be able to define your construct conceptually based on theory, and you need to be able to define the construct in a way that it can be studied. If you do not have enough information to do this, you may need to do further reading and research in order to better define your construct. Alternatively, you may wish to start with qualitative research studies, some of which are described in other chapters in this book, that can help you better understand people's experiences with the phenomena you are seeking to study and measure.

Sample Research Questions in Survey Design

Because survey design, as discussed in this chapter, has a specific purpose (i.e., developing and testing a new survey), this means that a practitioner is trying to answer specific questions about how well a new survey measures what it is supposed to measure (e.g., validity) and how reliable the new survey is at gaining information from clients. For example, if a practitioner wants to develop a new survey (or even evaluate an existing survey) to measure depression, some of the first questions that need to be answered are how well does the new survey actually measure depression (validity), and how consistent is the new survey at producing accurate information about depression (reliability)? Because such questions are very specific, the research questions may look different from other methodological approaches you read about in this book. Survey design tends to follow a series of steps in which you first develop the survey itself, and then you have clients (or students, if you work in schools) complete it so that you can research how well your survey holds up statistically. Research questions for survey design are usually homing in on those statistical tests with the sample of clients who completed the survey. This process is explained later in the chapter. Examples of research questions when designing a survey might include:

- To what extent is there evidence for construct validity?
- To what extent is there evidence for reliability among the subtests used to specify factors?
- To what extent is there evidence for convergent validity?
- To what extent is there discriminant validity?
- Is there evidence for social desirability or inattentive responding among individuals completing the survey?

If these research questions sound very specific and statistical, they are. However, they are not as intimidating as they may seem at first. Remember, when you design a survey, you are essentially creating a test of some aspect of the human condition that you hypothesize to exist (e.g., behaviors, thoughts, emotions, personality traits, relational processes) but typically cannot immediately be observed by you. The research questions and accompanying statistical tests are designed to provide you with evidence for how well your survey *actually* captures what you *think* it captures.

Tackling Survey Design: The Case of Meredith

To illustrate how surveys are designed and tested, consider the case of Meredith, a professional counselor working in a community mental health center. Meredith specialized in working with clients who engaged in nonsuicidal self-injury (NSSI; e.g., cutting, burning, scratching), and she noticed that many of her clients discussed using NSSI as a way to cope with overwhelming, negative thoughts and feelings. A pattern seemed to emerge in which clients would experience a wave of thoughts (e.g., "I am worthless," "My life will never get better") and/or emotions (e.g., sadness, anger, panic/anxiety), and these thoughts and emotions were experienced so intensely that clients could not bear them. As a result, Meredith's clients would use NSSI to relieve the intensity, and many reported feeling better after engaging in self-injury.

Meredith wanted to better understand these thoughts and feelings that seemed to spur NSSI behavior so she could help her clients learn to recognize and de-escalate them with healthier coping strategies, thereby releasing her clients of the perceived need to use NSSI. She recognized that she had no way to assess for these thoughts other than verbal self-report from her clients, which could sometimes be difficult for them to articulate aloud. She also wondered if other practitioners might encounter similar phenomena when working with clients who engage in NSSI. A survey might help her gather information from clients quickly, and it could help her study whether overwhelmingly negative thoughts and emotions prompt NSSI behavior.

Important Steps in Survey Design

This section breaks down the steps to designing a survey, and we will use Meredith's case as an example throughout the steps. There is no one way to design a survey, but there are some very important steps to take in order to do it correctly. In this chapter, we will draw from steps outlined by DeVellis (2017): (1) determine what to measure, (2) generate an item pool, (3) determine the format for measurement, (4) submit survey for expert review, (5) consider validation items, (6) administer items to a development sample and evaluate, and (7) optimize scale length.

Determine What to Measure

A seemingly obvious yet highly important first step in survey design is clearly establishing what will be measured by the survey. It is not enough to develop a survey to measure a construct without first clearly defining what the construct is. The challenge is that many of the phenomena of interest to practitioners may have different definitions. For example, some people define depression in cognitive terms characterized by negative thought patterns (e.g., Beck, 1979), while others may categorize it as an emotional experience (e.g., Greenberg & Watson, 2006) or as a diagnostic cluster of symptoms (American Psychiatric Association, 2013). No single definition or theory can capture a construct completely, and sometimes varying definitions overlap (see Figure 4.1). Some definitions cover the breadth of a construct, while others narrow in to capture the depth of a construct.

How you define a construct has implications for what goes on your survey, because survey items that are irrelevant to your defined construct will not help you better understand, define, and study the construct, yet too narrow a

Figure 4.1 Theory-Based Perspectives of Depression

view of a construct really limits one's understanding of what may be occurring. With our depression example, if you are focused on measuring depression from a cognitive perspective, then including items on your survey that measure emotions will not necessarily help you understand thought patterns. If you cannot clearly articulate what you want to measure, not only is it unlikely that people who might complete your survey would understand it, but ultimately you may find that the results you get are not actually about what you had been trying to study.

The key to clearly defining what you want to measure, particularly in capturing breadth versus depth, is to use a theoretical framework. This might be a counseling theory, but it can be more broad than that. Professionals in many disciplines use theories to define, predict, and explain things, and you may find a theory from a separate discipline best captures what you want to measure. A helpful guide to developing or discovering a theoretical framework is *Reason & Rigor: How Conceptual Frameworks Guide Research* (Ravitch & Riggan, 2017). Overall, the goal of this stage is to be able to articulate how your construct of interest can be measured by a survey. As mentioned previously in this chapter, if you struggle with this process, you might need to delve back into the professional literature to help you better understand the best way to operationalize your construct and what may need to be included on your survey.

In Meredith's case, she was interested in overwhelming thoughts and emotions that seemingly trigger clients to engage in NSSI behavior. If she thoroughly reviewed the available literature, she could find that other scholars and researchers have addressed this phenomenon (e.g., Chapman, Gratz, & Brown, 2006; Wester & McKibben, 2016), and she could use the conceptual frameworks and research to operationally define these thoughts and emotions in which she was interested. If we break down Meredith's interest in NSSI as we did with depression, there are two constructs at hand: overwhelming thoughts and overwhelming emotions. As with depression, these two constructs are likely not the sole definition of NSSI, and they also could overlap in different ways (see Figure 4.2).

Figure 4.2 Venn Diagram Illustrating Meredith's Constructs of Interest

In order for Meredith to concretely determine what her survey should include, she needs to decide how broad or how narrow she wants her survey to be. She can start by defining what exactly overwhelming thoughts and overwhelming emotions are. She likely can identify this relatively easily from reading what researchers have found and from her own experience working with her clients. Meredith also needs to consider more nuanced aspects related to capturing the depth of these experiences on her survey, such as what makes a thought or emotion overwhelming? How is intensity defined? At what point does a thought or emotion go from salient to overwhelming? Meredith also might wish to measure how frequently the overwhelming thoughts and emotions occur, as well as any precipitating events that evoke these thoughts and emotions. With these thoughts in mind, Meredith could better articulate the breadth (i.e., thoughts and emotions) and depth (i.e., intensity, frequency) of her constructs of interest, which would be a huge help as she develops items for her new survey.

Generate an Item Pool

After clearly defining what you want to measure, it is time to start developing items for the survey. This can be a tedious task to do correctly, and it is helpful to think of each item as a miniature test of the construct being measured. To that end, a helpful guide during item generation is Heppner, Kivlighan, and Wampold's (2008) MAXMINCON principle for research. Your overall goal is to *maximize* true score variance, *minimize* error variance, and *control* for as many confounds as possible. In classical test theory, an individual's response to any given item on a survey is assumed to consist of their true score plus an error score (Allen & Yen, 2002). Error in an individual's response may stem from a variety of sources (e.g., environmental distractions, ambiguous or confusing items, motivation to participate), and error obscures practitioners from measuring and observing the construct of interest in its purest form.

Try as we might, we cannot control all aspects of the research process. Thus, we cannot completely eliminate sources of error from survey responses.

Nevertheless, there are steps you can take in survey design that can help maximize the true score variance and minimize the error variance across individuals' responses. DeVellis (2017) recommended several useful strategies, such as choosing items that reflect the survey's purpose, writing items that are clear and concise, ensuring items are written at the appropriate reading level, and avoiding confusion in item wording (for examples of these strategies with a creativity survey, see Table 4.1).

Although it may seem obvious, you want to make sure that the items you draft are related to the construct(s) you are trying to measure. This can become more nuanced as your constructs of interest become more specific. For example, it seems obvious to say that Meredith should generate items related to NSSI, but what she needs to focus on in particular is capturing the emotional and cognitive processes or experiences that lead to NSSI. An item that is not related to these particular experiences would not help her test the notion of overwhelming emotions and thoughts. Meredith also needs to make sure she has a clear picture of what these emotions and thoughts look like so that her items are relevant and specific. Meredith will also want to generate as many relevant items as she possibly can at this phase. In this early phase of survey design, it is a good idea to generate as many relevant items as possible, even if some seem redundant (DeVellis, 2017).

Another consideration in maximizing true score variance is making sure your items are clear and free of ambiguity. The more a client has to guess or infer what you are asking, the more likely their response will contain error. Remember: what you think you are asking is not always what is interpreted by clients (this is true in counseling practice and in survey research!). This point

Table 4.1 Examples of Poorly and Strongly Worded Survey Items for a Survey of Creativity

Issue	Poorly Worded	Strongly Worded
Reflect the survey's purpose	"I believe that creative arts should be taught in schools."	"I enjoy engaging in art projects."
Item clarity	"The opposite of being creative is not expressing yourself."	"I use creativity to express myself."
Appropriate reading level	"I feel self-efficacious about engaging in the creative process."	"When I feel creative, I feel confident."
Double-barreled item wording	"I enjoy painting and sculpting."	"I enjoy painting." "I enjoy sculpting."
Biased/leading item wording	"How much do you agree with this statement: Creative people allow themselves to be open to new experiences?"	"I am comfortable with new experiences."

relates to another—try to make items as concise as possible. Wordy items can make it more difficult for a client to decipher what they are responding to, which again poses a risk for error. Notably, ambiguously worded items may not only confuse clients, but they may also increase risk for socially desirable responding (Fleming, 2012), a type of nonrandom error discussed later.

In seeking to reduce ambiguity, it is important to ensure that items are written at a level that is appropriate for the intended audience. For example, a survey written for children ages 5 to 8 years will have items at a reading level different from a survey written for adults over 18 years. Additionally, you want to avoid a common mistake of a double-barreled item. A double-barreled item essentially contains two ideas within one item, and it is impossible to know which idea is being endorsed in a client's response. For example, a double-barreled item on Meredith's survey might look like, "I engage in NSSI because I am overwhelmed by my emotions." On its face, the item sounds fine. However, if a client engages in NSSI, but not because they feel overwhelmed by their emotions (or vice versa), how should that person respond to this item? The item actually contains two ideas (i.e., engaging in NSSI and feeling overwhelmed by emotions), and when Meredith looks at the data, she will not be able to determine if her clients' responses are to one piece or both parts of the item.

Although intentionality is required to develop strong items, there is no right or wrong process for generating items. Some people may find it helpful to map out the theory or conceptual framework driving the survey design and then develop items from there. Others may wish to brainstorm as many items as possible before going back and evaluating them. It is also a good idea to talk to other practitioners, particularly those with experience or expertise in your construct of interest, to get ideas for generating items. Although it may not be feasible to seek ideas or feedback from your clients directly, it can be very helpful to seek ideas from those who might ultimately take your survey. Meredith, for example, might try to locate a few people who engage in NSSI, and she could potentially host a focus group to get feedback on the items she has been developing, to ask for new item ideas, or both. The keys are to work from your strengths and to engage your own creativity. Find what works for you and use that to be productive.

Determine Measurement Format

In addition to generating items, you must decide how individuals will respond to the items. Measurement formats are often referred to as scales, and there are a variety of options from which to choose. The most important factors in selecting a scale are that it fits with the wording of your items and that it provides you with the information you are seeking. Some of the more common measurement scales include Likert scales, binary scales, and visual analog scales (see Table 4.2 for examples of each). On a Likert scale, an individual is asked to indicate the extent of their agreement or disagreement with items. Accordingly, items written along with a Likert scale are declarative statements

Table 4.2 Examples of Common Measurement Formats

Scale	Example					
Likert	I am a nice person.	Strongly Disagree 1	Disagree 2	Neutral 3	Agree 4	Strongly Agree 5
Binary*	I am a nice person.	Yes	No		True	False
Visual Analog	I am a nice person.	Very Like Me				Not at All Like Me

Note. Two examples are offered for binary scales in this table: Yes/No and True/False.

rather than questions. The practitioner also must determine what the numbers on a Likert scale mean. A binary scale offers a person two options in response to an item (e.g., true/false, agree/disagree, yes/no). This type of scale is used when a practitioner is trying to concretely classify information into two categories. With a visual analog scale, a person is asked to indicate the extent of their agreement or disagreement with an item along a continuum with two end points. For a more comprehensive review of measurement format options, see the books in the Additional Resources list at the end of the chapter.

Expert Review

Once the items and the measurement format have been developed, it is a good idea to have other people look over the newly designed survey and provide feedback. When you are in the process of developing a survey, it can be easy to get "too close" to the topic, a bias that might limit a broader or more critical perspective. That is, you can easily spend a good deal of time reading, trying to narrow down and define your construct, writing out items, and arranging items with a response scale. All of that investment may make it difficult to see when something is not quite right on the survey, when you have overlooked something, or when something might make sense to you but not to others. Extra pairs of eyes from professionals with expertise in your topic of interest can help you uncover potential biases or blind spots you might have.

There is no standard for how many experts should review a survey under development, but more than one seems minimally necessary so that you can triangulate feedback from more than one source. The more experts that can review the survey the better; this may just create more work to integrate the feedback and possibly confusion about what to do if experts offer conflicting feedback. Ultimately, you must decide how to integrate expert feedback to improve your survey.

There are a few aspects to consider in the expert review process. First, you need to determine what constitutes an *expert* in the area(s) addressed on your survey. Who is qualified to offer substantive feedback that can help you improve or tweak your survey? Start by using more objective criteria to identify content experts, and then narrow in to people you might know who meet the criteria. For example, Meredith might start with criteria such as a licensed mental health practitioner with at least 10 years of experience working with nonsuicidal self-injury, or who has published at least five research studies on NSSI. Next, before you contact experts, clarify what you want feedback on and how they can assist. Common questions for experts are:

- Readability: Do the items make sense? Are any items confusing? How could any items be reworded for clarity? Will the population(s) likely to take this survey be able to understand the items?
- Validity: Do the items appear to relate to the construct(s) being measured? Do the items encompass all aspects of the construct(s)? Do any of the items contain biased, leading, or double-barreled wording?
- Instructional clarity: Do the survey instructions make sense?
- Measurement format: Is the selected measurement format appropriate for this survey? Can people respond to the items using the measurement format? Does the measurement format help me better understand my construct?
- Addition/Removal: Is there anything that should be added to or removed from the survey?

Validation Items

Previously, we discussed generating items in a way that maximizes true score variance and minimizes error variance, thereby gleaning information as purely as possible via a survey. Sometimes, a survey (or any study for that matter) can be solidly designed, yet despite best efforts, additional error can be introduced by individuals completing the survey. A common source of error is socially desirable responding, which occurs when someone attempts to present themselves in an overly positive way on a survey (Bäckström & Björklund, 2013). Depending on what a survey is attempting to measure, socially desirable responding may look like over- or underinflated scores. The problem with this is the information being provided on the survey is not accurate and can potentially lead practitioners to draw invalid or unreliable conclusions.

For example, it is possible that some of Meredith's clients deal with intensely aversive emotions that prompt them to engage in NSSI. However, when they take Meredith's new survey, they might respond to items by indicating that the intensity of their emotion is lower than is actually the case. This could be for any number of reasons, including that they do not want to admit to themselves that their emotions are intense and negative or because they do not want Meredith to know the true intensity of their aversive emotions. Regardless of the motivation, these clients have produced scores on Meredith's survey that are artificially lower than is actually the case. As a result, Meredith might draw inaccurate or unreliable conclusions from the data.

Unfortunately, you cannot read a person's mind to know for sure if they are accurately representing themselves on a survey. Because we cannot know for sure if someone is responding accurately, we cannot fully eradicate instances of social desirability. What we can do is try to detect it, and a common way to do that is by including a measure of social desirability. There are several popular, free social desirability scales available that have been used in hundreds of studies, including the Marlowe-Crowne Social Desirability Scale (Crowne & Marlowe, 1960) and its short forms (Reynolds, 1982). By including a social desirability scale along with your new survey when you administer it (in the next step), you can correlate scores on your survey with scores on the social desirability scale to see if there is a significant correlation. A significant result may indicate that social desirability is an issue in your data and you should use caution in interpreting the results of your survey. For a more nuanced discussion of social desirability, as well as another common source of error variance called inattentive responding, see McKibben and Silvia (2016) in the additional resources at the end of this chapter.

Administer to a Development Sample and Evaluate

At this point, you have clearly defined what you want to measure, you have developed items and an accompanying measurement format, you have had the items reviewed by experts and made any edits you deem necessary, and you may be including some validation items or scales to detect potential error. You are now ready to administer your survey to see just how well it holds up. Before sending out your survey for people to complete, an often overlooked yet notable consideration is the aesthetics of your survey. That is, how does the survey actually look? Is it easy to read? Is the layout visually appealing? A plain or convoluted survey layout may dissuade people from taking the survey or may make their process more difficult, which can increase the chances for error.

There are a few quick ways that you can check the aesthetics of your survey informally. You might hand out the survey to clients individually or in a group (or to a group of students in a classroom) and ask them to comment on the overall look and feel of the survey. If you work in an office that has a waiting area, then you might distribute your survey to clients who are waiting for their appointments. Assume, for example, that Meredith facilitates a dialectical behavior therapy skills group with some of her clients who engage in NSSI. Either prior to the group starting or at the end of a group, she might hand her survey to her clients in the group and ask them to give her some feedback on how her survey looks. Notably, this could also be an opportunity to ask clients some of the questions asked of experts during expert review, particularly around readability, instructional clarity, and measurement format.

Administering your survey to people is an exciting, and sometimes anxiety-inducing, step in the survey design process because you are putting your hard work out there for people to complete. This process is yet another vital and complex step in the overall survey design process, and it requires careful attention to do correctly. First, you need to select a population of people that you can sample with your survey. It is important to be intentional in defining to whom you will administer your survey. For whom did you design the survey? Is it for a broad audience or a more specific group? Who is most qualified to respond to the items on your survey? The answer(s) you come up with should be who you recruit. For example, Meredith's survey has grown out of her work at her community mental health center with clients who engage in nonsuicidal self-injury. A good population for her to test her survey with would probably be people who engage in nonsuicidal self-injury.

As a quick note on defining the most optimal population to sample, some researchers rely on convenience samples (i.e., a group of people that are easy to access, even if not the most relevant to the study), but this can be problematic if a group of people has no knowledge of or exposure to the content of a survey. In Meredith's case, she might have an easier time gathering a large number of people by partnering with a professor at a local university who could distribute her survey to college students. However, for those students who have not engaged in nonsuicidal self-injury or who have not sought counseling services, they may be confused by Meredith's survey, and their responses to the survey may not be particularly useful. Responses from people with no knowledge of Meredith's construct of interest are essentially noise that can complicate and distort the conclusions she can make about her survey's performance. Again, remember Heppner et al.'s (2008) MAXMINCON principle—selecting a group of people who are most qualified to speak to what your survey is about will help you maximize the true score variance on your survey.

Once you define your target population, you need to sample individuals from that population. The number of people you need depends on the statistics you plan to use to evaluate a survey (which have even deeper measurement theory guiding the statistical approaches), and there are varying perspectives on how many people are "enough" to adequately test factor structures. A common statistical approach in survey design is factor analysis, which is based in classical test theory. Although a comprehensive discussion of factor analysis and classical test theory exceeds the scope of this chapter, a common way to determine a sample size for factor analysis modeling is to calculate a sample size-to-variable ratio. Essentially, the more items on a survey, the more people you need in a sample to sufficiently evaluate the factor structure with factor analysis. Again, researchers and measurement theorists vary on an ideal ratio, but a ratio of 10 to 20 people to every one item may be appropriate (Crockett, 2012; Mvududu & Sink, 2013). Researchers also tend to agree that at least 200 people are needed to conduct factor analysis modeling (Crockett, 2012; Mvududu & Sink, 2013), even if there are only a handful of items. Another school of thought in evaluating surveys comes from item response theory (IRT), which involves a more nuanced evaluation of items. The implication for sample sizes is similar in IRT approaches—large sample sizes are required.

Once a survey has been administered and the data are in, you are ready to analyze the data. This step relates directly to research questions described near the beginning of this chapter. Evaluating a survey involves tests for evidence of validity (e.g., construct, convergent, discriminant) and reliability. In essence, how well does the statistical evidence support the theoretical structure and utility of your survey? Evaluating a survey often requires access to statistical software and proficiency at interpreting statistical output. If you are employed in a setting that does not have access to statistical software, or if you do not feel confident to evaluate a survey yourself, you may wish to seek assistance from a measurement expert. There are many statistical tests you could conduct to evaluate your survey; some of the more common approaches are listed in Table 4.3.

A quick note about testing for evidence of validity and reliability that may seem like semantics but is actually an important distinction: it is not uncommon in peer-reviewed journal articles involving survey design to see researchers state that they found evidence (or not) that the *survey* is valid or reliable. This is a misnomer. As Elmore (2010) pointed out, what is valid or reliable is not a statistical result itself but rather the conclusions that one infers from the result. Applied to survey design, a survey itself is not valid or reliable. Rather, validity and reliability refers to the conclusions one makes based on the survey responses. If this sounds unclear, remember that a survey is essentially a test of a hypothesized construct. By extension, each time you use a survey, you are basically retesting how well that survey performs in measuring the construct(s) with a new group of people. Each test with a new sample is an opportunity to infer conclusions about the human condition under study. In sum, what are valid and reliable (or not) are the decisions you make as the practitioner, not your survey. It is an inanimate object after all!

Optimize Scale Length

Assuming that your survey holds up under tests for validity evidence, a final step is to try to shorten the survey if possible. Before you do this, heed this word of caution: it is almost never worth dropping an item from a survey if doing so will impact the validity or overall reliability of your survey. You can make informed decisions about whether an item should stay or go by consulting results from an item analysis (see Table 4.3).

The statistical program SPSS (IBM Corp., 2016) offers useful and reader-friendly output that you can use to evaluate items, such as item–total correlations. EZAnalyze (n.d.), which was originally designed for school counselors, offers a free add-on to Microsoft Excel that all practitioners may find useful for this step. An item–total correlation essentially estimates the degree to which people's responses on any given item are related to all other items on the survey or subscale on a survey (Howard & Forehand, 1962). A weak correlation (e.g., less than .2 [Everit, 2002]) signals that an item may not really relate to other items and can probably be deleted. An additional piece of information that SPSS provides is a "Cronbach's alpha if item deleted" value. As noted in Table 4.3, Cronbach's alpha is an estimate of internal consistency of the survey (or subscale) items as a whole—that is, how well the items converge on a unidimensional construct. If you already know the Cronbach's alpha value

Table 4.3 Common Statistical Tests in Survey Design

Statistical Tests	What It Does	Provides Evidence For	What to Look For	Software Programs
Item analysis	Helps you identify statistically weak items and the normality of data	Data normality	Item means and standard deviations	SPSS (IBM Corp., 2016)
		Item strength/weakness	Item skew and kurtosis Item–total correlations	
Exploratory factor analysis (EFA)	Tells you how well items load onto your constructs/scales (CFA) or how well items load on scales that are extrapolated from the data (EFA)	Construct validity	Model fit indices	Mplus (Muthén & Muthén, 1998–2015)
Confirmatory factor analysis (CFA)			Factor loadings Residual values	Amos (Arbuckle, 2014) SPSS (IBM Corp., 2016) LISREL (Jöreskog & Sörbom, 2015)
Item response theory (IRT) models	Evaluates items as a function of item difficulty and people's ability to answer items	Construct validity	Model fit indices Item characteristic curve	ConQuest (Adams, Wu, & Wilson, 2015) R (R Core Team, 2016)
Pearson product moment correlation (r)	Tells you the extent to which scores on your survey overlap with scores on a theoretically similar or distinct survey	Convergent validity Discriminant validity	A correlation is considered statistically significant if $p < .05$. Also examine r for strength of correlation and whether r is +/-	SPSS (IBM Corp., 2016)
Cronbach's alpha (α) Kuder-Richardson Formula 20 (KR-20)	Tells you the extent to which item scores relate to one another in converging on an underlying construct	Internal consistency reliability	α values at or above .8 are considered evidence of good to strong internal consistency among items	SPSS (IBM Corp., 2016)

for your survey and/or any subscales on the survey, you can consult the Cronbach's alpha if item deleted for each item to see if dropping the item will impact the overall internal consistency of your survey.

Chapter Summary

Survey design is a robust area in counseling, and in many ways, it serves as the foundation for much of the research (particularly quantitative) and applied work that practitioners do. The steps outlined in this chapter, though not the sole authority on how to design a survey, can help start you on the path to designing a quality survey. By designing surveys that reliably measure what they are intended to measure, practitioners can make informed decisions about the work they do and about the clients they serve.

Resources for More Information

Peer-Reviewed Journal Articles

Crockett, S. A. (2012). A five-step guide to conducting SEM analysis in counseling research. *Counseling Outcome Research and Evaluation, 3*, 20–47. doi:10.1177/2150137811434142

Elmore, P. B. (2010). Reporting standards for research publications. *Counseling Outcome Research and Evaluation, 1*, 19–29. doi:10.1177/2150137810386108

Leech, N. L., Onwuegbuzie, A. J., & O'Conner, R. (2011). Assessing internal consistency in counseling research. *Counseling Outcome Research and Evaluation, 2*, 115–125. doi:10.1177/2150137811414873

McKibben, W. B., & Silvia, P. J. (2016). Inattentive and socially desirable responding: Addressing subtle threats to validity in quantitative counseling research. *Counseling Outcome Research and Evaluation, 7*, 53–64. doi:10.1177/2150137815613135

Mvududu, N. H., & Sink, C. A. (2013). Factor analysis in counseling research and practice. *Counseling Outcome Research and Evaluation, 4*, 75–98. doi:10.1177/2150137813494766

Books

DeVellis, R. F. (2017). *Scale development: Theory and applications* (4th ed.). Thousand Oaks, CA: Sage Publications.

Dillman, D. A., Smyth, J. D., & Christian, L. M. (2014). *Internet, phone, mail, and mixed-mode surveys: The tailored design method* (4th ed.). Hoboken, NJ: Wiley-Blackwell.

Fink, A. G. (2012). *How to conduct surveys: A step-by-step guide* (5th ed.). Thousand Oaks, CA: Sage Publications.

Ravitch, S. M., & Riggan, J. M. (2017). *Reason and rigor: How conceptual frameworks guide research* (2nd ed.). Thousand Oaks, CA: Sage Publications.

Questions for Further Review and Application

1. When is it appropriate to consider survey design? Think about a topic or topics you are interested in. What do you need to know about that topic in order to determine if survey design is needed in this area?

2.   What is the MAXMINCON principle, and how does it play into the survey design process? Why is it important that counselors adhere to this principle in survey design?
3.   What are potential sources of error that can show up in survey scores? How can counselors try to prevent/address these during the survey design process?
4.   What factors should one consider when administering and evaluating a newly designed survey?

References

Adams, R. J., Wu, M. L., & Wilson, M. R. (2015). *ACER ConQuest: Generalised Item response modelling software, Version 4* [Computer software]. Camberwell, Victoria: Australian Council for Educational Research.

Allen, M. J., & Yen, W. M. (2002). *Introduction to measurement theory*. Long Grove, IL: Waveland Press.

American Psychiatric Association. (2013). *Diagnostic and statistical manual of mental disorders* (5th ed.). Washington, DC: Author.

Arbuckle, J. L. (2014). *Amos, Version 23.0* [Computer software]. Chicago, IL: IBM SPSS.

Bäckström, M., & Björklund, F. (2013). Social desirability in personality inventories: Symptoms, diagnosis, and prescribed cure. *Scandinavian Journal of Psychology, 54*, 152–159.

Beck, A. T. (1979). *Cognitive therapy and the emotional disorders*. New York, NY: Meridian.

Chapman, A. L., Gratz, K. L., & Brown, M. Z. (2006). Solving the puzzle of deliberate self-harm: The experiential avoidance model. *Behaviour Research and Therapy, 44*, 371–394. doi:10.1016/j.brat.2005.03.005

Crockett, S. A. (2012). A five-step guide to conducting SEM analysis in counseling research. *Counseling Outcome Research and Evaluation, 3*, 20–47. doi:10.1177/2150137811434142

Crowne, D. P., & Marlowe, D. (1960). A new scale of social desirability independent of psychopathology. *Journal of Consulting Psychology, 24*, 349–354.

DeVellis, R. F. (2017). *Scale development: Theory and applications* (4th ed.). Thousand Oaks, CA: Sage Publications.

Elmore, P. B. (2010). Reporting standards for research publications. *Counseling Outcome Research and Evaluation, 1*, 19–29. doi:10.1177/2150137810386108

Everit, B. S. (2002). *Cambridge dictionary of statistics* (2nd ed.). New York, NY: Cambridge University Press.

EZAnalyze. (n.d.). *Excel-based tools for educators*. Retrieved from www.ezanalyze.com

Fleming, P. (2012). Social desirability, not what it seems: A review of the implications for self reports. *The International Journal of Educational and Psychological Assessment, 11*, 3–22.

Greenberg, L. S., & Watson, J. C. (2006). *Emotion-focused therapy for depression*. Washington, DC: American Psychological Association.

Heppner, P. P., Kivlighan, D. M., & Wampold, B. E. (2008). *Research design in counseling* (3rd ed.). Belmont, CA: Thomson Brooks/Cole.

Howard, K. I., & Forehand, G. A. (1962). A method for correcting item-total correlations for the effect of relevant item inclusion. *Educational & Psychological Measurement, 22,* 731–735.

IBM Corporation. (2016). *SPSS statistics for windows, Version 24.0* [Computer software].Armonk, NY: Author.

Jöreskog, K. G., & Sörbom, D. (2015). *LISREL 9.20 for windows* [Computer software]. Skokie, IL: Scientific Software International, Inc.

McKibben, W. B., & Silvia, P. J. (2016). Inattentive and socially desirable responding: Addressing subtle threats to validity in quantitative counseling research. *Counseling Outcome Research and Evaluation, 7,* 53–64. doi:10.1177/2150137815613135

Muthén, L. K., & Muthén, B. O. (1998–2015). *Mplus user's guide* (7th ed.). Los Angeles, CA: Author.

Mvududu, N. H., & Sink, C. A. (2013). Factor analysis in counseling research and practice. *Counseling Outcome Research and Evaluation, 4,* 75–98. doi:10.1177/2150137813494766

R Core Team. (2016). *R: A language and environment for statistical computing* [Computer software]. Vienna, Austria: R Foundation for Statistical Computing.

Ravitch, S. M., & Riggan, J. M. (2017). *Reason and rigor: How conceptual frameworks guide Research* (2nd ed.). Thousand Oaks, CA: Sage Publications.

Reynolds, W. M. (1982). Development of reliable and valid short forms of the Marlowe-Crowne social desirability scale. *Journal of Clinical Psychology, 38,* 119–125.

Wester, K. L., & McKibben, W. B. (2016). Participants' experiences of non-suicidal self-injury: Supporting existing theory and emerging conceptual pathways. *Journal of Mental Health Counseling, 38,* 12–27. doi:10.17744/mehc.38.1.02

5 Case Study

Holly Downs

When doing research, inevitably someone will ask, "What do you want to research?" usually followed by the question, "How do you plan to do that?" In tackling a research project, one of the most challenging topics is how to get started in the design of the study. Qualitative designs are typically used in research to provide in-depth descriptions of a specific program, practice, or setting (Denzin & Lincoln, 2011). One of the most popular types of social science research related to qualitative inquiry is case study. Although not always solely qualitative, case study does seek to provide an in-depth view of a case or phenomenon. According to one of the leading case study researchers, Robert Yin (2014), doing case study research "remains one of the most challenging of all social science endeavors" (p. 3). While this sounds daunting, one of the rewards of doing a case study well is that you are given insights into your data that otherwise would have remained uncovered; much like an iceberg in the ocean, case study can help reveal what is under the surface of the water that is not as readily evident at first glance. This chapter will review case study research, including an introduction to case study research, when to use case study research, an example of a case study, case study methodology including case study designs, analysis activities, and presentation of case study findings to provide you with guidance as you design your own case study.

What Is Case Study?

The definition of case study research is not as simple as one would think because the term has been bandied about at times incorrectly. Before talking about what case study is, it is important to dispel some myths by covering what case study is not.

Case Study Is Not Solely Used in One Field of Study

Case study is not field specific, as case studies have been used in counseling (Hill, Carter, & O'Farrell, 1983; Wester, Downs, & Trepal, 2016), psychology (Cosmides & Tooby, 1989), traditional and online education (Cann, 2005; Downs, 2014; McAdams, Hess, & Viteritti, 1999), health (Luo & Wang,

2003; van Oort, Schröder, & French, 2011), engineering (Wieringa, 2014), and business (Berson & Avolio, 2004; Eisenhardt & Graebner, 2007; Garrett & Vogt, 2003; Perren & Ram, 2004) as well as others. Even though fields may privilege or favor one type of data collection or analysis over another, case study is valuable to all fields when the researcher seeks to do deeper exploration of a topic.

Case Study Is Not Just Qualitative Data and Analysis

Case study is also not solely qualitative, as some believe. Rather, it includes many different data collection techniques and analysis strategies that are both qualitative and quantitative in nature. While most are familiar with the common qualitative data sources like interviews and observations that are potentially rich data sources for a case study, omitting numeric data and analysis is shortsighted. Many case study authors assert that having both qualitative and quantitative data actually increases credibility (Bickman & Rog, 2009; Korzilius, 2010; Yin, 2014), as it creates "a strong evidentiary base." With that base, "methodically analyzing these data using qualitative or quantitative methods will then lead to more defensible findings and solutions" (Bickman & Rog, 2009, p. 279).

Case Study Does Not Have to Be a Single Case

Case study can be a single case or multiple cases. One of the most prominent case study researchers, Robert Stake, says case study "is the study of particularly and complexity of a single case, coming to understand its activity within important circumstances" (p. xi) that is driven by the interest of the researcher in the case (Stake, 1995). While Stake emphasizes a single case being the focus of a study, others talk about the possibilities of including in-depth exploration of multiple cases for more comparative purposes and richer findings. Linda Chmiliar (2010) asserts that multiple-case design is "more powerful than single-case designs as it provides more extensive descriptions and explanations of the phenomenon or issue" (p. 583).

Regardless of whether single- or multiple-case studies are used, at the heart of a good case study is that it is "an empirical inquiry that investigates a contemporary phenomenon (the 'case') in depth and within its real-world context, especially when the boundaries between phenomenon and context may not be clearly evident" (Yin, 2014, p. 18). It is the depth of the study that truly defines the value of what quality case study research should do and be.

When to Use Case Study

A number of factors may suggest that case study is appropriate for a research method for your study. Ultimately, the best way to determine the type of research to do, regardless of whether it is case study, is by positing the research questions you want to answer (which is discussed in the next section). However, there are several general characteristics agreed upon by most case study researchers. Yin (2014) asserts that a case study design should be specifically considered when the researcher (a) seeks to answer "how" and "why" research questions, (b) will not manipulate the behavior of those involved in the study, (c) wants to fully explore the context because it is relevant to the phenomenon being studied, or (d) cannot separate the case from the context. For instance, conducting a case study on how graduate students are making decisions on their dissertation research methodology might result in very different findings depending on factors like their personal experience, coursework, and dissertation advisor preferences. Without considering the full context, it would be impossible for this case study researcher to have a true picture of the case without it.

Research Questions Best Suited for Case Study

As suggested by the National Research Council, posing carefully designed, significant questions that can be tested is the first guiding principle in conducting rigorous, quality research regardless of the approach (Shavelson & Towne, 2002). Looking across the literature, typically case study is used to answer "how" or "why" questions that fit into three different category types and purposes, including descriptive, process, or issue questions (see Table 5.1). The first two purposes are the typical purposes in almost all research projects (Shavelson & Towne, 2002). First, **descriptive questions** come from the need to pose questions for informational gathering purposes. Next, **process questions** look more deeply into how or why something happened to try to find associations or factors that may have influenced the outcome. The third type

Table 5.1 Types of Research Questions for Case Studies

Research Question Purpose	Definition	Research Question Example
Descriptive	This question is for informational purposes that seeks to answer "What is happening or has happened?"	How are graduate students trained on research methods?
Process	This question is for process purposes that seeks to answer "How or why did something happen?"	How do graduate students decide what type of research methods to use for their dissertations?
Issues	This question is for raising attention to potential issues that seeks to answer "What are some potential problems that might be important to explore?"	How does the power structure of the graduate advisor and graduate student influence the decisions on the types of research methods they use?

are ~~issue questions, which may be posed to get at more cause-and-effect rela-tionships, but this can sometimes be controversial given the case study nature of the design~~. Stake (1995) talks about the need to raise issue questions, which are used in order to "force attention to complexity and contextuality . . . iden-tification of issues draws attention to problems and concerns" (p. 16). He goes on to describe issue questions as "intricately wired to political, social, histori-cal, and especially personal contexts" (p. 17).

Case Study of Digital Online Degree Programs

To illustrate the application of the methodological concepts, an example of a study that undertook a multiple-case study approach to probe how three prom-inent science, technology, engineering, and mathematics (STEM) programs with entirely online graduate degree programs were evaluating their programs (Downs, 2014). This case study included a combination of document review, surveys ($n = 107$), and interviews ($n = 27$) with program administrators, fac-ulty, and students from the three established STEM online master's degree programs, including the departments of natural resources and environmental sciences (NRES), crop sciences (CRSC), and mechanical science and engi-neering (MechSE) at a midwestern university. The study probed the core research question of:

> *How are the online graduate programs from the various STEM fields discerning the quality of their programs?*

Case Study Methodology

This section will discuss the characteristics and common designs used when implementing case study research and specifically how these applied to the case study of the aforementioned three STEM online degree programs. Design and data analysis considerations are also discussed.

Characteristics of Case Studies

In case study research, a few key elements across all case studies are fundamen-tal to their success that almost all researchers agree upon regardless of their field of study. Some of the most important elements to consider include the concepts of bounding a case, defining case study type and design, and deter-mining the unit of analysis.

Bounding a Case

A critical early step in conducting a case study is to define or bound the "case" that is going to be studied (Creswell, 2009; Stake, 1995; Yin, 2014). This is more than the sheer identification of a general topic area but truly looking to define the boundary between the case and with other phenomena surrounding it. For instance, several authors have suggested bounding a case by (a) time and activity and uniqueness (Stake, 1995), (b) time and place (Creswell, 2009), (c) definition and context (Miles & Huberman, 1994), or by (d) other factors like unit of analysis, group, organization, or geographic area (Yin, 2014). Bounding the case will not only help strengthen the understanding of the case but will also guard against the scope of the project becoming too broad or too big, which is really important to all researchers but particularly to novices. Stake (1995) also recommends considering the historical background, the economic, political, and legal contexts, and the multiple stakeholder groups that make up the case.

For the STEM study sample mentioned earlier, it was important to establish the boundaries of the cases, particularly since it was in the digital realm. In order to be a part of this study, programs needed to meet five criteria, including being (a) an online degree program affiliated with the midwestern university in the fall of 2009, (b) a complete master's degree program, (c) an established program housed in a department for at least 5 years at the main campus at Midwestern University, (d) one of the nine STEM departments identified by the National Science Foundation, and (e) an online program in which all of the content is delivered online (Downs, 2014). Thus, the cases were bounded by the degree requirements, departments, and time.

Defining the Case Study Type and Design

A second critical piece in conducting a case study is to define the type of case study that is going to be used. Some cases can be more complex, and therefore it is harder to define what type of case study is being done. While choosing an individual might be an easy way to define the case, case study research involving multiple people like in a program, organization, population, clinic, or geographic region can be more difficult to define. First, it is important to identify the type of case study a researcher is undertaking, which is closely related to a researcher's overarching purpose. Stake (1995) categorizes the types of case study research as intrinsic and instrumental, while Yin (2014) categorizes these as explanatory, exploratory, or descriptive. Evident from Table 5.2, these case study types for research purposes are distinct, but they also overlap and can be used in tandem.

Further, these case study types can primarily be further separated into two design categories of either single- or multiple-case study designs. In deciding between single- or multiple-case studies, it is important to understand what they are. A single-case study is comparable to single-subject experimental research designs in which the individual him or herself is the focus of the study and the focus of analysis (Bickman & Rog, 2009; Creswell, 2009; Egel & Barthold, 2010). Typical justifications for doing single-case studies include if the case seems to represent a critical test to existing theory, an extreme case, a typical case, or a longitudinal case (Yin, 2014). However, some researchers

Table 5.2 Case Study Types for Research Purposes

Case Study Types	Use If a Researcher. . .
Intrinsic	Has an interest in the particular case chosen because it illustrates a particular trait or issue of interest; the case is of primary interest. For instance, the case is explored because the researcher seeks deeper knowledge of the case itself.
Instrumental	Wants to provide insight into an issue or support for a theory in which the case is of secondary interest. For instance, the case is explored because it helps the researcher pursue knowledge of an external interest.
Explanatory	Seeks to explain causal links in interventions (in experimental and quasi-experimental designs). For instance, the case is explored because it has outcomes set, and the study seeks to explain how the process links with the outcomes. This also can include pre–post designs in which two time points are separated by some critical event.
Exploratory	Desires to explore cases in which the outcomes in interventions are unknown. For instance, the case is studied to explore and identify what the outcomes are.
Descriptive	Aspires to describe an intervention or phenomenon and the real-life context in which it occurred. For instance, the case is explored primarily to describe how it exists and interacts with the environment and immediate context.

suggest that doing single-subject research is limiting (Cook & Campbell, 1979), but researchers like Stake (1995) posit that this perceived limitation is precisely the strength of this design—it maximizes what we can learn about this single case without trying to force the assertions to be applied or generalized to other cases.

Multiple-case studies are the other overarching option in case study design and give the researcher the option to explore similarities and differences within and between cases. In other words, multiple cases are oftentimes done for replication to find similar results (sometimes referenced as direct or literal replication) or contrasting results for anticipated reasons (theoretical replication; Yin, 2014). It is believed that

> Multiple-case design allows examination of processes and outcomes across many cases, identification of how individual cases might be affected by different environments, and the specific conditions under which a finding might occur. It may also help to form more general categories of how the specific conditions might be related.
>
> (Chmiliar, 2010, p. 583)

While the evidence created from a multiple-case study design can be more robust and reliable than just looking at one case, it can be more time consuming and expensive to conduct because it deals with multiple sites. For instance, rather than doing extensive data collection with one site, doing this with multiple sites usually requires more researcher time to do the data collection and analysis.

The second limitation of the multiple-case studies is that there are no quick rules or tests like power analysis to justify the sample size or number of cases in a multiple-case study. Qualitative research specialists like Merriam and Tisdell (2015, p. 101) admit,

> Unfortunately for those with a low tolerance for ambiguity, there is no answer. It always depends on the questions being asked, the data being gathered, the analysis in progress, and the resources you have to support the study. What is needed is an adequate number of participants, sites, or activities to answer the question posed at the beginning of the study.

Yin (2014, p. 61) recommends,

> [Y]ou may want to settle for two or three literal replications when your theory is straightforward . . . However, if your theory is subtle or if you want a higher degree of certainty, you may press for five, six, or more replications.

Ultimately, it is up to the researcher to decide and justify the design decisions and assertions that they make. In other words, the more contentious your case, theory, or assertion, the more evidence or support you will need to justify your findings so that other people find the evidence compelling and credible. For instance, the STEM example referenced before was done for descriptive purposes utilizing a multiple-case study design. In many ways, it would have been easier to just focus on one online class or program, but because the study sought to build not only an understanding but also a model for meta-analysis that could be applied to more than one program, focusing on just one program was insufficient for the assertions, so three entire degree programs were chosen. Moreover, the digital delivery was different, so using one program would not have given the breadth and depth of information that was required to deliver a more compelling in-depth study of the programs.

Determining the Unit of Analysis

After the type of research design is established, it is then important to determine the unit of analysis (Patton, 2015). Because both single- and multiple-case designs may have one to several units of analysis depending on the findings and the research questions, case study researchers usually describe the unit of analysis as either *holistic* or *embedded* (Berg, 2004; Gall, Borg, & Gall, 1996; Yin, 2014). For a case study using a holistic unit of analysis, this means that you can choose a single or main unit for analyzing the overall case or cases. A case study using an embedded unit of analysis translates into looking at the main unit as well as other subunits for the analysis of the case.

For instance, if you wanted to look at a single case such as a single leadership training program in one school or a single unit within multiple cases such as the same leadership training program within different schools, then this would be a holistic unit of analysis. However, if a case is the training program and the researcher also wanted to investigate individual subunits such as participants in the program by demographics such as gender, then this would be an embedded unit of analysis. It's much like looking at an onion—you could either look at the onion in its entirety or multiple whole onions in their different contexts (like from homes, gardens, and stores), or you could look at the onion and the different sublayers in that single onion or those sublayers in multiple onions. For the STEM example, each program was looked at individually, so it was a multiple-case study design with a holistic unit of analysis. If the researcher would have looked at individuals or subunits within the three programs, this could have been an embedded unit of analysis, because the overall program and subunits within would have represented multiple layers of analysis.

Additional Design Considerations

In addition to the considerations mentioned, within any case study design, some additional decisions should be made including deciding whether to develop a formal theoretical framework and considering the quality of the case study research, including the concepts of validity and reliability.

Deciding Whether to Develop a Formal Theoretical Framework

Similar to the other topics that we've discussed on case study, the use of theory is driven by the design and purpose decisions you make. Theory can help you complete the other important steps like developing your research questions, bounding your case, making your design decision, or defining the unit of analysis that you're interested in exploring (Yin, 2014). Additionally, it is the hope that this will benefit the precision and the ability of others to replicate the analysis to yield similar findings on other similar research. However, having an initial theoretical map or perspective about your case may not fit directly with your purpose. For example, having an initial theoretical perspective about metrics of success in a training program might be very helpful to know at the onset of a study in order to attempt to build, extend, or challenge this framework and your study in order to support hypothesis testing. However, it is the belief of some case study researchers that this may limit your ability to make discoveries about the case in its individual context and may bias the researcher to focus too much on one aspect of the picture. This does not mean that preparation work is not necessary, but it means that it might take a more generalized or exploratory approach to preparing to do systematic data collection (Stake, 1995). The general advice that one should take is that if you are looking to convince others that your study has produced findings that contribute to your field, developing a theoretical framework is advisable and necessary.

Considering the Quality of Case Study

Despite the commonness of using case study research, there is trepidation about using case study as a method of choice because of the question of the credibility or "trustworthiness" of the method, the instruments, the data, and the findings. Quality case study research should be done by using systematic procedures in terms of case study data collection and analysis procedures. If anyone tells you that case study research is "easier" because you can "just do it," they are sorely mistaken. While a number of concepts have been offered for judging the quality of any research, two main concepts are common for judging social science research and should be addressed in case study research: validity and reliability (see Figure 5.1).

Validity refers to the extent to which the study measures what it is intended to measure (Cho & Trent, 2006; Maxwell, 1992; Miles & Huberman, 1994; Patton, 2015) and the interpretations are appropriate, meaningful, and useful (Messick, 1989; Patton, 2015; Stake, 1995). Important to all research, validity in case study can be particularly difficult to justify. Qualitative data and findings may be suspect of researcher bias, instrument weakness, and individual interpretation, which limit confirmatory replicability (Mertens, 2010; Patton, 2015). However, strategies have been proposed by case study researchers to strengthen the validity of findings in case study, including:

- Collecting multiple sources of evidence,
- Checking data to see if methods support a single conclusion, known as triangulation,
- Inviting persons who were sources of data to review the data collected and reports, known as member checking,
- Utilizing multiple data sources for triangulation,
- Using replication logic in multiple cases (Denzin & Lincoln, 2011; Maxwell, 2013; Patton, 2015).

Validity	**Reliability**
The study measures what it is intended to measure and the interpretations are appropriate.	Study operations (i.e., data collection & analysis) can be repeated to provide consistent results.
Multiple Sources	Acknowledge researcher role
Triangulation	Case study protocols
Member Checks	Databases

Figure 5.1 Strategies to Increasing Validity and Reliability in Case Study Research

Reliability is the extent to which the study operations like data collection and analysis can be repeated to provide consistent results (Yin, 2014). Ultimately, reliability should seek to minimize the errors and biases in any study. As Stake (1995) suggests, the case study researcher can play many roles including teacher, observer, advocate, evaluator, and interpreter, among others. Not acknowledging these roles can threaten the reliability of the findings you present. For instance, if you are playing an "advocate" role for the program you are studying and the report becomes more of a promotional piece, this causes major problems to the reader of the case to believe what you are saying. Instead, clearly stating your role and then discovering the best arguments against your assertions then providing data that either are supportive of or contrary to those assertions can be better in terms of the reliability.

The case study report should adopt the following suggestions to improve reliability: clearly acknowledging your role as a case study researcher, developing and using case study protocols, and using databases and keeping detailed fieldnotes and memos to track fidelity (Miles & Huberman, 1994; Schwandt, 2007; Stake, 1995; Yin, 2014). The most important thing to note is that you as a researcher cannot just go onsite somewhere and start collecting data to have adequate reliability in the study. Having plans for meta-analysis and review at the conclusion can also help in increasing the reliability of the findings (Yin, 2014).

Data Collection

As suggested earlier in this chapter, certain qualitative data collection approaches are often associated with case study research. However, approaches to data collection can range from fairly simple to more complex. Numerous textbooks and courses cover all of these data collection strategies, but the typical approaches used with case study outlined in Table 5.3 can include document review, interviews, observations, artifact review, and surveys (Berg, 2004; Stake, 1995; Yin, 2014).

Data Analysis and Interpretation

Obviously, certain data analysis approaches are better suited to answer certain types of research questions with the type of data that is collected, as "the aim of analysis is to convert a mass of raw data into a coherent account" (Weiss, 1998, p. 271). Analysis in developing an understanding of the case is an ongoing process. Stake (1995) asserts, "There is no particular moment when data analysis begins. Analysis is a matter of giving meaning to first impressions as well as to final compilations" (p. 71). Moreover, because the case can have so many different types of data collection, you need to have an idea about analysis from the onset to prevent becoming overwhelmed with the data. In my experience, it takes approximately three to five times as long to clean and analyze the data as it does to collect it. Meaning if you do a 1-hour interview it will take approximately 3 to 5 hours to transcribe verbatim or summarize your notes, to put it into a format that you can use, and to analyze the actual interview data. While advances have been made in transcription services and

Table 5.3 Common Data Collection Strategies

Data Collection Strategy	Overview	Some Possible Sources
Document Review	Includes collecting documents previously produced by or about the case	Any documents current or past about the case produced by various stakeholders including letters, websites, articles, promotional materials, photography, video, social media, databases, personal correspondence, or administrative documents
Interviews	Incorporates question-and-answer direct conversations using structured and/or open prompts and questions	Targeted individuals or focus groups, interviewees might be directly or indirectly aware and involved in the case. These should seek to uncover in depth data about expectations and reflections about the case.
Observations	Involves observing or watching the case in its typical setting or state	Direct observations of the entire case or subunits of the case
Artifact Review	Consists of collecting tools, objects, instruments generated by or used in the direct observations	Physical artifacts (like observed and unobserved work, assessments) generated by participants or used by stakeholders in the case
Surveys	Incorporates questions and answers in a questionnaire type format using simple descriptive research for longitudinal purposes	Large-scale surveys from national and international governing bodies, topic-specific surveys commonly used in the field of study, customized questions directly created to study the case

software programs for analyzing qualitative and quantitative data, it still takes researcher time and effort to get to know your data. Some common analytic techniques in case study research include trend or pattern analysis, explanation or theory building, and time series analysis.

Trend or Pattern Analysis

The purpose of trend or pattern matching is to compare the theoretical patterns to empirical outcomes (Weiss, 1998). Pattern analysis is not always solely based on consistencies, as this type of analysis can be commonly categorized to summarize (a) convergence or similarity, (b) divergence or difference, (c) frequency, (d) order or sequence, (e) correspondence, or (f) causation (Hatch, 2002; Patton, 2015; Saldaña, 2015; Weiss, 1998). The goal of trend or pattern matching is to compare the pattern with the predicted one so that this does not simply become a quantitative exercise with qualitative data (Yin, 2014).

Explanation or Theory Building

It is more complicated than pattern matching, as it is used "to 'explain' a phenomenon to stipulate a presumed set of causal links about it, or 'how' or 'why' something happened" (Yin, 2014, p. 147). Yin (2014) stresses that this type of analysis should be an iterative, systematic process in which a theoretical framework is proposed, an initial case study is done, a revision is done to the original theoretical framework, additional case studies are done and compared to the original framework, and then final explanations and frameworks are proposed.

Time Series Analysis

The final analytic technique is the same for any time-series analysis conducted in experimental and quasi-experimental studies in which you compare data from one time period to data from other periods (see Bickman & Rog, 2009 and Cook & Campbell, 1979). These can range from simple to complex designs. When adequate numbers of data are appropriate and available about the case, simple to complex statistical analysis can be used if it adds to the richness of the case (Yin, 2014). For instance, in a simple pre–post design, Wester and associates (2016) wanted to explore the data they collected on nonsuicidal self-injury (NSSI), where descriptive statistics and frequencies were generated from eight individuals to explore their NSSI frequency and methods from intake to termination in outpatient counseling. An example of more complex design is the case study done by Berson and Avolio (2004), in which they used hierarchical linear modeling (HLM) to do a case study of a large telecommunications organization in order to examine group-level effects and relationships between aggregates in their study about leadership style of top- and middle-level managers and their ability to convey organizational goals.

Reporting a Case Study

Depending on the data that are generated, case study affords you the opportunity to utilize many strategies for data presentation. Academic writers like Wolcott (1990) assert that "You cannot begin the writing process early enough" (p. 20) because of the potential large amount of data that you can collect with case study. Stake (1995) warns, "a 20-page case study is likely to run 50 if the researcher doesn't 'ruthlessly winnow and sift'" (p. 121). So decisions about audience and reporting formats are crucial in case study.

Traditionally, writing reports is what most case study researchers within academia discuss in the literature. However, giving thought to your case study audience as well as reporting formats "serves as a good starting point for composing your case study" (Yin, 2014, p. 179). The overarching goal of reporting case study research is "to describe the study in a manner to enable the reader to feel as if they had been an active participant in the research and can determine whether or not the study findings could be applied to their own situation" (Baxter & Jack, 2008, p. 555). Yin (2014) encourages case study researchers to consider that case study reporting might be received by multiple audiences, such as those that are academic colleagues as well as nonspecialists.

Most case study reporting is delivered via a traditional report structure of some sort. Stake (1995) talks about the importance of using story formats in case study reporting to engage the reader and illustrate what is happening with vignettes, which are short descriptions of an issue or episode to illustrate something about the case. He recommends a report structure of having an entry vignette, background and purpose discussion, issue development, narrative about data analysis and triangulation discussion, assertions, and then closing vignettes. Yin (2014) also talks about six different types of compositional structures for case study report, including the standard research reporting style he identifies, linear-analytic structure. This structure commonly used by journal articles would start with an introduction to the issue or problem being studied, a review of the literature, methods, data collection, data analysis and findings, and conclusions and implications.

While the traditional case study reporting approaches are great for certain audiences, sometimes additional pieces should be considered for nonspecialists. Adapting communication and reporting to think about potentially making them more interactive is important in getting different audiences to understand and use the research (Patton, 2015; Torres, Preskill, & Piontek, 2005; Yin, 2014). Looking at Figure 5.2, there are examples of traditional and nontraditional pieces to help discussion. For instance, in doing a larger case study research project on digital learning within an organization, we needed to produce a data visualization infographic (see Figure 5.3) in addition to the traditional report in order to help communicate about the interview results with a broader audience (see Evergreen, 2014).

Least Interactive	Potentially Interactive	Most Interactive
Memos, Emails, newsletters, bulletins, briefs, brochures, websites	Verbal presentations (visual slides and flipcharts)	Working discussion sessions (skits, group sense making)
Paper reports (interim and comprehensive)	Video and multimedia presentations	Interactive dashboards
Executive summaries	Data visualizations and posters (live or digitized)	Webinar presentations (i.e., chat rooms, interactive whiteboards, web conferences)

Figure 5.2 Communication and Reporting Formats by Level of Potential Interaction
Credit line: adapted from Torres et al., 2005

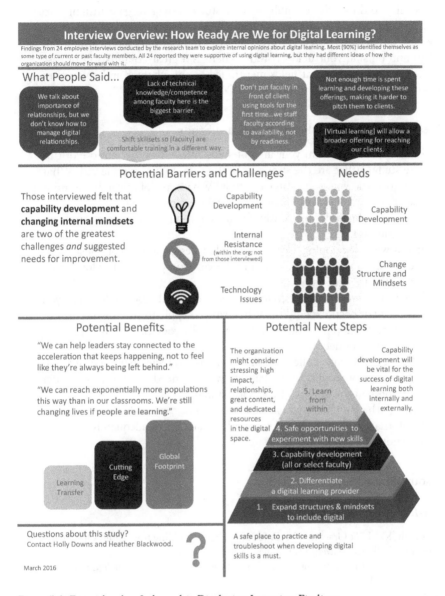

Figure 5.3 Example of an Infographic Displaying Interview Findings

Continuing to Apply

Evident from the discussion, case study research is more than conducting qualitative research on a single individual or situation. This approach can be simple or complex, encouraging the researcher to ask different types of questions in order to study phenomena in depth within their own contexts. For new researchers, case study can be very informative, as it provides a rich opportunity to do single- or multiple-case study designs to gain insight into the case using myriad data sources and analyses to inform multiple audiences. The best way to get started is to review case studies from empirical journals within and outside your field of study. There is a great compilation of case studies from many different fields mentioned in this chapter and covered in Yin's book, *The Case Study Anthology* (2004).

Questions for Further Review on Case Study

1. Find a case study from your area of study. What was the purpose of this case study? What are the strengths of the case study you reviewed? What limitations do you see in this case study? What types of research questions (i.e., descriptive, process, issue questions) were presented?
2. What would you do differently if you were to undertake a case study on the same case?
3. If you were developing a case study, what design would you most likely use? Would you use a single- or multiple-case study approach? How would you justify this decision?
4. What are some common characteristics across all case studies that you have read or been exposed to? What can you apply to your own research?
5. Will you develop a theoretical framework for your case study? How will you justify your decision?
6. What are the data collection and analysis strategies being considered? What issues of validity and reliability will you need to attend to in order to strengthen the quality of your case study?
7. Identify the audiences you anticipate for your case study report. Do you think that one report would serve all the audiences adequately? Why or why not?

Resources for More Information

Peer-Reviewed Journal Articles

Eisenhardt, K. M., & Graebner, M. E. (2007). Theory building from cases: Opportunities and challenges. *Academy of Management Journal, 50*(1), 25–32.

Flyvbjerg, B. (2006). Five misunderstandings of case-study research. *Qualitative Inquiry, 12*(2), 219–245.

Nespor, J. (2000). Anonymity and place in qualitative inquiry. *Qualitative Inquiry, 6,* 546–571.

Stringfield, S. C., & Yakimowski-Srebnick, M. E. (2005). Promise, progress, problems, and paradoxes of three phases of accountability: A longitudinal case study of the Baltimore City public schools. *American Educational Research Journal, 42*(1), 43–75.

Wells, A. S., Hirshberg, D., Lipton, M., & Oaks, J. (1995). Bounding the case within its context: A constructivist approach to studying detracking reform. *Educational Researcher, 24,* 18–24.

Books

Hancock, D. R., & Algozzine, B. (2015). *Doing case study research: A practical guide for beginning researchers.* New York, NY: Teachers College Press.
Stake, R. E. (1995). *The art of case study research.* Thousand Oaks, CA: Sage Publications.
Yin, R. K. (2004). *The case study anthology.* Thousand Oaks, CA: Sage Publications.
Yin, R. K. (2014). *Case study research: Design and methods* (5th ed.). Thousand Oaks, CA: Sage Publications.

References

Baxter, P., & Jack, S. (2008). Qualitative case study methodology: Study design and implementation for novice researchers. *The Qualitative Report, 13*(4), 544–559.
Berg, B. L. (2004). *Qualitative research methods for the social sciences* (Vol. 5): Boston, MA: Pearson.
Berson, Y., & Avolio, B. J. (2004). Transformational leadership and the dissemination of organizational goals: A case study of a telecommunication firm. *The Leadership Quarterly, 15*(5), 625–646. doi:http://dx.doi.org/10.1016/j.leaqua.2004.07.003
Bickman, L., & Rog, D. J. (2009). *The SAGE handbook of applied social research methods.* Los Angeles, CA: Sage Publications.
Cann, A. (2005). Extended matching sets questions for online numeracy assessments: A case study. *Assessment & Evaluation in Higher Education, 30*(6), 633.
Chmiliar, L. (2010). Multiple-case designs. *Encyclopedia of Case Study Research,* 1–2.
Cho, J., & Trent, A. (2006). Validity in qualitative research revisited. *Qualitative Research, 6*(3), 319–340.
Cook, T. D., & Campbell, D. T. (1979). *Quasi-experimentation: Design & analysis issues for field settings.* Chicago: Rand McNally & Co.
Cosmides, L., & Tooby, J. (1989). Evolutionary psychology and the generation of culture, part II: Case study: A computational theory of social exchange. *Ethology and Sociobiology, 10*(1–3), 51–97.
Creswell, J. W. (2009). *Research design: Qualitative, quantitative, and mixed method approaches* (3rd ed.). Thousand Oaks, CA: Sage Publications.
Denzin, N. K., & Lincoln, Y. S. (2011). *The Sage handbook of qualitative research.* Thousand Oaks, CA: Sage Publications.
Downs, H. A. (2014). Evaluation in STEM online graduate degree programs in agricultural sciences and engineering. *Journal of Case Studies in Education, 5,* 1.
Egel, A. L., & Barthold, C. H. (2010). Single subject design and analysis. *The Reviewer's Guide to Quantitative Methods in the Social Sciences,* 357–370.
Eisenhardt, K. M., & Graebner, M. E. (2007). Theory building from cases: Opportunities and challenges. *Academy of Management Journal, 50*(1), 25–32.
Evergreen, S. D. (2014). *Presenting data effectively: Communicating your findings for maximum impact.* Thousand Oaks, CA: SAGE Publications.
Gall, M. D., Borg, W. R., & Gall, J. P. (1996). *Educational research: An introduction.* White Plains, NY: Longman Publishing.
Garrett, L. A., & Vogt, C. L. (2003). Meeting the needs of consumers: Lessons from business and industry. *New Directions for Adult and Continuing Education,* (100), 89–101.
Hatch, J. A. (2002). *Doing qualitative research in education settings.* Albany: SUNY Press.

Hill, C. E., Carter, J. A., & O'Farrell, M. K. (1983). A case study of the process and outcome of time-limited counseling. *Journal of Counseling Psychology, 30*(1), 3.

Korzilius, H. (2010). Quantitative analysis in case study. *Encyclopedia of Case Study Research, 2.*

Luo, W., & Wang, F. (2003). Measures of spatial accessibility to health care in a GIS environment: Synthesis and a case study in the Chicago region. *Environment and Planning B: Planning and Design, 30*(6), 865–884.

Maxwell, J. (1992). Understanding and validity in qualitative research. *Harvard Educational Review, 62*(3), 279–301.

Maxwell, J. (2013). *Qualitative research design: An interactive approach* (3rd ed.). Thousand Oaks, CA: Sage publications.

McAdams, D. R., Hess, G. A., & Viteritti, J. P. (1999). Lessons from Houston. *Brookings Papers on Education Policy,* (2), 129–183.

Merriam, S. B., & Tisdell, E. J. (2015). *Qualitative research: A guide to design and implementation.* San Francisco, CA: John Wiley & Sons.

Mertens, D. M. (2010). *Research and evaluation in education and psychology* (3rd ed.). Thousand Oaks, CA: Sage Publications.

Messick, S. (1989). Meaning and values in test validation: The science and ethics of assessment. *Educational Researcher, 18*(2), 5–11. doi:10.3102/0013189x018002005

Miles, M. B., & Huberman, A. M. (1994). *Qualitative data analysis* (2nd ed.). Thousand Oaks, CA: Sage Publications.

Patton, M. Q. (2015). *Qualitative research and evaluation methods* (4th ed.). Thousand Oaks, CA: Sage Publications.

Perren, L., & Ram, M. (2004). Case-study method in small business and entrepreneurial research mapping boundaries and perspectives. *International Small Business Journal, 22*(1), 83–101.

Saldaña, J. (2015). *The coding manual for qualitative researchers.* Thousand Oaks, CA: Sage Publications.

Schwandt, T. A. (2007). *The Sage dictionary of qualitative inquiry* (3rd ed.). Thousand Oaks, CA: Sage Publications.

Shavelson, R., & Towne, L. (2002). *Scientific inquiry in education.* Washington, DC: National Academy Press.

Stake, R. E. (1995). *The art of case study research.* Thousand Oaks, CA: Sage Publications.

Torres, R. T., Preskill, H., & Piontek, M. E. (2005). *Evaluation strategies for communicating and reporting: Enhancing learning in organizations* (2nd ed.). Thousand Oaks, CA: Sage Publications.

van Oort, L., Schröder, C., & French, D. P. (2011). What do people think about when they answer the brief illness perception questionnaire? A 'think-aloud' study. *British Journal of Health Psychology, 16*(2), 231–245. doi:10.1348/135910710x500819

Weiss, C. H. (1998). *Evaluation* (2nd ed.). Upper Saddle River, NJ: Prentice Hall.

Wester, K. L., Downs, H. A., & Trepal, H. C. (2016). Factors linked with increases in nonsuicidal self-injury: A case study. *Counseling Outcome Research and Evaluation, 7*(1), 3–20.

Wieringa, R. J. (2014). Observational case studies. In *Design science methodology for information systems and software engineering* (pp. 225–245). Berlin: Springer.

Wolcott, H. F. (1990). *Writing up qualitative research* (Vol. 20). Newbury Park, CA: Sage Publications.

Yin, R. K. (2004). *The case study anthology.* Thousand Oaks, CA: Sage Publications.

Yin, R. K. (2014). *Case study research: Design and methods* (5th ed.). Beverly Hills, CA: Sage Publications.

6   Using Single-Case Research Designs to Evaluate Outcomes

A. Stephen Lenz & Karisse A. Callender

So far, you have reviewed some important ways that researchers determine how efficacious interventions or programs are when looking at desired effects. In this chapter, we will review single-case research designs (SCRDs), one of two approaches that have been endorsed as able to demonstrate what works, for whom, how, and under what circumstances (Chambless et al., 1996, 1998). The purpose of this chapter is to orient you to the general activities associated with SCRDs and get you started on the road to designing your own. Within this discussion, you will begin to understand how foundational concepts, design and analysis activities, and prudent interpretation of findings contribute to a defensible depiction of relationships between interventions and associated outcomes. Following, we have provided you with some resources that provide a more comprehensive discussion of these topics.

What Are SCRDs?

Single-case research designs (SCRDs) are a practical way to evaluate the efficacy of an intervention, establish preliminary support for novel practices, and assess applications of established programs with low incidence or understudied populations. Similar to the other experimental methods (e.g., Randomized Controlled Trials, Chapter 9) well-designed SCRDs can demonstrate a cause-and-effect relationship between an intervention and dependent variables; unlike other experimental designs, in SCRDs, participants function as their unit for analysis, and progress is determined on an individual level instead of across groups (Cook, Codding, Silva, & Hayden, 2017; Lenz, 2015; O'Neill, McDonnell, Billingsley, & Jenson, 2011). Within these designs, the *single case* of interest is not bound to an individual and instead can be representative of an individual client, family, group, or system (Morgan & Morgan, 2009; O'Neill et al., 2011). Regardless of how your case is defined, your participants will always serve as their own comparison through the process of contrasting data collected during and after the intervention with those collected prior to the introduction of an independent variable (Egel & Barthold, 2010; Rubin & Belamy, 2012). As a result, SCRD analyses provide a wealth of information related to the unique magnitude and course of outcomes that individuals experience during an intervention. Although the data collected for a single participant's experience can be useful, the power of SCRDs lies in the accumulation of many cases whose data can be visually inspected and statistically aggregated to depict an overall effect (Lenz, 2013; Bowman-Perrott, Davis, Vannest, Williams, Greenwood, & Parker, 2013).

The beauty of using SCRDs to evaluate the outcome of interventions lies in their many practical advantages related to sample size, self as control, flexibility and responsiveness, ease of analysis, and type of data yielded. For example, the minimum sample size required for an SCRD is one, but most will include between three and 10 participants as a precaution against attrition. Also, being able to compare participant performance during and after an intervention with their experiences prior to it starting provides the basis for a functional relationship and thus causal inferences about outcomes. Within an SCRD, the repeated and consistent assessment of participant performance allows researchers to adjust their interventions so that people who may not respond to an intervention will have the chance to do so. Once an SCRD is completed, there are many statistically based approaches available to estimate intervention effect; however, the many trustworthy approaches require little more than a graph of your data, a straightedge, a pencil, and some basic arithmetic. As you will see in our discussion of situating SCRD results to participant context, the data yielded from these inquiries provides a depiction of the course of intervention effects and the amount of dosage that may be required to meet the intended criterion. What emerges from well-designed SCRDs is a body of empirical literature that can support practitioners in monitoring the progress of individual clients, completing larger program evaluations, maintaining evidence-based practice, and completing stakeholder reporting.

Situations Most Appropriate for SCRDs

Earlier in this chapter, we identified SCRDs as being a practical way to evaluate the efficacy of interventions and assess how programs are applied with underrepresented populations. One of the great things about using SCRDs is the ability to apply this design in a variety of settings such as inpatient, outpatient, partial hospitalization, private practice, community agencies, institutions of learning, and within your community. The results from SCRDs can be useful when reporting to stakeholders about treatment efficacy and the impact on the community. Kazdin (2011) also identified SCRDs as being applicable across several disciplines including education, psychology, social work, business, counseling, law enforcement, medicine, and corrections. SCRDs are appropriate when you have a low number of participants in your research, as the design is not likely to fail, because the minimum number of participants needed for SCRDs is one. In addition, researchers who desire to identify the course of treatment and observe for efficacy will find SCRDs an appropriate design.

Types of Research Questions Best Suited for SCRDs

Although a number of case study approaches are suitable for answering myriad research questions, the quantitative SCRDs discussed in this chapter are particularly well-suited to answer two general types of research questions—those that estimate the degree of intervention effect and those related to exploring how individuals respond to an intervention. Research questions concerning degree of treatment effect should include language that establishes a causal relationship between a participant's experience with a dependent variable before your intervention and after it is introduced. Examples of these prompts include, "To what degree does an in-home reading intervention increase reading comprehension among school-aged children following a traumatic brain injury?", "How effective is a Graston treatment for increasing hip mobility among collegiate volleyball players?", and "How efficacious is a 12-week child-centered play therapy intervention for increasing on-task behavior in children with attention deficit hyperactivity disorder?" In each of these examples, the introduction of the interventions (i.e., in-home reading intervention, Graston treatment, and play therapy) is situated in a way that is intended to cause desired change among outcomes of interest (i.e., reading comprehension, hip mobility, and on-task behavior).

Research questions concerning how individuals respond to an intervention should include language related to important concepts such as immediacy of effect, course of response to intervention, and time until a desired criterion is met. Examples of these prompts include, "How many sessions are required to increase reading comprehension?", "What is the course of hip mobility gains during treatment?", and "How many sessions of play therapy are required for participants to no longer meet criteria for hyperactivity?" In each of these examples, the interest is associated with understanding the participant's personal response to the intervention. The answers to research questions related to intervention effect are best inferred from inspection of quantitative estimates of treatment effect and effect size, such as the nonoverlap and regression-based approaches discussed ahead. By contrast, the answers to questions related to how someone responds to an intervention are best inferred by using strategies for visual analysis of graphical data. We will address both approaches in our discussion of methodology, but first, let's consider an illustrative case example.

Case Example: Treating Response to Interpersonal Violence

To illustrate the application of methodological concepts, we present an example evaluating a 12-week, community-based, trauma-focused cognitive behavior therapy (TF-CBT) (Cohen, Mannarino, & Deblinger, 2017) program for adolescents who have been the victim of repeated interpersonal violence at school. The five participants range from ages 13 to 15, and all met the criteria for a diagnosis of posttraumatic stress disorder (PTSD) following a clinical interview and converging evidence from formal PTSD assessments.

Participant symptoms were monitored weekly for 3 weeks (N = 3) and 5 weeks (N = 2) across participants. Once treatment began, participants completed the Child PTSD Scale one time a week while waiting for their scheduled appointment. As part of the TF-CBT treatment, all participants received a manualized series of coping skills training modules during the first 7 weeks with the remaining 5 weeks oriented to completing a trauma narrative and safety planning for posttermination life.

SCRD Methodology

This section will discuss the characteristics and common designs used when implementing SCRDs. You will also learn about considerations for designs and what is involved in data analysis.

Characteristics Across All SCRDs

In SCRDs, inferences about the efficacy of interventions are made by comparing observations of an outcome across various phases of the study. A few key characteristics across all SCRDs are fundamental to their experimental nature. Among some of the most important to be familiar with are the concepts of baseline assessment, continuous assessment, performance stability, self as comparison, minimal sample size, and flexibility/responsiveness.

Baseline Assessment

In SCRDs, data is collected prior to any intervention during what is referred to as a *baseline phase*. Through baseline data, researchers can gather information about the level of particular behaviors before introducing an intervention. This initial period of observation serves two important functions. The first function, referred to as the *descriptive function*, describes the extent to which a participant engages in the behavior being studied. The second function is *prediction* of the immediate level of performance when intervention is not administered. This data serves as the comparison to all other data in an SCRD.

Continuous Assessment

One of the central requirements of an SCRD is the dependence on outcome variables being continually assessed over time. The researcher observes the participant's behavior across several occasions, occurring pre- and postintervention. Continuous assessment is a basic requirement of SCRDs, as this design examines the efficacy of interventions across time. Researchers can establish trends and patterns of behavior before implementing an intervention.

Performance Stability

Stability of performance can be explained by the absence of a slope in the data. The slope of data refers to the increase or decrease in performance over time. In addition, stability can be determined based on the level of variability of performance over time. Increased variability may adversely impact any conclusions about treatment efficacy.

Self as Comparison

Researchers utilizing an SCRD also have the ability to observe and evaluate the impact of interventions on overt behavior through the use of visual inspection. Additionally, researchers are able to use the participant as their own control in an SCRD. This means the participant is their own comparison condition when comparing their scores during and after the implementation of an intervention. The researcher is then able to observe for cause-and-effect relationship between the intervention and behavior being observed.

Minimal Sample Size

One characteristic central to SCRDs is the focus on one or a few participants. These designs are referred to as *small N research, single-case design*, or *N = 1 designs*. Since these designs are developed to study individual behavior over time, SCRDs can be implemented with one participant; however, in order to account for attrition, at least three to five participants are recommended.

Flexibility and Responsiveness

SCRDs can be implemented with diverse or unique populations in a variety of settings. SCRDs are not limited to a single set of standards or protocols; therefore, researchers have the ability to be flexible and adaptive in their approach to capture as many participants as needed. In addition, accommodation can be made for the amount of intervention needed across phases.

Common Designs

We have discussed the idea that SCRDs are used to evaluate the efficacy of an intervention over a period of time. SCRDs begin with repeated measurement of an outcome before introducing the intervention, but what happens afterward can take various forms in the effort to answer your research questions. Two general categories of SCRDs are those that are best suited for monitoring and those that are well-suited for garnering evidentiary support.

Designs Suitable for Monitoring

The most basic SCRD, the A-B design, can be used to document change in target behaviors at a single point and is the foundation of all SCRDs. In this design, the researcher collects baseline data (A) until stability is observed, then the intervention is implemented (B) while continuously observing the target outcome.

Figure 6.1 A-B Design

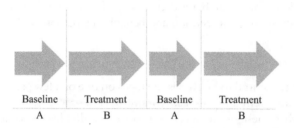

Figure 6.2 A-B-A-B Design

Researchers may make inferences from visual analysis of the graphed data while observing for any change in trends and patterns. Although important details about participants' experience can be observed using an A-B design, they are less defensible for demonstrating a cause-and-effect relationship between an intervention and the outcome of interest. In order to ease concerns about the threats to internal validity, researchers can implement another baseline (A) at the end, resulting in an A-B-A design. However, it should be noted that even with an A-B-A design, the threats-to-interval validity associated with an absence of replication persist.

Designs Suitable for Garnering Evidentiary Support

One of the characteristics of SCRDs is continuous assessment, in which the participant's behavior can be monitored across several occasions, as the intervention is repeated or replicated over time. Replication designs strengthen the conclusion that improvement can be attributed to the intervention. Examples of replication designs include A-B-A-B or A-B-A-B-A-B. Within these designs, the withdrawal of an intervention and reintroduction of it demonstrates a truer effect over time on participant experience, and thus, there is more internal validity as an effect is observed with every replication.

Replications may be difficult to pull off, or, in some settings, withdrawing an intervention may be unethical; therefore, using a multiple baseline design is a prudent alternative. Multiple-baseline designs comprise a series of A-B designs repeated in numerous ways: with the same individuals across various behaviors (multiple baselines across behaviors), the same behavior across various individuals (multiple baseline across subjects), or same individual across different settings (multiple baseline across settings). With multiple baselines, researchers collect baseline data at the same time across several participants, introducing the intervention only at systematic times when stability has been established. Baseline data can be collected on two or more behaviors, and the effect of an intervention is demonstrated by showing that the participant's behavior changes only when the intervention is applied. Multiple baselines do not require withdrawal or reversal of interventions; therefore, this is an appropriate design for establishing new behaviors.

Design Considerations

The best SCRDs clearly depict functional relationships between an intervention and the dependent variable of interest. When this relationship is clearly established through multiple baselines or replication designs, the design is thought to be more defensible to scrutiny than when those characteristics are present to a lesser degree. Within any design, some important considerations should be addressed, including those related to sample size, homogeneity of the sample, sensitivity of measurements, and fidelity of the intervention.

Sample Size

As mentioned, some useful information can be garnered from an SCRD with a sample size of one. However, guidelines for demonstrating evidentiary support require demonstration of treatment effect across three to nine participants to be regarded as having modest support and 10 or more to be considered well-established (Chambless et al., 1996, 1998). In either scenario, evidence is most robust when findings converge across at least two different research teams residing at different sites. In the example of our illustrative case, there are five participants; therefore, even if the results depicted a clear picture of efficacy, the quality of support yielded would be modest at most.

Homogeneity of the Sample

Because there is a small number of participants within an SCRD, those participants should be similar in important ways. The amount of similarity across participants, referred to as the homogeneity of the sample, is directly related to the defensibility of inferences about the intervention effect. In our case example, the participants were all boys who were about the same age and experiencing the same response (PTSD symptoms) to a common problem (bullying). When making inferences, the findings from this sample are more trustworthy than a sample of five participants from a wide range of ages (e.g., 8 to 17 years) and genders with different types of trauma and presenting symptoms (PTSD versus depression and self-injury).

Sensitivity of Measurements

The consistent, repeated nature of outcome measurement in SCRDs presents a unique consideration for researchers. Approaches to measuring outcomes should closely align with the phenomena intended to influence. In our case example, the target change was PTSD symptoms, and the associated measurement, the Child PTSD Symptom Scale (CPSS), was developed to reflect diagnostic criteria for PTSD. Several informal and formal assessments are available to facilitate this practice, but guidelines for use and adaptation-intended use should be considered in relationship to the frequency of your measurement interval. For example, the Direct Observation Form (Achenbach & Rescorla, 2001) is designed to rate observations of children's behavior and can be administered with some amount of regularity, whereas the Beck Anxiety Inventory (BAI; Beck & Steer, 1990; Beck, Epstein, Brown, & Steer, 1988) captures symptom expression over the last month and is not intended for multiple uses within the same week. In the case example, the instructions of the CPSS were modified from reporting changes in the previous 2 weeks to reflect progress in between sessions (1 week).

Fidelity of Intervention

Although flexibility is a prominent strength of SCRDs, the intervention should share some important commonalities across participants. Approaches to promote fidelity include demonstrating provider competence, using manualized approaches, and documenting adherence to essential intervention content and processes. In our case example, the providers were master's-level mental health counselors with at least 5 years of experience working with adolescents and advanced training in TF-CBT. Additionally, they were using a manualized approach to treating PTSD among adolescents (TF-CBT), and they were documenting completion of program modules weekly. It is important to remember that fidelity is not categorical (i.e., you have it or you do not); instead it is an estimate of credibility upon which we can infer degrees of internal and external validity.

Taken together, when SCRDs have a sufficient sample that is homogeneous, features sensitive measurements, and accounts for fidelity of the intervention, the design is more likely to depict the actual intervention effect rather than influences from other extraneous influences.

Data Analysis and Interpretation

We suggested earlier in this chapter that certain data analysis approaches are best suited to answer certain types of SCRD research questions. We also mentioned that approaches to data analysis ranged from fairly simple to more complex. In either case, important inferences can be made about the effectiveness of an intervention. Regardless, we submit that the data analysis used in an

SCRD should be based on at least two things: (a) the nature of your research question and (b) the characteristics of your baseline data. Among the bevy of available analysis options, most can be clustered within the general categories of visual analysis, measures of treatment effect, and estimates of effect size.

Visual Analysis

Visual analysis is the process of making determinations about intervention effects based on impressions derived from graphical representation of data, such as that represented in Figure 6.3. Brossart, Parker, Olson, and Mahadevan (2006) suggested that depictions of data should include information to place findings in context (target behavior, time frame, instrument used), be considered in terms of practical effect, lead to impressions about degree of effect, and be accompanied by quantitative metrics. At a minimum, visual analysis takes into consideration characteristics referred to as level, variability, and trend.

LEVEL

Evaluation of the level refers to comparing general representations of data in each intervention phase, typically represented by either the mean or median. When baseline data are stable, the mean of data points across phases is indicated; however, in the presence of an unstable baseline data trend or a notable outlier, use of the median value may be prudent. Consider the example of Chris in Figure 6.3, whose baseline data (34, 36, 35) appear relatively stable. Therefore, we can compare the range of distance between average scores in the baseline (35) and intervention (24) phases and estimate the practical usefulness of this 11-point difference.

VARIABILITY

Interpretations of visual data should consider the degree of variability versus stability of data within baseline and intervention phases. When data in the baseline phase is highly variable, inferences about the way that the intervention influences the outcome is less defensible. Similarly, intervention-phase data is more reliable when the desired change is stable and not vacillating greatly from observation to observation. In our case example data (Figure 6.3), Chris's baseline data shows distinctive stability, whereas Earl's baseline data features comparatively more variability.

TREND

Evaluating the trend of data denotes identifying the pattern of data in the baseline and intervention phases in ways that range from simple (increasing or decreasing) to complex (cyclical, curvilinear, erratic). The trend provides useful information about the course and nature of treatment, which can be

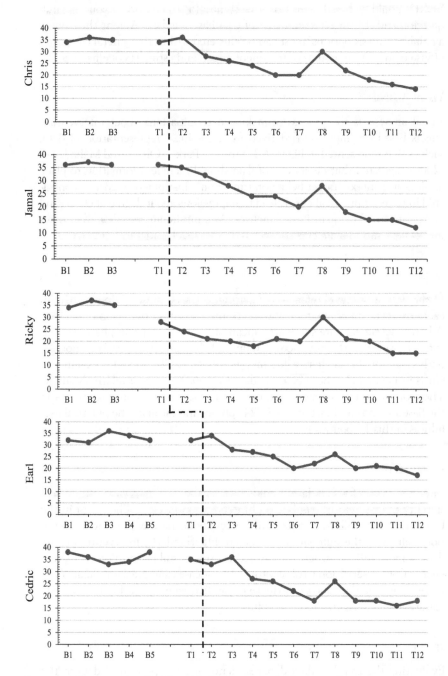

Figure 6.3 Scores on the Childhood PTSD Symptom Scale Across Baseline and Treatment Phases

supplemented with narrative accounts to explain complexities, such as apparently spurious peaks and valleys in the data. For example, all participants in our case example had seemingly linear and decreasing data trends with exception of a peak in T8. Accounts from the researcher can share that this is the phase of TF-CBT at which the focus moves from coping skills training and practice to developing a trauma narrative and more directly and concretely confronting traumatic material.

Measures of Treatment Effect Whereas visual analysis has a longstanding history within SCRD traditions, their complementary use with quantitative measures of treatment effect has become a standard of practice. One of the most enduring approaches is to compute an estimate based on the proportion that results when comparing the number of data points in an intervention phase to those that overlap with data in a baseline phase. Two of the more predominate and easy to use, in our opinion, are the percentage of nonoverlapping data (PND; Scruggs, Mastropieri, & Casto, 1987) and the percentage of data points exceeding the median (PEM; Ma, 2006). In PND and PEM, the number of data points in the intervention phase that do not overlap with an identified point in the baseline phase is divided by the total number of observations in the intervention phase. For PND, the identified datum point is the most therapeutic value, and for PEM, that value is the median among scores. In either case, the resulting values are interpreted using a handy rubric suggested by Scruggs and Mastropieri (2001), wherein scores greater than 90% represent very effective treatments, scores ranging from 70 to 90% represent effective treatments, scores from 50 to 70% are debatable, and scores below 50% are regarded as ineffective.

Estimates of Effect Size In contrast to providing estimates of treatment effect that are based on proportions of overlap, more true estimates of effect size are available such as those based in linear regression of scores, standardization of mean gain (Hedges, Pustejovsky, & Shadish, 2012), and statistically combining nonoverlap with trend analysis (Parker, Vannest, Davis, & Sauber, 2011). Although all of these can be computed by hand, use of Excel or a related program is recommended. Each of these choices provides important information that explains the amount and direction of change between baseline and intervention phases.

Putting It All Together

SCRDs are a wonderful addition to the researcher's toolbox because they allow for the evaluation of outcomes in a way that requires small samples yet still yields causal data. Just like any other approach to research, there are strengths and limitations, and some designs are more robust than others. When done well, SCRDs can give voice to the experience of low-incidence populations, depict the utility of novel interventions, and support evaluation of existing programs that may not have access to large numbers of participants needed for a between-groups comparison. The body of literature related to SCRDs is growing month to month, and we have included some resources in what follows that may support your curiosity and application within your setting.

Continuing to Apply

Now that you have walked through the possibilities of SCRD, more specifically A-B and A-B-A designs, consider other methods or applications. First, consider if either of these designs might fit into your clinical experiences or setting. Is there an intervention or program that would be helpful for you to evaluate using an SCRD? Now consider other designs. While the most common SCRD are A-B and A-B-A designs, other designs exist as well, such as A-B-C designs or A-B-A-C-A designs. These designs would be examples of when you may have more than one intervention to test, such as trying to determine if one intervention or treatment is more impactful or efficacious than another. How might you set up an A-B-A-C-A design?

Resources for More Information

Online

Computing measures of treatment effect and effect size. Retrieved from www.singlecaser esearch.org/

List of resources and seminal references. Retrieved from http://ethics.iit.edu/projects/ single-subject-research

Peer-Reviewed Journal Articles

Bowman-Perrott, L., Davis, H., Vannest, K., Williams, L., Greenwood, C., & Parker, R. (2013). Academic benefits of peer tutoring: A meta-analytic review of single-case research. School Psychology Review, 42, 39–55.

Cook, A., Codding, R., Silva, M., & Hayden, L. (2017). Enhancing school counselor research and practice in data-based assessment through single-case research design. Counseling Outcome Research and Evaluation, 8, 48-62. doi:10.1080/21501378.20 17.1327746

Egel, A. L., & Barthold, C. H. (2010). Single subject design and analysis. In G. R. Hancock & R. O. Mueller (Eds.), The reviewer's guide to quantitative methods in the social sciences (pp. 357–370). New York, NY: Routledge.

Foster, L. H. (2010). A best kept secret: Single-subject research design in counseling. Counseling Outcome Research and Evaluation, 1, 30–39. doi:10.1177/21501378103 87130

Lenz, A. S. (2015). Single-case research: Using single-case research designs demonstrate evidence for counseling practices. Journal of Counseling & Development, 93, 387–393. doi:10.1002/jcad.12036

Ray, D. (2015). Single-case research design and analysis: Counseling applications. Journal of Counseling & Development, 93, 394–402. doi:10.1002/jcad.12037

Books

Barlow, D. H., Nock, M. K., & Hersen, M. (2009). *Single case experimental designs: Strategies for studying behavior change* (3rd ed.). Boston, MA: Pearson.

Kazdin, A. E. (2011). *Single-case research designs: Methods for clinical and applied settings.* (2nd ed.). New York, NY: Oxford University Press.

Morgan, D. L., & Morgan, R. K. (2009). *Single-case research methods for the behavioral and health sciences.* Thousand Oaks, CA: Sage Publications.

O'Neill, R. E., McDonnell, J. J., Billingsley, F. F., & Jenson, W. R. (2011). *Single case research designs in educational and community settings.* Boston, MA: Pearson.

Vannest, K. J., Davis, J. L., & Parker, R. I. (2013). *Single case research in schools: Practical guidelines for school-based professionals.* New York, NY: Routledge.

Questions for Further Review and Application

1. SCRDs are useful for answering two categories of research questions. What are the two categories? Develop a research question for each one based on your interests.
2. SCRDs are helpful for evaluating the effect of an intervention across a single individual. If you were developing a study, what design would you use? What would your outcome variable be? How long would you collect data at baseline? How long would your intervention phase be?
3. What are some common characteristics across all SCRDs? How do they each support cause-and-effect inferences?
4. What are some design considerations for all SCRDs? How do they each support cause-and-effect inferences?
5. What are the three approaches to visual analysis, and what are some aspects of those analysis that are important to consider?

References

Achenbach, T. M., & Rescorla, L. A. (2001). *Manual for the ASEBA school-age forms & profiles.* Burlington, VT: Achenbach Research Center for Children, Youth, and Families.

Barlow, D. H., Nock, M. K., & Hersen, M. (2009). *Single case experimental designs: Strategies for studying behavior change* (3rd ed.). Boston, MA: Pearson.

Beck, A. T., Epstein, N., Brown, G., & Steer, R. A. (1988). An inventory for measuring clinical anxiety: Psychometric properties. *Journal of Consulting and Clinical Psychology, 56,* 893–897.

Beck, A. T., & Steer, R. A. (1990). *Manual for the Beck Anxiety Inventory.* San Antonio, TX: Psychological Corporation.

Bowman-Perrott, L., Davis, H., Vannest, K., Williams, L., Greenwood, C., & Parker, R. (2013). Academic benefits of peer tutoring: A meta-analytic review of single-case research. *School Psychology Review, 42,* 39–55.

Brossart, D. F., Parker, R. I., Olson, E. A., & Mahadevan, L. (2006). The relationship between visual analysis and five statistical analyses in a simple AB single-case research design. *Behavior Modification, 30,* 531–563.

Chambless, D. L., Baker, M., Baucom, D. H., Beutler, L. E., Calhoun, K. S., Crits-Christoph, P.,. . . . Woody, S. R. (1998). Update on empirically validated therapies, II. *The Clinical Psychologist, 51*, 3–16.

Chambless, D. L., Sanderson, W. C., Shoham, V., Johnson, S. B., Pope, K. S., Crits-Christoph, P.,. . . . McCurry, S. M. (1996). An update on empirically validated therapies. *The Clinical Psychologist, 49*, 5–18.

Cohen, J. A., Mannarino, A. P., & Deblinger, E. (2017). *Treating trauma and traumatic grief in children and adolescents*. New York, NY: Guilford Press.

Cook, A., Codding, R., Silva, M., & Hayden, L. (2017). Enhancing school counselor research and practice in data-based assessment through single-case research design. *Counseling Outcome Research and Evaluation, 8*, 48–62. doi:10.1080/21501378.2017.1327746

Hedges, L. V., Pustejovsky, J. E., & Shadish, W. R. (2012). A standardized mean difference effect size for single case designs. *Research Synthesis Methods, 3*, 224–239.

Kazdin, A. E. (2011). *Single-case research designs: Methods for clinical and applied settings.* (2nd ed.). New York, NY: Oxford University Press.

Lenz, A. S. (2013). Calculating effect size in single-case research: A comparison of nonoverlap methods. *Measurement and Evaluation in Counseling and Development, 46*, 64–73. doi:10.1177/0748175612456401

Lenz, A. S. (2015). Single-case research: Using single-case research designs to demonstrate evidence for counseling practices. *Journal of Counseling & Development, 93*, 387–393. doi:10.1002/jcad.12036

Ma, H. H. (2006). An alternative method for quantitative synthesis of single-subject research: Percentage of data points exceeding the median. *Behavior Modification, 30*, 598–617.

Morgan, D. L., & Morgan, R. K. (2009). *Single-case research methods for the behavioral and health sciences*. Thousand Oaks, CA: Sage Publications.

O'Neill, R. E., McDonnell, J. J., Billingsley, F. F., & Jenson, W. R. (2011). *Single case research designs in educational and community settings*. Boston, MA: Pearson.

Parker, R. I., Vannest, K. J., Davis, J. L., & Sauber, S. B. (2011). Combining nonoverlap and trend for single case research: Tau-U. *Behavior Therapy, 42*, 284–299.

Rubin, A., & Bellamy, J. (2012). *Practitioner's guide to using research for evidence-based practice* (2nd ed.). Hoboken, NJ: John Wiley & Sons, Inc.

Scruggs, T. E., & Mastropieri, M. A. (2001). How to summarize single-participant research: Ideas and applications. *Exceptionality, 9*, 227–244. doi:10.1207/S15327035EX0904_5

Scruggs, T. E., Mastropieri, M. A., & Casto, G. (1987). The quantitative synthesis of single subject research: Methodology and validation. *Remedial and Special Education, 8*, 24–33.

Sharpley, C. F. (2007). So why aren't counselors reporting $n = 1$ research designs? *Journal of Counseling and Development, 85*, 349–356.

7 Using Correlational and Causal-Comparative Research Designs in Practice

Exploring Relations Among Client Variables

Lindsey K. Umstead & Heather Mayton

As practitioners, we typically have questions about our services or clients. These may include questions such as why does some classroom guidance impact students more than others, why do female clients self-injure more than male clients, or why do children who attend counseling with their parents fare better than those who do not? Different research methodologies are used to answer different questions. In this chapter, we provide an overview of both correlational and causal-comparative research methods, which are used when you want to examine the relationship between two or more variables without any manipulation. Put simply, these research designs involve looking at two or more variables, as they currently exist, to determine if they are related in some way. In other words, manipulation is when you change something, such as an intervention, educational guidance, or medication, to see if that change works better or differently than what was done previously. While this manipulation is important to answer some research questions, through these two designs, you would not manipulate or change anything that you are currently doing with your students or clients; you would simply be examining how things relate or how groups differ based on how they currently exist. The purpose of this chapter is to expose you to each design in order to help you to understand and practically apply this in your own clinical setting. By the end of the chapter, you will have a foundational understanding of both correlational and causal-comparative research designs with regard to their methodologies, data analyses, specific types of research questions, and interpretation of your findings in addition to an understanding of the similarities and differences between the two methods. Additionally, you will learn how to design your own correlational and/or causal-comparative design, interpret the results, and determine if there is a relationship that exists between two or more different variables of interest.

Introduction to Correlational and Causal-Comparative Research Designs

Correlational and causal-comparative research designs are two types of quantitative descriptive methods that seek to define the existence and characteristics of various phenomena (Heppner, Wampold, & Kivlighan, 2008). Specifically, these two particular research designs aim to explore and identify associations, or relationships, between and among variables. While they are similar in what they are seeking to do, they also differ. Let's take a moment and start first with correlational research designs. With correlational designs, you are seeking to determine whether two variables are connected in such a way that as one increases, the other one either increases or decreases, or whether these two variables are not connected at all, thus unrelated. For example, you might notice that as clients spend more hours in counseling, they begin to acquire more healthy coping skills. Here, you would use a correlational research design to see if there is a positive relationship between the number of hours in therapy and the number of healthy coping skills acquired. This works similarly to exploring whether a negative relationship would exist between the number of hours spent in group counseling and behavioral disruptions in the classroom for students in a school; thus as the number of hours spent in group counseling increases, the frequency of behavioral disruption decreases.

Causal-comparative research, on the other hand, would be used to examine whether individuals in one group are different on one or more variables than individuals in at least one other group. For example, you might observe in your practice that clients who abuse substances use more maladaptive coping strategies than individuals who do not abuse substances. To see if a difference between these groups actually exists, you could use a causal-comparative design to see if clients who abuse substances use a significantly higher number of maladaptive coping strategies than clients who do not abuse substances.

A key difference between correlational and causal-comparative research involves the number of variables and the number of groups being studied (Gay & Airasian, 2000). Correlational research involves examining relationships among two or more independent and dependent variables for a single group in order to describe how these variables are related. Alternatively, causal-comparative research seeks to compare two or more groups on one or more dependent variables of interest. The groups you choose to examine serve as your independent variable, or the variable you change. By using causal-comparative designs, a researcher aims to determine whether the independent variable(s) (i.e., the group status or assignment one is in) causes the difference in the dependent variable(s)—or the outcome variable you are interested in. In general, correlational research aims to describe the relationship among variables, whereas causal-comparative research aims to identify whether an independent variable acts as the cause or reason for differences in one or more dependent variable of interest. Table 7.1 outlines the differences between these research designs.

On the other hand, there are some important similarities between correlational and causal-comparative research designs. First, both of these designs are considered *ex post facto*, or "after-the-fact," research designs. This means that the relationships between and among the variables you are studying are thought to have been present prior to the research being conducted and not due to any manipulation of the variables by the researchers. Consequently, correlational research would be considered *ex post facto* because you are

Table 7.1 Similarities and Differences Between Correlational and Causal-Comparative Research

Similarities	Differences	
	Correlational	Causal Comparative
• Descriptive quantitative designs	• Aims to understand relation between dependent variables	• Aims to begin understanding a causal relation between independent and dependent variables
• Examine relationships between and among variables	• Does not attempt to understand cause and effect	
• Lack of control over variables – neither is experimental	• One group	• Two or more groups (independent variable)
• Cannot infer direct causality from results	• Two or more dependent variables	• One or more dependent variables
• Results may lead to experimental research to test a hypothesis	• Requires a numerical score for each variable of interest for every person	• Involves at least one categorical variable (e.g., gender, race, ethnicity)

investigating a relationship between variables in a group that existed prior to the research being conducted. Similarly, causal-comparative research is also a type of *ex post facto* research due to the fact that the groups being looked at are predetermined, or already existing (e.g., gender, race, ethnicity, classrooms), as opposed to having been determined by the researcher (Heppner et al., 2008); thus, in both correlational and causal-comparative research designs, you are studying relationships that are between or among variables for groups that were present before your study began rather than being manipulated during your study (as you would in the experimental or quasi-experimental designs).

Another important similarity shared by correlational and causal-comparative research is that neither design allows you to infer direct causality from the results. With regard to correlational research, although you may find results showing a positive relationship between x and y variables, you cannot say that x causes y, and you also cannot say that y causes x. In other words, correlational research does not allow you to establish the *direction of causality*, or the path of a causal effect, between two variables (Aron, Aron, & Coups, 2008). For example, you may find that as clients' anxiety levels increase, their happiness levels decrease; however, from this, you do not know whether increased anxiety directly leads to decreased happiness or if decreased happiness directly leads to increased anxiety. Here, you cannot establish a direct causal relationship between increased anxiety and decreased happiness because there may be other factors influencing anxiety and happiness levels. Similarly, if you find in a correlational research study that a positive relationship exists between clients' stress levels and the number of positive coping skills they use, you would not be able to say that stress causes an increase in the number of positive coping skills they use, nor would you be able to say that the number of positive coping skills they use causes an increase in stress level. Instead, you simply understand that as one of these variables increases, the other one also increases.

Likewise, although the goal of causal-comparative research is to determine a causal relationship between an independent variable and a dependent variable, you cannot establish a true cause-and-effect relationship between these variables. That is, even though you may observe a difference between groups on a variable of interest, you cannot say that the groups themselves directly cause this difference. For example, in your practice, you may find that female clients report lower levels of workplace satisfaction than male clients; however, you would not be able to infer that being a female causes lower levels of workplace satisfaction. It may be that there are other factors contributing to lower levels of workplace satisfaction, such as more sexual harassment experienced in the workplace or receiving lower salaries than male coworkers. Additionally, because the groups you examine in causal-comparative research are preexisting before your study, you cannot say that a group status directly created or caused the difference in the dependent variable. In fact, for both correlational and causal-comparative research designs, you collect data on groups that were determined before your study instead of collecting data as groups are being manipulated or determined by you during the study. Due to this limitation, you would not be able to say that one variable truly causes the other because you did not manipulate or change anything or control other variables that might have influenced your results (Mitchell & Jolly, 2010).

When to Use Correlational and Causal-Comparative Methods

As we discussed earlier in this chapter, correlational and causal-comparative research are useful quantitative descriptive designs when you are interested in increasing your understanding of phenomena that you may observe in your clinical practice (Heppner et al., 2008). Specifically, these designs allow you to identify whether one thing relates to another, such as how hours spent in classroom guidance relates to student academic achievement. For counseling practitioners, these research designs may be used in multiple settings to explore client variables (e.g., race, gender), treatment variables (e.g., type of intervention used), and client outcomes (e.g., anxiety level), ultimately providing us with answers as to how these variables are related. While you may want to know if time in counseling *causes* decreases in depression, it may seem silly to use these research designs that will not provide you the degree to which that is true; however, research using these particular designs can serve as the foundation for experimental research or more exploration of cause and effect without needing the same levels of control or time and effort needed to manipulate how counseling is offered, or the length and time spent in counseling, but allows you to explore what currently exists among all of your clients at the same time. While limitations to these designs exist, correlational and causal-comparative research can be used to increase the effectiveness of counseling interventions used in your practice or school. Another way to think about the utility of correlational and causal-comparative research is to consider the bigger picture for your results. That is, what might be the implications for the results you find using a correlational or causal-comparative design? Subsequently, this may lead to better outcomes for the clients you serve in your practice. Even though cause and effect cannot be determined with these designs, relationships can, and this information about these relationships can apply to what you do with the clients you serve.

While earlier it was noted that similarities and differences exist between these designs, the question becomes when you would select correlational versus causal-comparative. Reflecting, if you have a question that is asking about the differences between two or more groups—such as what is the difference in disciplinary referrals from students in Ms. Smith's class versus Mr. Martin's class—you would select a causal-comparative design. But if you were interested in knowing how food insecurity related to disciplinary referrals, thus the relationship between two or more variables within groups as a whole, you would select correlational design.

Finally, these research designs may be used in any setting to answer important research questions. When considering where to use these research designs, consider settings such as community agencies, schools, colleges and universities, and inpatient or outpatient settings, where you can gather data from several clients or students in these settings to answer correlational or causal-comparative questions. Later in this chapter, we will discuss the importance of your sample size, or how many clients you observe in your study, when conducting correlational and causal-comparative research.

Research Questions Answered by Correlational and Causal-Comparative Designs

When developing research questions, you should first observe or identify your dependent variable(s), or the variable(s) you want to measure. The next step involves hypothesizing that your dependent variable is related to either another variable (in the case of a correlational research design) or a group status (in the case of a causal-comparative research design). For example, if you are interested in the depression level of adolescent females, this would be considered your dependent variable, which you may measure using a depression inventory, such as the Beck Depression Scale. Subsequently, you may hypothesize that social support (measured by counts of the number of friends and family members who provide support) has an influence on depression levels; therefore, this would be your independent variable.

It is important to note that how you measure any of the variables you are interested in will determine how you can answer your questions. This provides a specific way to define, or operationalize, your variable so that you are able to measure it according to that definition. It is important to note that in the case of both correlational and causal-comparative research, you need to use appropriate ways of measuring or assessing your variables of interest; however, that discussion is outside of the scope of this chapter and can be found more specifically in Chapter 4, "Evaluating and Designing Surveys."

When you are simply asking whether a relationship between two or more variables exists, you are asking a research question that would fit nicely within correlational research design. When developing a correlational research question, it is important to use language that establishes a relationship between the different variables you are studying. Here are some examples of research questions for correlational research:

- Is the number of hours spent practicing yoga related to counselor burnout?
- Is there a positive association between positive client outcomes and social support among African American women?
- Are there relationships among the hours of classroom guidance received, hours spent doing homework, and academic achievement in middle school students?

On the other hand, for a causal-comparative research design, you would be asking about differences between two or more different groups on one or more dependent variables. When developing this type of research question, it is important to use language that establishes an intent to compare two or more groups for differences. Example questions might include:

- Is there a difference between females' and males' depression scores after receiving outpatient therapy?
- Does the number of incidents per week of self-harm differ among Caucasian clients, African American clients, and Latino clients who present with depression?
- Are there differences in standardized test scores and number of days absent among high school students who report low, moderate, and high parental involvement?

Case Example: Is Social Support Related to Anxiety? Exploring Differences Between Male and Female Clients

The following case study will illustrate the application of both correlational and causal-comparative research methods. Imagine that you are a practitioner at a community mental health agency. Recently, you have noticed some differences between male and female clients with regard to the amount of social support they have and their levels of anxiety. You want to compare a sample of the agency's male clients to a sample of female clients on their social support and anxiety. Specifically, you are interested in (1) whether social support is related to anxiety levels across all clients (i.e., including both men and women) and (2) if there are differences between men and women in the amount of social support they have and in their anxiety levels. You will select similar-sized groups of men and women from your community agency, and you will collect their social support and anxiety scores.

For this study, you need to operationally define each variable. This means you need to determine the scope of what you want to know and how to measure it. For the sake of this case example, social support will be defined as the number of friends and family that provide some form of support to the individual each week, and this construct will be measured informally using the intake form clients complete before beginning mental health services. Anxiety will operationally be defined and measured according to the Beck Anxiety Inventory (BAI; Beck & Steer, 1993). Each client selected by you to participate in this study, to answer your research questions, will complete the BAI, in addition to the information they provided originally at intake about their social support. To answer your research questions, you will use a correlational research design to see if there is a relationship between social support and anxiety for both men and women combined as one group. If you were interested in exploring the differences between men and women, then you will use a causal-comparative research design to determine whether men and women differ both social support and anxiety. For the purposes of this chapter, we are staying with simpler designs, but these can also be used to explore more complex practice-oriented questions. For example, you could explore how social support impacts the differences in anxiety between men and women. Answering this question involves mediating and moderating relationships, which you can learn to use once you master the basics of research design. Just know that this ability to combine relationships and group differences does exist.

Methodology

Now that you have your research question outlining what you want to know, and you have your samples of men and women and understand how you are collecting this information through various measures, let's walk through the methodology of both of these designs.

Research Questions

It is important to determine your research questions before setting out to conduct your study, because the questions will determine the methodology you use.

Textbox 7.1 Research Questions

Correlational Research Questions

1. Is there a relationship between social support and anxiety in male clients?
2. Is there a relationship between social support and anxiety in female clients?

Causal-Comparative Research Questions

3. Is there a difference in the amount of social support between male and female clients?
4. Is there a difference in anxiety level between male and female clients?

As you can see in Textbox 7.1, the language used in these research questions indicates the type of research design you will use. Specifically, research questions 1 and 2 use a correlational design, and research questions 3 and 4 use a causal-comparative design.

Hypotheses

For each of these designs, it is important that you establish *hypotheses*, or predictions about what you expect to find in your results. The hypotheses can be directional, where you are predicting that there is a positive or negative relationship between two variables. Alternatively, your hypotheses can be nondirectional, where you are predicting that there is a relationship between the two variables, but you are not certain what kind of relationship. For example, a directional hypothesis would imply that there is a positive relationship between social support and anxiety, whereas a nondirectional hypothesis would imply that there is a relationship between social support and anxiety, but you are not clear on the direction. Notice that there is one hypothesis for each research question originally noted.

Textbox 7.2 Hypotheses

1. There is a relationship between social support and anxiety in male clients (nondirectional).
2. There is a positive linear relationship between social support and anxiety in female clients (directional).
3. Female clients have more social support than male clients (directional).
4. There is a difference in the level of anxiety between male and female clients (nondirectional).

Sample Size

There are many different ways to sample, including random sampling (selecting randomly from your clients) or convenience sampling (selecting specific clients, or the first few clients who walk into your office to complete the BAI). You may even use volunteer sampling (posting an advertisement or flier in your agency asking clients if they would like to participate). While there are pros and cons of each of these sampling methods, for this case example, your sample will consist of 35 males and 35 females from your community agency. While you could randomly sample, in this case you decide to simply use convenience sampling, and you sample the first males and females who come to your agency this month *and* agree to participate. It is important to note the impact of sample size, as the number of people you get to participate in a study influences what you may find and is influenced by a combination of factors including the statistic needed to answer your question, your measurement of the variables, the number of groups, and the number of variables, among many others. However, your sample may also be bound by the number of clients you have or who decides to participate. If you are running the statistical analysis to answer your question, know that in quantitative designs such as correlational and causal-comparative, it is important to determine your sample size through determining your statistical power. We are not going to spend time talking about that in this chapter, but know that it is important to determining final sample size.

Confounding Variables

In addition to determining the independent and dependent variables, you should consider if there is anything other than the independent variable (social support in this case) that might be influencing the dependent variable (anxiety). For example, while you believe social support may be one of the main reasons why anxiety is increasing or decreasing, you also believe that the number of sessions your clients have attended with you is also important to control, as it may confound (or change/alter) the relationship between social support and anxiety. In order to prevent this from happening, you would want to either control for these irrelevant variables (such as selecting only clients who have attended 30 counseling sessions with you, a homogenous sample) or randomly select clients from your practice, which controls for the possible effect through the sampling method or you could control for the confounding nature of number of counseling sessions by collecting this information and including it in your analysis.

Statistical Significance

In order to say that a relationship exists between two variables, you need to achieve statistical significance. Achieving statistical significance means that the relationship you observe in your results is likely not due to chance alone (Mitchell & Jolley, 2010). To determine this, you will refer to the appropriate test statistic for the statistical analysis you use. For both correlational and causal-comparative research, you will typically set an alpha level of 0.05 or lower to determine whether your results are statistically significant. Once you get your results, you compare the p-value determined by the statistical analysis you use to your preestablished alpha value in order to know whether your results are significant.

Data Analysis: Correlational Research Design

Many different analyses are appropriate for a correlational research design. These include but are not limited to correlations, regressions, and path analysis. We will not go in depth into all of these analyses, but know that they are all used for different reasons and ultimately may depend on how many variables you are comparing. What underlies each of these analyses is the correlation, so we are going to focus solely on the Pearson correlation coefficient (but note that there are many other correlation coefficients available as well).

Pearson Correlation Coefficient (r)

This is a measure of the strength of the relationship between two variables. The r-value will consist of (1) a numerical value ranging from -1 to 1 and (2) a positive or negative sign. These values correspond to the strength and the direction of the relationship. More specifically, a positive or negative sign indicates the *direction* of the association, and the r-value itself indicates the *strength* of the association; thus, the higher the absolute numerical value the stronger the relationship, with an r-value of (0.00) representing no relationship, an r-value of (±0.50) representing a moderate relationship, and an r-value of (±0.90) representing a strong relationship.

Visual Expression of Your Data

Providing your data in a scatterplot will allow for a visual understanding of the strength and direction of the relationship. The scatterplot graph can be created by plotting both values of social support and anxiety for each individual. There is no specific requirement for which variable goes on which axis. After the data have been plotted, the best-fit line will be drawn to visually see the linear relationship between the two variables more clearly (see Figure 7.1).

Interpreting Your Results

The interpretation of the results is structured based on the strength and direction of the relationship of the correlation. For a positive relationship, as one variable increases, the other variable increases as well. For a negative relationship, as one variable increases, the other variable decreases. The results of a correlational design can only inform researcher about the relationship, but the results do not infer causality of the relationship. In other words, a correlation would not imply that one variable causes another variable but rather would describe the relationship between the two.

Figure 7.1 Examples of Correlations

Note: (a) no correlation, (b) strong positive correlation, (c) strong negative correlation

Data Analysis: Causal-Comparative Research Design

Descriptive Statistics

Descriptive statistics are used to describe your data. Typically, these statistics include the mean, mode, and median for your groups. For example, when conducting a causal-comparative study, you are testing whether there is a difference in the *mean* scores of each of your groups. In the case of the present example, you would test whether there is a difference in the mean scores of social support and anxiety between male and female clients. Descriptive statistics do not typically allow you to draw inferences or conclusions based on the mean scores but simply provide you a visual of whether one group is, on average, greater or less than another group.

Inferential Statistics

Inferential statistics are used in a causal-comparative research to demonstrate a relation between your independent and dependent variables (Brewer & Kubn, 2012). Unlike descriptive statistics, inferential statistics allow you to make inferences, or conclusions, about your results. There are several types of statistical analyses that may be used when conducting causal-comparative research; however, the three most commonly used statistical tests for causal-comparative research designs include the chi-square test, paired-samples and independent *t*-tests, and a statistical test from the analysis of variance (ANOVA) family (e.g., ANOVA, multiple ANOVA [MANOVA], or analysis of covariance [ANCOVA]). The analysis you use depends on the number and type of independent and dependent variables you observe in your study and the number of groups you are comparing.

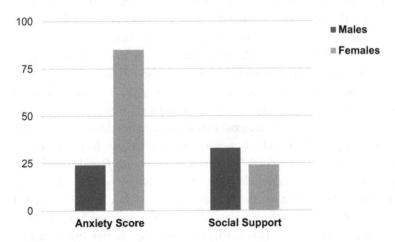

Figure 7.2 Bar Graph of Anxiety and Social Support Scores

Visual Expression of Your Data

When you use a causal-comparative design, there are various means by which to display your data and the results of your analysis. While most researchers may report the data simply using the statistics provided by the inferential analysis, another common way to present your data is through the use of bar or line graphs. These charts allow you to visually depict the descriptive statistics that show that a difference exists between your two groups (see Figure 7.2).

Interpreting Your Results

How you interpret your results will vary depending on the type of statistical analysis you use to answer your research question. Generally speaking, however, your results will inform you as to whether your groups are significantly different from each other and how your variables are related to one another. Specifically, for causal-comparative research designs, you will be able to determine from your results whether there is a difference between the groups you observe on your variable(s) of interest in order to infer that the difference you find is a result of an effect of the group.

Threats to Validity

In both correlational and causal-comparative designs, validity means that your data are accurate and that your findings reflect what they are intended to reflect. In causal-comparative research, there are various threats to the validity of your results. Because you are unable to randomly assign your clients to groups, the external validity of your results is limited. External validity refers to whether you can generalize your findings to those not included in your actual study or to clients that you did not collect data from. When your external validity is limited, this means that you cannot generalize, or apply, your results to all clients because your sample might not accurately represent your group of interest. Internal validity is also a consideration when it comes to these designs. Internal validity is the degree to which your results are actually true. As an example, if you found a difference in anxiety between males and females from your practice, to have internal validity would mean that you are confident that this difference found is truly due to being a male or a female. However, it may also be possible that some other innate difference may exist between groups, such as females attended more counseling sessions than males, which brings into question the internal validity of your study. This is why determining confounding variables is important.

Putting It All Together

Correlational and causal-comparative research designs both belong under the large umbrella of descriptive research studies and can be applied in any mental health setting to understand the relationship between two variables. Whether to use one design over the other depends on the specific research questions that are to be addressed. Despite the similarities and differences between these two specific designs, attempting to conduct this type of descriptive research has the potential to provide practitioners with valuable information concerning their clients, clients' outcomes, and clients' presenting concerns. In addition, correlational and causal-comparative research designs can provide the foundational step toward experimental designs that provide answers to causality of variables; therefore, these designs not only offer answers to your research questions, but they also provide insight into the bigger picture such as the effectiveness of treatment based on outcomes you observe. Looking beyond the possible benefits for clients, utilizing research methods allows practitioners to develop their own research skills and integrate their roles as both practitioners and researchers.

Continuing to Apply What You Have Learned

In this chapter, you have learned about correlational and causal-comparative designs, the types of research questions you can answer using these designs, and specific methodological considerations for each design. You have read through a case example illustrating how these research designs might be used in a counseling setting. Now it is your turn to think about applications for these research designs using your own experiences and interests as a counselor. First, consider how you might use one or both of these designs in your counseling setting. Are there two or more groups of clients that appear to show differences on a presenting issue that interests you (e.g., depression, anxiety, substance use)? Are you curious about whether a variable relates in some way to a certain issue for one group of your clients? As you work in your setting, begin to notice possible relationships between client groups, treatments, and outcomes.

Resources for More Information

Online

Correlation sample size calculator. Retrieved from www.sample-size.net/correlation-sample-size/

Fraenkel, J. R., & Wallen, N. E. (2017). *How to design and evaluate research in education*. Retrieved from http://highered.mheducation.com/sites/0072981369/student_view0/index.html

Peer-Reviewed Journal articles

Moinester, M., & Gottfried, R. (2014). Sample size estimation for correlations with pre-specified confidence interval. *The Quantitative Methods for Psychology, 10*, 124–130. doi:10.20982/tqmp.10.2.p124

Book Chapters

Brewer, E. W., & Kubn, J. (2012). Causal-comparative design. In *Encyclopedia of research design* (pp. 125–131). Thousand Oaks, CA: Sage Publications.

Questions for Further Review and Application

1. What are the similarities between correlational and causal-comparative research designs? What are the differences?
2. What are the design considerations for correlational research?
3. What are the design considerations for causal-comparative research?
4. Consider the setting in which you practice. How might you use correlational and/or causal-comparative research to understand two variables of interest to you?
5. What is an example of a correlational research question? What is an example of a causal-comparative research question?

References

Aron, A., Aron, E. N., & Coups, E. J. (2008). *Statistics for the behavioral and social sciences: A brief course* (4th ed.). Upper Saddle River, NJ: Pearson.

Beck, A. T., & Steer, R. A. (1993). *Beck anxiety inventory manual.* San Antonio, TX: Psychological Corporation.

Brewer, E. W., & Kubn, J. (2012). Causal-comparative design. In *Encyclopedia of research design* (pp. 125–131). Thousand Oaks, CA: Sage Publications.

Gay, L. R., & Airasian, P. W. (2000). *Educational research: Competencies for analysis and application* (6th ed.). Upper Saddle River, NJ: Pearson.

Heppner, P. P., Wampold, D. M., & Kivlighan, B. E. (2008). *Research design in counseling* (3rd ed.). Belmont, CA: Thomson Brooks-Cole.

Mitchell, M. L., & Jolly, J. L. (2010). *Research design explained* (7th ed.). Belmont, CA: Wadsworth.

8   Quasi-Experimental Methods

Casey A. Barrio Minton

As you are learning, there are many ways to investigate relationships in the helping professions. Quasi-experimental designs allow researchers to examine impact of an event or intervention on groups of individuals, families, or organizations in a practical, feasible manner. The purpose of this chapter is to introduce you to quasi-experimental methods and their role in mental health and human services professions. This chapter begins with an overview of quasi-experimental methods, situations most appropriate for the design, and types of research questions researchers can address with quasi-experimental methods. After presenting a practice-based case study, we will turn attention to specific characteristics, design considerations, and data analysis procedures utilized within quasi-experimental methodology. The chapter concludes with additional research and questions for application or reflection.

What Are Quasi-Experimental Methods?

Before exploring quasi-experimental methods specifically, it is important to understand the broader continuum of experimental designs. Most simply, experimental designs involve making causal inferences regarding the impact of an experience or intervention on one or more groups. It may help to think of a group as a collection of units; for example, we may have groups of individuals, families, classrooms, schools, or organizations. In human services and mental health professions, we most often focus on individuals or families as the unit of study.

There are three broad types of experimental designs: preexperiments, quasi-experiments, and true experiments (Thyer, 2012). **Preexperiments** investigate the impact of an experience or intervention on just one group without comparison to other groups. For example, a researcher may provide a bullying intervention to a group of students, measuring students' likelihood to intervene as bystanders before and after the intervention. Although simple, preexperimental designs do not allow researchers to determine whether interventions caused changes. It is possible that participants in the preexperiment started thinking about their role as bystanders when they completed the initial assessment, there was a widely publicized community event between measurements, or participants naturally matured over time. Without careful comparison, it would be nearly impossible to determine what caused the observed changes.

True experiments, including randomized control trials (RCTs) or randomized control designs (see Chapter 9), involve manipulating treatment conditions or interventions and randomly assigning units of study to groups in ways that allow researchers to conclude that the interventions caused changes among groups (Grant & Wall, 2009). For example, researchers may identify a group of individuals eligible for a bullying intervention, assess likelihood to intervene as bystanders before the intervention, randomly assign so half of participants engage in the intervention while the other half does treatment as usual through the school counseling curriculum, and compare changes in scores between groups. The controls taken in assessing pre- and postchanges and assigning groups helps researchers be relatively certain that the intervention is responsible for the changes observed.

As you will learn in this chapter, quasi-experiments "involve comparing outcomes of one group receiving a treatment that is the focus of evaluation to one or more groups of clients who receive either nothing or an alternative real treatment, or to a group receiving a placebo-type treatment" (Thyer, 2012, p. 9). In contrast to true experiments, quasi-experiments do not feature random assignment, most often due to practical or ethical constraints (Baldwin & Berkeljon, 2010; Grant & Wall, 2009). Rather, researchers create comparison groups on the basis of self-selection (e.g., participants sign up to attend a certain group or at a certain setting), administrator selection, or self- and administrator selection (White & Sabarwal, 2014). Some quasi-experimental methodologists also find opportunities to investigate the impact of naturally occurring phenomena in ways that do not involve researcher-controlled manipulation of the intervention or experience (Grant & Wall, 2009). For example, a researcher may compare changes in mental health among individuals in communities directly impacted by a natural disaster to those in communities that only heard about the disaster on the news.

The task of the quasi-experimental researcher is to design studies in ways that demonstrate that the intervention or experience, not a plausible alternative explanation, is most likely responsible for changes observed (Baldwin & Berkeljon, 2010). To continue the example, researchers may identify a group of students eligible for a bullying intervention, assess likelihood to intervene as bystanders, and then assign students on one schedule to the intervention group and students on another schedule to treatment as usual through the school counseling curriculum. This method may have a reasonable chance of providing valuable information provided assignment to groups was done in a thoughtful manner; for example, that there were no meaningful preexisting differences in classroom composition or assignment based on schedules.

As we will explore later in this chapter, there are a number of unique quasi-experimental designs. These designs vary with regard to (1) use of no-treatment, comparison, or alternative-treatment interventions, (2) use of posttest only or pretest-posttest data, and (3) timing of interventions and observations. In addition, quasi-experimental researchers can utilize a variety of procedures for enrolling participants and assigning them to groups. For now, I turn attention to situations most appropriate for quasi-experimental methods.

Situations Most Appropriate for Quasi-Experimental Methods

Although many researchers consider quasi-experimental methods to be less rigorous than true experimental designs, quasi-experimental designs tend to be more practical and feasible for real-world practice settings. In other words, wherein quasi-experimental designs may have less internal validity due to lack of random assignment and control, they gain external validity in terms of ability to be carried out and practiced in real-world settings that are rarely as controlled as laboratory settings.

Thyer (2012) outlined a number of situations in which quasi-experimental designs might be the most appropriate method available. These included initial screening or piloting of interventions before investing in more time- and cost-intensive RCTs, testing and advancing theory, developing generalizable knowledge in contexts where it is not possible to conduct true RCTs, and as a teaching tool for those first learning experimental methods.

Grant and Wall (2009) argued convincingly that quasi-experimental methods may be superior to other designs when considering impossibilities or ethical quandaries raised by random assignment and controlled manipulation in some situations, collaboration with field-based practitioners, and need for exploration of conflicting or inconsistent findings. For these reasons, quasi-experimental designs are particularly relevant to mental health and human services professionals and settings.

Types of Research Questions Best Suited for Quasi-Experimental Methods

In short, quasi-experimental designs are most appropriate when researchers want to understand the effect of an experience or event, including a mental health intervention, on two or more groups. As will be explored later in this chapter, the effect must be able to be assessed quantitatively, and the researcher must have a large enough sample to compare groups in a way that allows for detection of changes over time.

To understand construction of research questions best suited for quasi-experimental methods, it is important to understand a few general concepts as applied to this design. The **independent variable** is the treatment, event, or experience being investigated in the study. In quasi-experimental design, the independent variable is comprised of two or more groups (e.g., treatment group, no-treatment control group, or comparison group). The **dependent variable** is the outcome the researcher believes will change as a result of exposure to the independent variable.

Quasi-experimental methods help researchers answer the general question *Do those who experience [independent variable/experimental condition] report changes in [dependent variable] compared to those who [independent variable control/comparison condition]?* In the bullying example, the research question might read, "To what degree do students who engaged in a bullying intervention report changes in likeliness to intervene as bystanders compared to students who participated in treatment as usual through the district's school counseling curriculum?" In this case, the research question makes clear both the independent variable (bullying intervention vs. treatment as usual) and the dependent variable (likelihood to intervene as a bystander).

Quasi-experimental research questions may be simple or complex. For example, quasi-experimental designs can assess effectiveness of multiple treatment conditions on multiple dependent variables. In the case study that follows, a sexual violence response center decides to evaluate impact of a mindfulness-based stress reduction (MBSR) group for waitlist clients (independent variable) on symptoms of posttraumatic stress disorder and overall outcome (two dependent variables). Their research question was **"To what degree do survivors who participate in an MBSR group demonstrate improvements in PTSD, symptom distress, interpersonal relations, and social functioning compared to waitlist clients who have access to a peer support group only?"**

Case Study: Sexual Violence Recovery

The Sexual Violence Recovery Center is a nonprofit organization that serves adolescents and adults who self-report as having survived sexual assault. The center employs five full-time clinicians and two part-time interns and uses a trauma-informed approach to care. Historically, the center has offered individual counseling services to clients, and the average time on waitlist is 2 months. To provide initial support for clients on the waitlist, the center offers unstructured, weekly peer support groups facilitated by volunteer advocates.

Recently, the staff has been exploring evidence-based approaches to trauma and decided to implement an MBSR group in which participants would learn skills for noticing, accepting, and managing symptoms of traumatic stress (see www.ptsd.va.gov/professional/treatment/overview/mindful-PTSD.asp). The center is exploring new sources of grant funding and wonders whether it can develop a rationale for state funding to fully implement the intervention as part of their treatment menu.

Center staff contact a local university researcher who has interest in trauma-based services to develop a study that would provide preliminary evidence for effectiveness of the services offered. The research team identifies symptoms of posttraumatic stress as assessed by the PTSD Checklist 5 (PCL-5; Blevins, Weathers, Davis, Witte, & Domino, 2015) and overall outcome as assessed by the Outcome Questionnaire (OQ-45.2; Lambert et al., 1996) as dependent variables. Based on an a priori power analysis, discussed in what follows, the researchers determine they need complete data for at least 14 people in each group.

Given the number of individuals needed for the MBSR groups, the staff decides to invite all new clients to participate in the MBSR group on Tuesday nights, and they continue this practice until the new group is full and ready to begin. On the first and last night of the 6-week group, clients complete the PCL-5 and the OQ-45.2. If new clients are not available on Tuesday nights, the staff invites them to join one of two ongoing peer-support groups instead; they complete instruments the first day of group and again after 6 weeks. Once the MBSR group is filled, the staff invites all new clients to the peer support groups; they complete the instruments as described.

Quasi-Experimental Methods

This section delineates technical characteristics and design considerations for quasi-experimental research designs. This includes attention to nomenclature, development of experimental conditions, observations of dependent variable(s), and strategies to rule out plausible alternative explanations. The section ends with attention to data analysis in quasi-experimental methods.

Nomenclature

In order to understand design considerations and options, it is important to understand common nomenclature and symptoms used when writing about various experimental methods. The following nomenclature and symbols are adapted from Thyer (2012).

- X is used to refer to the independent variable of focus and most often refers to the **novel treatment or experimental group** in which the researcher is most interested.
- Y (and sometimes Z) is also used to refer to the independent variable; in this case, it most often refers to **comparison situations or conditions**.
- O stands for **observation** and refers to measurement of the dependent or outcome variable of interest. Quasi-experimental designs vary in the number of observations utilized, so a subscript is used to denote the order of observations. For example, O_1 refers to the first time a researcher measures the dependent variable. O_2 refers to the second time a researcher measures the dependent variable. O_3 refers to the third time a researcher measures the dependent variable, and so forth.
- N refers to the size of the **population** from which the sample was obtained.
- n refers to the size of a group or a **sample**, for example, the number of individuals in condition X, Y, or Z.

Researchers often use these symbols to denote specific types of quasi-experimental designs. For now, refer to Table 8.1 to see the various design configurations possible with quasi-experimental methods (see Thyer, 2012, for a complete discussion). For simplicity, each example in the table includes

Table 8.1 Quasi-Experimental Design Considerations

Notation	Name	Brief Description
$X\,O_1$ $Y\,O_1$	Posttest-only comparison/ control design	Compares whether individuals in two conditions have different scores after an intervention or experience
$O_1\,X\,O_2$ $O_1\,Y\,O_2$	Pretest-posttest comparison/ control design	Compares degree of change experienced before and after two or more interventions or experiences
$O_1\,X\,O_2\,O_3$ $O_1\,O_2\,X\,O_3$	Switching-replications design (also known as delayed treatment or lagged-groups design)	Provides the same intervention to different groups at different points in time; allows researchers two chances to show change based on a single intervention; introduces the ability to assess for maintenance of change over time
$O_1\,X\,O_2$ $O_1\,X{-}_1\,O_2$	Dismantling study	Creates comparison condition in which the same intervention, minus one component, is delivered to groups; allows researchers to determine the importance of different parts of treatment

just two levels of the independent variable (X and Y). Note that any of the interventions could compare more than two levels of the independent variable (X, Y, and Z). Additionally, any of the designs could have additional measures of the dependent variable during or after treatment.

Treatment or Experimental Conditions

As discussed previously, all quasi-experimental studies feature an independent variable comprised of at least two different treatment or experimental conditions. Quasi-experimental designs are unique in that they use nonrandom assignment to experimental conditions. The types of conditions to which participants may be assigned include novel/experimental group, no-treatment control group, treatment-as-usual or placebo group, and competing or dismantled interventions group.

Novel or Experimental Group

Most often, researchers are interested in one approach or experience, that which is represented by X in the nomenclature from earlier. The literature most often refers to this as the **novel or experimental group.** In this chapter, the bullying bystander intervention and MBSR groups are two specific examples of possible treatments of focus.

No-Treatment Control Group

Quasi-experiments differ from preexperiments because they include some type of comparison or control group to help rule out other plausible explanations for change. Researchers can choose from a number of possible configurations for this level of the independent variable. The simplest option is to use a **no-treatment control group** in which those receiving an intervention are compared to those who do not receive any intervention or treatment, perhaps those on a waitlist for services. In helping professions, withholding treatment for those in emotional distress or with worsening conditions may go against fundamental ethical principles to do no harm. Although the use of a no treatment control group may help answer the question *Is this treatment better than nothing at all?*, it cannot answer whether the treatment is better than current practices.

Treatment-as-Usual or Placebo Group

For reasons noted already, researchers may prefer to compare those in the novel or experimental group with those who are having some other sort of experience. There are several options for comparison groups. One option would be to compare the novel or experimental group with effectiveness of **treatment as usual**. In the examples within this chapter, researchers compared a novel bullying program to curricula already provided to school counselors. Similarly, counselors at the sexual assault violence center realized that long waitlists for their clients were problematic, so they had already implemented the peer-support group. In the proposed design, researchers compared the MBSR intervention to treatment as usual. Alternately, researchers could decide to compare the novel treatment with a **placebo** experience designed to elicit hope for change and provide a degree of attention to participants but not, in theory, assumed to facilitate change.

Competing or Dismantled Interventions Group

In more advanced quasi-experimental designs, researchers may compare the novel or experimental group with other carefully designed conditions. For example, you may design a competing intervention or intentionally manipulate an intervention to determine the degree to which specific elements of the treatment are important. Manipulation could involve adding a specific element to the intervention or taking away a different component of the intervention. For example, individuals researching a play therapy intervention for which parent/caregiver consultation is considered an important element may decide to compare outcomes of those in the traditional condition with those in a condition offering no parent consultation. Results of that study could confirm the importance of that element of treatment or, if not supported, indicate an opportunity to save time and resources by not offering an element of care that does not make a practical difference to client outcome.

Observations of Dependent Variables

All quasi-experimental designs involve observations of at least one dependent variable; however, they vary with regard to the number of times dependent variables are assessed. At the most basic level, researchers may observe the dependent variable only at posttest or both pretest and posttest. As you will see in this section, there are many creative opportunities to observe dependent variables.

Posttest-Only Designs

Posttest-only designs involve observation of the dependent variable for two or more nonrandomly assigned groups only after the groups have experienced the independent variable. These studies can answer whether individuals in condition X have different outcomes than individuals in condition Y. A posttest-only design could be useful when assessing changes in naturally occurring, noncontrollable events (Grant & Wall, 2009). This might be particularly helpful in assessing impacts of crisis and disaster or taking a broader look at the impact of widespread educational policy or preventative programming.

There are a number of limitations to posttest-only designs. Because there is no pretest comparison, one can only compare *how different* groups are from each other after the event rather than comparing *the degree of change* each group experienced related to the intervention. This distinction becomes particularly important because researchers are responsible for making a strong case that pre-existing, uncontrolled factors or differences between the groups did not account for differences observed (Baldwin & Berkeljon, 2010; Sheppard, 2004; Thyer, 2012). This may be particularly difficult to do in the absence of pretest data.

Pretest-Posttest Designs

Pretest-posttest designs involve assessing participants in all groups at least once before and at least once after experiencing the experimental condition. These studies allow you to compare *the degree of change* each group experienced related to the intervention. In addition, the studies allow you the opportunity to *explore possible preexisting differences* across groups that might impact response to the experimental condition.

Although researchers may assess each group just once pre- and postintervention, there are a number of reasons to include more frequent observations of dependent variables. In longer interventions, you may be interested regarding whether there are periods of time during which the most change occurs. For example, if the most change occurred during the first 4 weeks of the MBSR group, the agency might offer shorter groups to serve more clients; if the most change occurred between weeks 4 and 6, they would have a data-based rationale for keeping the groups longer. Similarly, you may be interested in understanding whether participants maintain changes after the intervention is over. Thus, they may decide to integrate one or more follow-up posttests in the design. From a statistical perspective, having a greater number of observations means researchers need fewer participants to yield meaningful data. This may be important in settings in which access to participants or clients is limited.

Strategies to Eliminate Alternate Explanations

When researchers use random assignment in true experimental designs, they engage in a process that increases internal validity and, with it, the likelihood that any changes or differences observed between groups were due to the intervention. By definition, quasi-experimental designs do not involve random assignment. This means researchers have a special responsibility to take steps demonstrating that "cause must precede effect; cause must be related to effect; and, aside from the cause, no alternative explanation for the effect must be plausible" (Baldwin & Berkeljon, 2010, para. 2). In this section, I explore several strategies and considerations researchers may use to rule out alternative explanations. These include treatment fidelity, assignment to groups, demonstrating equivalence of groups, measurement sensitivity, and statistical sensitivity.

Treatment Fidelity

Treatment fidelity refers the degree to which treatments or conditions in the independent variable are designed and delivered in an intentional, replicable manner. When treatments are designed and delivered with fidelity, researchers are better able to conclude the degree to which the interventions were responsible for changes. If researchers do not provide interventions as they were intended, they may contaminate the design in such a way that one cannot determine what actually happened and contributed to change or lack of change. The most common treatment fidelity strategies used in helping professions include use of standardized manuals or curricula and video monitoring of interventions for compliance with the manual.

The National Institute of Health Behavior Change Consortium (Bellg et al., 2004) delineated a number of treatment fidelity goals and strategies. Many focused on ensuring equivalence of designs (e.g., length of contact, number of sessions) within and between conditions, standardizing treatment protocols, monitoring provider implementation, and ensuring designs were appropriate to the participant population. The report provides an excellent, in-depth exploration regarding steps researchers can take to improve treatment fidelity.

In the case study presented earlier, fidelity steps related to MBSR may include ensuring adequate provider training, using published MBSR curricula, and utilizing an outside observer to ensure the curricula are delivered as planned. In addition, the center may monitor the peer support group so a well-intentioned volunteer does not hear about the new MBSR material and find ways to bring in little doses or exercises for the groups, thus altering their experiences.

Assignment to Groups

As noted previously, there are a number of options for assigning participants to groups. These may include allowing participants to self-select into groups, assigning to groups by an administrator, or using a combination of self- and administrator selection (White & Sabarwal, 2014). You should consider carefully potential benefits and drawbacks of each design. If using self-selection, for example, it is possible that participants will self-select into a condition on the basis of a characteristic, belief, or preference that might influence their experience and, ultimately, their outcomes. Similarly, those who engage in administrative assignment should consider whether there may be meaningful differences as they make their assignments. For example, if conducting the treatment condition at one center and the control condition at another center, one should ask whether the centers vary on basis of provider experience or populations served. Similarly, if using intact classrooms for an intervention, you will want to make sure there was not an outside factor guiding student assignment to classes (e.g., student achievement or special needs).

When creating groups, you must also decide whether to hold initial data collection until all groups are established and then implement concurrently, stagger implementation so data collection within groups begins at one time but data collection between groups begins at another time, or engage in rolling enrollment wherein each individual starts as he or she is ready and completes instruments on a set schedule. As with all design considerations, there are positives and negatives to each decision. Although engaging in simultaneous implementation might be strongest from a design perspective, it might not be practical given the number of participants available at any given time and the nature of the phenomenon being addressed. For example, it might take the sexual violence center 3 months to collect enough people for the group design; by then, the potential participants will be enrolled in counseling services, have sought treatment elsewhere, or perhaps have experienced a degree of healing on their own. Thus, the staff decided to use a modified rolling enrollment design for their study.

When you choose to collect data at different points in time, you should also consider how outside, seemingly unrelated events might influence the groups differently (Thyer, 2012). Sometimes these influences may be as simple as the natural ebbs and flows of academic semesters or seasonal change. Imagine, for example, that researchers were implementing a stress-management program in a school. They collected data for the group in the fall, and they implemented the experimental condition in weeks leading up to standardized testing in the spring. Although groups looked equivalent at pretest, timing of examinations may have influenced students' stress in ways that made it appear the intervention was not effective.

Other times, communities may experience disasters, unrest, turmoil, or significant changes that influence participants. Imagine, for example, that the sexual violence center was in the midst of data collection when news broke that a major political figurehead had been accused of sexual violence *and* was planning to defund a number of grant-funded organizations like the one they were attending. Participants may have found themselves reliving elements of their assaults through incessant media reports and wondering where they could go for support and safety. As a result of these confounds, the interventions may have appeared ineffective (or not as effective). If data collection for the comparison and intervention group was occurring on different schedules, the impact of these outside events on study findings could be even more profound.

Demonstrating Equivalence of Groups

Because the ways in which researchers create groups may have a profound impact on quasi-experimental designs, researchers are responsible for presenting a strong case regarding the equivalence of groups. By showing that groups are as equivalent as possible before the intervention, researchers are able to be more certain that the intervention led to changes between groups at the end of the intervention.

The first step toward demonstrating equivalence of groups is being intentional regarding selection of data collection sites and participant profiles. If collecting data across centers or schools, you should take care to ensure that the experimental and control/comparison groups do not vary on important elements such as participant gender, age, race/ethnicity, socioeconomic status, resources, and general design. Similarly, if using intact classrooms within a school, you would not want to compare effectiveness of an intervention for students in a gifted and talented classroom with a control group of students in a self-contained classroom, as preexisting differences may influence the study outcome.

In some cases, researchers may decide to use nonrandom matching to assign participants or units to groups (Sheppard, 2004). For example, researchers may gather demographic and pretest data and systematically assign individuals to conditions so the groups are as balanced as possible in terms of important characteristics. In the classroom example, researchers may examine classroom composition and divide up assignments so that each group contains one gifted and talented classroom, three general education classrooms, and one self-contained classroom.

Even if researchers do not intentionally match group assignments, they should provide evidence of group equivalence when conducting data analysis. For example, you might provide demographic descriptives and pretest profiles for each group, showing that they were roughly equivalent at pretest. Some researchers also engage in advanced methods to consider how to handle dropouts (e.g., efficacy subset analyses, intention-to-treat analyses; Thyer, 2012). White and Sabarwal (2014) presented advanced techniques such as regression discontinuity design and propensity score matching procedures to make the case for similarity of groups at baseline. Across all examples, you need to monitor and report characteristics of groups, design studies to ensure optimal equivalence, and interpret findings with attention to this fundamental consideration.

Measurement Sensitivity

Although not unique to quasi-experimental designs, the repeated-measures nature of most quasi-experimental designs makes measurement sensitivity particularly important. Researchers who are conducting pre–post designs should ensure that they are selecting instruments that are (1) related to the dependent variable, (2) appropriate for the population of focus, (3) designed to be used at intervals relevant to the study, and (4) sensitive to change. Most simply, measurements that assess experience over a long period of time (e.g., 6 months, 1 year, or a lifetime) or trait-like characteristics are not designed to be sensitive to change over time. In addition, you will want to select instruments that provide meaningful information for the group of participants under study.

For example, I once conducted a study regarding empathy in counselors-in-training; however, I selected an instrument on which my sample scored nearly two standard deviations above the normed mean. This created a ceiling effect in which the instrument was not able to detect changes in participants' already high levels of empathy. In our running example, researchers should carefully consider how the population tends to score on the PCL-5. If initial measures of client symptoms are below threshold at the beginning, it will be unlikely to discern meaningful change from the intervention. On the other hand, if participants score in clinical or higher ranges, the assessment tool is sensitive enough to detect change over the 6-week intervention. In the sexual violence example, both the OQ-45.2 and PCL-5 were designed to detect clinically meaningful change of periods of weeks to 1 month, and their manuals included reliable change metrics and cutpoints that provided support for interpreting degree of meaningful change on the scales.

Statistical Sensitivity

Statistical sensitivity relates to the degree to which one can use statistical tests to detect changes between groups. Although it is a concept related to data analysis and interpretation, it is an important consideration when designing quasi-experimental studies. Those who design quasi-experimental research need to consider a unique interplay between number of participants, number of groups in the independent variable, number of measurements of the dependent variable(s), degree of change they wish to be able to observe, and amount of error they are willing to accept in their tests of statistical significance.

In order to do this, researchers will often use a program such as G*power (Faul, Erdfelder, Lang, & Buchner, 2007) to conduct an a priori power analysis. The program calls for researchers to enter a variety of design factors (e.g., level of Type I error, level of Type II error, anticipated effect size, number of groups, number of measurements, correlations between measures, and statistical test to be used). In turn, the program generates an estimate regarding number of participants needed to run the analysis. Researchers can use G*power to see how design decisions influence number of individuals needed for different designs. Being intentional about number of participants during the design stage sets researchers up to be able to make accurate conclusions about the impact of their independent variable on the dependent variable(s) when it comes time for data analysis and interpretation. Certainly, you do not want to leave an intervention wondering whether the intervention really did not work or whether you simply did not have enough participants or use the right instruments to conclude whether it worked.

Data Analysis and Interpretation

There are a broad range of statistical procedures available to researchers, and intricacies of these decisions depend on level and nature of measurement, sample size, and overall sophistication of the design. In this section, I review the most common and typical data analysis considerations including exploration of descriptives, inferential tests of statistical significance, effect size, and clinical significance.

Exploration of Descriptives

Researchers should begin data analysis by exploring their dataset as a whole. This would include looking at score ranges, means, and standard deviations for groups as a whole and exploring the dataset for individual cases or outliers that might indicate errors in scoring, extreme cases, or other problems in the dataset. Researchers may find it helpful to examine scatterplots for each group and time of measurement as well as graphics showing each group mean at each time of measurement. Exploration of distributions also helps researchers to determine whether certain assumptions are met for statistical tests.

Inferential Tests of Statistical Significance

Quasi-experimental researchers may use a variety of inferential statistics that test for changes between groups over time. The appropriate test depends on number of groups, number of independent variables, number of dependent variables, type of data (e.g., nominal, ordinal, or interval-ratio), and special characteristics of the data (e.g., normality). Most commonly, *t*-tests allow researchers to determine whether there are mean differences among two independent groups, including groups with pre–post data. **Analysis of variance**

(ANOVA) is used to test for mean differences among two or more independent groups on one interval and can answer more complex questions including whether there are changes in mean differences by group, by time, and by group and time. **Multivariate analysis of variance (MANOVA)** is similar to ANOVA, but it has capacity to test for differences among multiple, theoretically related dependent variables at one point in time. These are just three of many available statistical procedures that are beyond the scope of this chapter. In all, these tests help researchers answer whether two or more groups are different in a way that is not likely due to chance.

Effect Size

While statistical tests answer the question if/whether a change is present, researchers need to use measures of effect size or practical significance to determine the degree or size of the changes observed (Thompson, 2002). This consideration is particularly important because results of inferential statistical tests are heavily influenced by sample size. The specific type of effect size used depends on the statistical test of interest. Often, researchers will report effect sizes such as Cohen's d, eta^2, or Adjusted R^2, which they then determine to account for small, medium, or large degrees of change.

Clinical Significance

Finally, clinical significance refers to the idea that interventions should result in real-life changes for real-life people (Thompson, 2002). Imagine, for example, that the MBSR intervention earlier in this chapter was tested and found to produce statistically significant changes compared to the peer-support group, and the effect size was decided to be moderate (both good things!). Now, imagine that participants started with severe levels of PTSD as assessed on the PCL-5. Although scores went down at posttest, participants still mostly fell in the severe range. We would have to ask whether the participants actually felt or experienced meaningful change. If, however, half of the group moved from severe to mild range on the PCL-5, one might conclude that the intervention had a very real impact on some clients' well-being. It might also open up exploration regarding why some participants benefited when others did not. In short, researchers have a responsibility for exploring individual-level impacts even within group comparison designs.

Summary

You may use quasi-experimental designs to navigate a delicate balance between rigorous, laboratory-based research and the real, complex world of practice many helping professionals encounter. By building designs in ways that help rule out plausible alternative explanations, you may build an evidence base for practice that deepens both theoretical, academic understanding and practical, field-based implementation.

Resources for More Information

Bellg, A. J., Borrelli, B., Resnick, B., Hecht, J., Minicucci, D. Sl., Ory, M., ... Czajkowski, C. (2004). Enhancing treatment fidelity in health behavior change studies: Best practices and recommendations from the NIH behavior change consortium. *Health Psychology, 23,* 443–451. doi:10.1037/0278–6133.23.5.443

Grant, A. M., & Wall, T. D. (2009). The neglected science and art of quasi-experimentation: Why-to, when-to, and how-to advice for organizational researchers. *Organizational Research Methods, 12,* 653–686. doi:10.1177/1094428108320737

Thyer, B. A. (2012). *Pocket guide to social work research methods: Quasi-experimental research designs.* New York, NY: Oxford University Press.

Web Center for Social Research Methods. (2006). *Quasi-experimental design.* Retrieved from www.socialresearchmethods.net/kb/quasiexp.php

White, H., & Sabarwal, S. (2014). Quasi-experimental design and methods. In *Methodological briefs: Impact evaluation No. 8.* Florence: UNICEF Office of Research. Retrieved from www.unicef-irc.org/publications/pdf/brief_8_quasi-experimental%20design_eng.pdf

Questions for Further Review and Application

1. Quasi-experimental design exists on a continuum from preexperiments to a true experimental design. What are the primary features distinguishing these three types of designs?
2. In which situations might a quasi-experimental design be favorable to a true experimental design?
3. What are the options for assigning participants to groups in quasi-experimental designs? What are the strengths and limitations of each option?
4. Imagine you are designing a quasi-experimental study for implementation in your work setting. Write a research question and use standardized notation to indicate your design. Then specify each design decision. What groups will you use for your independent variable? How will you assign participants to groups? What dependent variable(s) will you explore? How will you work to rule out plausible alternative explanations? Justify your decisions.

References

Baldwin, S., & Berkeljon, A. (2010). Quasi-experimental design. In N. J. Salkind (Ed.), *Encyclopedia of research design* (pp. 1172–1176). Thousand Oaks, CA: Sage Publications. doi:10.4135/9781412961288

Bellg, A. J., Borrelli, B., Resnick, B., Hecht, J., Minicucci, D. Sl., Ory, M., . . . Czajkowski, C. (2004). Enhancing treatment fidelity in health behavior change studies: Best practices and recommendations from the NIH behavior change consortium. *Health Psychology, 23* 443–451. doi:10.1037/0278–6133.23.5.443

Blevins, C. A., Weathers, F. W., Davis, M. T., Witte, T. K., & Domino, J. L. (2015). The posttraumatic stress disorder checklist for DSM-5 (PCL-5): Development and initial psychometric evaluation. *Journal of Traumatic Stress, 28,* 489–498. doi:10.1002/jts.22059

Faul, F., Erdfelder, E., Lang, A. G., & Buchner, A. (2007). G*Power 3: A flexible statistical power analysis program for the social, behavioral, and biomedical sciences. *Behavior Research Methods, 39*, 175–191.

Grant, A. M., & Wall, T. D. (2009). The neglected science and art of quasi-experimentation: Why-to, when-to, and how-to advice for organizational researchers. *Organizational Research Methods, 12*, 653–686. doi:10.1177/1094428108320737

Lambert, M. J., Hansen, N. B., Umphress, V., Lumen, K., Okiishi, J., Burlingame, G. M., & Reisenger, C. W. (1996). *Administration and scoring manual for the OQ-45.2*. Stevenson, MD: American Professional Credentialing Services LLC.

Sheppard, M. (2004). *Appraising and using social research in the human services: An introduction for social work and health professionals*. Philadelphia: Jessica Kingsley Publishers.

Thompson, B. (2002). "Statistical," "practical," and "clinical": How many kinds of significance do counselors need to consider? *Journal of Counseling & Development, 80*, 64–71. doi:10.1002/j.1556–6678.2002.tb00167.x

Thyer, B. A. (2012). *Pocket guide to social work research methods: Quasi-experimental research designs*. New York, NY: Oxford University Press.

White, H., & Sabarwal, S. (2014). Quasi-experimental design and methods. In *Methodological briefs: Impact evaluation No. 8*. Florence: UNICEF Office of Research. Retrieved from www.unicef-irc.org/publications/pdf/brief_8_quasi-experimental%20design_eng.pdf

9 Randomized Controlled Trials

Dee C. Ray

Randomized controlled trials (RCTs) are considered the "gold standard" of research designs for the purposes of evaluating effectiveness of intervention. As indicated by the design title, RCTs are characterized by the random assignment of a sample into comparison groups receiving or not receiving the tested intervention in the context of a controlled environment. Both random assignment and internal validity controls serve to allow the exploration and conclusion of effectiveness related to a given intervention. In this chapter, I will discuss the required components and methods involved in RCTs for research. Although the process of conducting an RCT may seem daunting to practitioners, this chapter presents clear steps for implementation of an RCT or possibly as criteria for reviewing published RCTs to determine evidence-based practices.

Public and government organizations typically emphasize RCTs as the highest level of evidence to support mental health interventions (e.g., American Psychological Association, 2006; California Evidence-Based Clearinghouse, 2017; Substance Abuse and Mental Health Services Administration, 2017; What Works Clearinghouse, 2017). In order for interventions to be noted as evidence based, they must be supported by research studies in which effectiveness is proven. Effectiveness is determined by outcome studies in which variables that may interfere with results are controlled for and positive outcomes can reasonably be attributed to participation in treatment. For example, if a university counseling center wanted to test whether a specific type of orientation activity was more effective for building knowledge about mental health resources on campus, the staff could work with the orientation office to select students at random who will participate in that activity during the normal orientation period. Other students not selected might not receive anything during that time or might participate in an alternative activity. After the orientation, all students might fill out a survey that assesses their knowledge about mental health resources on campus.

Due to the random assignment, RCT designs offer the most control over variables that may interfere with outcomes (internal validity) in combination with ability to generalize findings to the greater population (external validity). The rigor necessary to offer acceptable levels of internal and external validity is found within the well-designed RCT. Hence, RCT design is well-regarded, carefully scrutinized for thoroughness, and lauded as an exemplary design under which to test intervention. Although other intervention research designs such as single-case and quasi-experimental designs are considered contributory to evidence-based practice, the RCT is respected as the most appropriate design for determining effectiveness.

The well-designed RCT includes several components that contribute to rigor and to internal validity. Specifically, if you use RCT, you seek to isolate intervention as the most likely cause of change for participants through controlling for passage of time, client expectation of change, therapist attention, repeated assessments, and regression to the mean (Kendall, Comer, & Chow, 2013). In other words, clients participating in a research study with few variable controls may demonstrate improvement for a wide range of reasons. It may have been due to getting older or time passing, or because they believe that they will get better, or just because a therapist spent time with them. Maybe they become more sophisticated about instruments that are provided and how to best answer items, or they moved away from the more severe ends of the symptom spectrum to a more middle ground. These are just a few factors that have been shown to interfere with credibility of results. In order to control for these possibilities, RCTs employ the use of random assignment of participants to treatment conditions and measure change over time. By randomly assigning participants, you most likely control the internal validity factors (e.g., for every participant assigned to the treatment group who improves by passage of time, there is a participant in the control group who improves simply through time passage who serves as a counterbalance). Internal validity controls such as random assignment and comparison conditions help to rule out factors that interfere with treatment outcome (Kazdin, 2017).

When an RCT's findings result in favorable outcomes related to the intervention and internal validity has been established, indicating that results can be considered credible, external validity should also be addressed. External validity refers to the ability to generalize findings across other people, units, outcomes, and settings (Heppner, Wampold, Owen, Wang, & Thompson, 2016). External validity for an individual RCT is likely accounted for by conclusions drawn by researchers regarding the applicability of their findings to other groups or populations. For example, if an RCT results in decreased depressive symptoms for participants in the treatment group and all participants were college-educated White American females, conclusions that treatment is broadly effective across gender and race would be inappropriate and a violation of external validity. However, researchers could offer implications that treatment appears effective for college-educated White American females whose situations are similar to those of study participants. As discussed, the concepts of internal and external validity are central to the RCT design, establishing the context for the detailed components necessary for an RCT to be considered for evidence-based decision making.

Appropriate Contexts for RCTs

The RCT design is used when you desire to explore the effectiveness of an intervention or program. The design and statistical analyses used in RCTs serve to compare the effects of receiving an intervention when compared with not receiving the specified intervention or receiving another form of intervention. The design determines cause and effect, thereby allowing for conclusions regarding the impact of the intervention on targeted outcomes. Typically, when you use RCT, you embark on research with a defined intervention and a specific outcome of interest. Simply put, you want to know if an intervention works, with whom it works, and with what problems or issues. The RCT is designed to answer these questions from a positivistic philosophical framework (Heppner et al., 2016) with a yes or no, an objective truth. For example, RCT design is used to determine if Intervention X is effective with female adults who have been sexually abused in reducing their trauma symptoms. The RCT design is useful in clinical settings, as well as other institutions such as schools and workplaces, where subgroups can be defined and then assigned to different conditions.

Alternately, in some contexts, RCTs are inappropriate and possibly an ethical challenge to client service. When RCT designs employ experimental conditions that withhold or delay treatment, clients who have substantial needs may be negatively affected. In a community clinic, counselors may determine that it would be unethical to withhold services from a client in crisis who is randomly assigned to a control condition, especially if resources are available. In these settings, you must determine ethical practice, which may include the use of a non-RCT design or your willingness to accept higher attrition (dropout) rates when a person who is delayed service is determined to be in greater need and is terminated from the study in order to receive services. Institutions legally and morally committed to equitable services, such as schools, may also struggle with the concept of no-treatment control conditions. In these settings, the use of waitlist-control conditions and alternative services may help institutional administrators be more favorable to RCT conditions.

Types of Research Questions and Hypotheses Related to RCTs

Because the purpose of the RCT is to test the effectiveness of an intervention, research questions suitable for RCTs focus on determining the impact of the intervention on the targeted variable. The research question encompasses variables that are measurable and clearly interpretable regarding effectiveness. Additionally, RCT research questions include a "compared to what" feature in which the intervention will be compared to another condition (Solomon, Cavanaugh, & Draine, 2009, p. 87) in order to conclude effectiveness. Some examples of research questions include: "For parents of foster-care children, is ABC parent education more effective in teaching parenting skills than the current agency curriculum?" "For adult clients who are clinically depressed and seeking mental health services in a community-based clinic, does participation in XYZ counseling intervention result in reduced depressive symptoms when compared to symptoms of clients who do not participate in XYZ?"

In addition to stated research questions, RCT designs often generate testable hypotheses in order to drive the statistical analysis of data. Because of the positivistic nature of RCT design and goals, hypotheses are suitable to the discovery of an objective truth regarding the relationship between intervention and outcomes. RCT hypotheses consist of statements that correlate intervention delivery with measurable outcomes. Examples of testable RCT hypotheses generated from the previous research questions include: "Parents of foster-care children who participate in ABC parent education will demonstrate no significant difference in attainment of parenting skills when compared to parents of foster children who participate in current agency curriculum (null hypothesis)." "Adult clients who qualify as clinically depressed and participate in XYZ counseling will demonstrate a significant reduction in depressive symptoms when compared to adult clients who qualify as clinically depressed but do not participate in XYZ (directional hypothesis)." In these hypotheses, the relationship between the independent variable (intervention) and dependent variable (target outcome) is well-defined and measureable through data analysis.

Case Study

In order to highlight the detailed components involved in designing and implementing an RCT, I will present a case in which a researcher wants to explore the effectiveness of child-centered play therapy (CCPT) in reduction of aggressive behaviors among children who are enrolled in first through third grade in a public school setting. The research question for this study is: Do young children identified as exhibiting clinical levels of aggressive behaviors who participate in 16 sessions of CCPT demonstrate a reduction in aggressive symptoms in comparison with children who do not participate in CCPT? In the following listed steps (see Table 9.1), I will address issues related to the implementation step and present the specific procedures followed for this case study.

Table 9.1 Steps to Conduct RCTs

Step 1	Define Intervention
Step 2	Target Outcomes
Step 3	Define Experimental Conditions
Step 4	Identify Valid and Reliable Measures
Step 5	Define Inclusion Criteria
Step 6	Implement Recruitment and Informed Consent Procedures
Step 7	Conduct Criterion and Baseline Testing
Step 8	Perform Random Assignment
Step 9	Monitor Intervention and Control Conditions
Step 10	Monitor Participant Flow
Step 11	Conduct Posttest and Follow-Up
Step 12	Explore Statistical, Practical, and Clinical Significance

Step 1. Define Intervention

The first step in RCT design is to decide what intervention will be explored. In this case, the intervention is identified within the research question as CCPT. Because the intervention itself is what will be manipulated through delivery or nondelivery to participants, it is considered the independent variable in an RCT. In order for RCTs to be deemed credible evidence of an intervention, intervention must be specified in a manual or detailed protocol of procedures (APA Publications and Communications Board Working Group on Journal Article Reporting Standards, 2008). The length and format of intervention should also be specified. Although intervention manuals or rich description of treatment is required for a credible RCT, they may consist of guidelines to treatment and not necessarily detailed instruction of intervention delivery (Carroll & Rounsaville, 2008; Solomon et al., 2009). In this case study, CCPT will be delivered according to the published CCPT manual (Ray, 2011) and, as the research question specifies, over the course of 16 sessions (30 minutes each) delivered twice a week for 8 weeks. Additionally, the qualifications and training of treatment providers should be detailed. For this case, the counselors are doctoral-level students who are state-licensed interns and have completed three courses in CCPT as well as a 2-day training on the CCPT protocol.

Step 2. Target Outcomes

The second step in RCT is the identification of a target outcome or multiple outcomes, also referred to as the dependent variables. In this case, as in most RCTs, step 2 is conducted simultaneously with step 1. The example research question identifies the target outcome as reduction in aggressive symptoms. Because RCTs are conducted to test what intervention works with what types of issues, the identification of treatment and outcome variable occurs concurrently. Best practices in RCT encourage the limiting of outcome target variables to a minimal number of constructs (Kazdin, 2017). The tendency to cast a broad net by attempting to target multiple and diverse outcomes indicates that the researcher may have limited theoretical rationale for how the intervention works and is on a "fishing" expedition to find any possible positive outcome. RCTs are ideally grounded in the conceptual framework that defines the role of intervention in behavioral or emotional change (Solomon et al., 2009).

Step 3. Define Experimental Conditions

Once the intervention and target outcomes are well-defined, the researcher determines the control condition from which to compare the treatment condition. Kendall et al. (2013) identified four control conditions in treatment outcome research that include a no-treatment control, waitlist control, attention-placebo/nonspecific control, and standard treatment (treatment as usual) control. In the no-treatment control condition, participants assigned to this group receive assessments on repeated occasions at the same time as the treatment group, but they do not receive treatment. In the same procedures as the no-treatment control, the waitlist control does not receive treatment and participates in assessment, but they will be scheduled to receive treatment following final data collection. The attention-placebo control receives a treatment that involves attention or contact at the same time as the treatment group; however, the treatment is not intended to address the target outcome. In the standard treatment control, participants receive an intervention that is already in place but not the intervention being tested. For this case study, wherein the research was scheduled to take place in a school setting, the researchers selected a waitlist control condition as the experimental condition from which to compare the treatment group. Administrators at the school agreed to participation in the study with the stipulation that every child who qualified for the study would eventually receive treatment. The waitlist control group seemed most suitable to meet this requirement.

Step 4. Identify Valid and Reliable Measures

The fourth step involves the identification of valid and reliable measures in order to assess changes in the target outcomes. Prior to implementation of an RCT, researchers will select instruments with strong psychometric properties that capture the construct of the targeted outcomes. Although researchers may be tempted to create an assessment to more fully match their RCT design, this practice is discouraged. The development of reasonably valid and reliable assessments is a research agenda in and of itself (see Chapter 4) and should be embarked on with caution and care. For most outcomes, assessments with solid psychometric properties can be identified. Using inadequately supported instruments to measure dependent variables in an RCT results in credibility and interpretation limitations. Kazdin (2017) recommended the use of multiple measures in order to operationalize a construct. Limiting assessment of a key construct to one instrument may result in the inability to fully interpret change in the construct.

In the case study, researchers identified aggressive symptoms as the target dependent variable. In order to capture the construct of aggression fully, the RCT design included the use of the Children's Aggression Scale (CAS; Halperin & McKay, 2008) for both parents and teachers, as well as the Aggression Scale on the Child Behavior Checklist and Teacher Report Form (CBCL/TRF; Achenbach & Rescorla, 2001). Thereby, change in aggression was captured by two different reporters (parent and teacher) and two instruments, resulting in a fuller picture of how aggression was affected by participation in CCPT.

Measurement preference for RCTs is the utilization of objective raters to report and assess behavioral changes. RCTs often employ objective raters who are trained in an assessment protocol and establish interrater reliability prior to observation or participant interview. This type of measurement is considered most objective and of highest credibility. However, RCTs more frequently utilize self-report and other-report on reasonably valid and reliable instruments due to the lack of availability of objective measurements, as well as the high interest in change of emotional status for mental health interventions, normally only captured through self-report.

Step 5. Define Inclusion Criteria

Once design features regarding independent variable (intervention), dependent variable (targeted outcomes), control conditions, and measures of change have been determined, the RCT researcher must establish criteria for participant inclusion and necessary sample size. RCT researchers seek participants that have a connection with the target outcome and favorable candidates for the intervention. In the case study, because CCPT is an intervention that is directed to younger children, sample children needed to be between first and third grade. Because the dependent variable of interest was aggression, a clinical score on the parent or teacher aggression scales was required for participant inclusion. In order to extend external validity, children of both genders and various ethnicities were recruited across three elementary schools. In all, inclusion criteria for the case study required that children were (1) enrolled in first through third grade at one of the recruiting schools, (2) scored by a parent or teacher in the clinical range on one aggression scale, and (3) not participating in any other mental health intervention over the course of the study.

Prior to recruitment for an RCT, researchers must determine the sample size necessary for results from statistical analysis to be credible. This procedure is referred to as a power analysis. In order to conduct a power analysis, the researcher determines the magnitude of the desired effect size, the alpha level at which the null hypothesis will be rejected, and the likelihood that you want to reject the null hypothesis if there is a relationship between intervention and outcome, known as power (Cooper, 2011). Traditionally, the alpha level is set at .05 and power is set at .80 or above. Desired effect sizes are ideally selected based on previous research, but researchers often default to a medium effect size (e.g., $d = .5$). Power analysis also requires that the researcher has decided the type of statistical analysis that will be used to test differences in treatment conditions. G*power is one online program to help run a power analysis (www.gpower.hhu.de/). The result of running a power analysis is the determination of how many participants a researcher will need to recruit for adequate power to run analyses and find credibility in results. Power analysis for a factorial analysis of variance based on .95 power, .05 alpha level, and medium effect size of $d = .5$ indicated that 36 participants were needed for the CCPT RCT example study.

Step 6. Implement Recruitment and Informed Consent Procedures

Up to this point, the RCT has been in the planning stages. Prior to making contact with potential participants, the researcher has organized a plan for intervention, targeted outcomes, determined a comparison design, selected reasonably valid and reliable measures, set criteria for participant inclusion, and analyzed the number of participants necessary to address the research question. The delineation of steps emphasizes the detailed planning and organization required prior to implementation of an RCT design. Now that the researcher has a plan of action, recruitment can begin. Because RCTs involve human subjects by virtue of the design, human subjects approval from an institutional review board is a prerequisite for research implementation. Human subjects approval involves the development of a recruitment plan and participant informed consent that notifies the potential participants of the nature of the study, extent of participation, address of confidentiality, benefits, and risks. Upon human subjects approval, the researcher can embark on participant recruitment.

When recruiting, the RCT researcher works within the context setting to inform potential participants of the upcoming RCT and criteria for participation. Often, researchers will design a simple statement of recruitment disseminated to staff or clients in order to identify participants. For this particular case study, the researchers sent out a notice to parents and teachers that play therapy services were being offered in their schools through a research study. If parents or teachers were concerned about a child being aggressive or defiant, the child might qualify for free services. Once the parent contacted the researcher, the researcher explained the use of the waitlist control group and that children may not immediately receive services but they would be guaranteed services immediately following posttest data collection. If parents were still interested, the researcher reviewed the informed consent with the parent and acquired signature for participation.

Step 7. Conduct Criterion and Baseline Testing (Pretest)

Participants have now been recruited, and it is time to determine whether they meet the qualification criteria stated necessary for the RCT. Recruitment procedures generally limit participants to those who meet some criteria. In the case study, only parents and teachers of children who were between first and third grade in the recruiting schools were notified of the study. Hence, most potential participants met some criteria at initiation of the study. However, criteria for qualification that requires assessment may only be met through the potential participant's inclusion in preliminary procedures. For example, although potential child participants may have met age and referral criteria, it is unknown whether they would qualify as clinical on the selected instruments. Therefore, pretest instruments were administered to parents of all potential participants. Inclusion could not be determined until all pretest assessments were scored. Once scored, the researchers identified participants who met all inclusion criteria, as well as those who did not. According to RCT procedures and human subjects approval, it is common to dismiss potential participants who do not meet full criteria. However, RCT researchers should consider the demoralization possible for participants who become excited about participation and then are rejected for inclusion. In this circumstance, it is recommended that when RCT researchers recruit, there should be an alternate plan for how to serve potential participants who do not meet criteria.

Step 8. Perform Random Assignment

In this step, participants have been screened for inclusion, met criteria, and are now ready for assignment to an experimental condition. Random assignment is the crucial component of a credible RCT. Random assignment is the key distinguishing feature between conducting an experimental design and a quasi-experimental design. Ideally, random assignment would occur directly following the identification of all participants so that the sample is equally and simultaneously distributed, referred to as simple random assignment (Hsu, 2008). However, the identification of all participants is often not possible, and random assignment occurs in block assignments in which the researcher decides a priori how many participants will be blocked at a time before random assignment occurs, referred to as randomized blocks assignment (Kendall et al., 2013). In the case study example, upon the identification of 12 children who met inclusion criteria, those 12 were randomly assigned to the treatment or waitlist control groups. Hence, random assignment took place at three different points in order to reach the desired number of 36 participants. Further ideas regarding types of random assignment can be found in Hsu (2008).

Proper random assignment includes the use of a mathematical procedure to determine assignment to conditions (Solomon et al., 2009). Although some random assignment procedures are described informally, such as every other participant is assigned to a group or participants are assigned according to the first initial of their last name, these types of procedures are considered unacceptable in ensuring the equality of groups. Credible procedures include the use of a table of random numbers or computerized random number generator. For the case study, once 12 participants had met inclusion criteria, the research team employed the website Research Randomizer (randomizer.org) to generate assignment to groups.

The purpose of random assignment is ensuring that participants in experimental conditions are comparable. Using credible procedures for random assignment allows the researcher to assume that groups are similar, start approximately in the same place, and can be compared to one another. However, even with random assignment, there are likely to be slight differences among groups such as small non–statistically significant variances in pretest data. Even though researchers may be encouraged to demonstrate equivalence of groups through pretest analyses, this type of analysis is considered superfluous and unnecessary (de Boer, Waterlander, Kuijper, Steenhuis, & Twisk, 2015) when proper assignment procedures have been used. Exceptions to this guideline may occur when attrition rates are high throughout the study, and pretest analysis would ensure comparability of the intact groups at follow-up testing.

Step 9. Monitor Intervention and Control Conditions

Once participants have been assigned to an experimental condition, treatment intervention is implemented. For participants who are assigned to the treatment group, they will begin intervention for the set amount of time as designated by the researcher prior to design implementation. As previously discussed, intervention is delivered according to protocol or manualized procedures by qualified and trained facilitators. Adherence to treatment is a critical piece of conducting solid research, and it has been shown that without monitoring, researchers will drift from manualized treatments (Nathan, Stuart, & Dolan, 2003). Monitoring of treatment goes beyond the general supervision and training of treatment providers in a given study. RCTs require the use of fidelity checks to confirm that intervention is being delivered as intended in the RCT design (APA, 2008). Fidelity checks include objective evaluation that intervention is facilitated as designed such as employing objective raters to visually inspect and rate intervention delivery. For the example RCT case study, researchers enlisted two raters unaffiliated with the study to use the Play Therapy Skills Checklist (Ray, 2011) to rate the therapist responses in video-recorded sessions for adherence to protocol, resulting in a percentage adherence. The researchers had previously cited an acceptable adherence percentage at 80%, meaning that 80% of the therapist's responses in the evaluated session must match with protocol response categories to be considered as meeting fidelity standards.

In addition to monitoring the treatment condition, the RCT researcher also monitors the comparison or control condition. Comparison groups are typically subjected to the same types of fidelity checks used for the experimental group. For example, if the comparison group is supposed to be receiving a reading intervention, the RCT researcher ensures that the reader is not initiating discussions or engaging in therapeutic techniques with participants assigned to that condition. For no-intervention control conditions, the RCT researcher ensures that there is no cross-contamination of treatment to the control participants and that participants in that condition are not receiving other mental health services during the course of the experiment. For the case study, the researcher checked in with the school administrators, counselors, and teachers to monitor that the waitlist control group participants received no additional mental health services.

Step 10. Monitor Participant Flow

Throughout recruitment, inclusion, data collection, and treatment delivery, RCTs report an account of participant flow. Participant flow indicates how many participants were initially involved in the study, assigned to experimental conditions, dismissed or dropped out of the study, failed to provide usable data, and completed the study. A visual flowchart is recommended for publication to diagram the specifics of participant flow (Cooper, 2011). Transparency related to participant flow lends credibility to final results through the acknowledgment of limitations in participant completion. For the case study, the following description is an example of monitoring participant flow: Thirty-eight participants were recruited for the study who appeared to meet criteria. At pretest, two participants did not qualify due to lack of clinical ratings on the assessments. Thirty-six participants were randomly assigned to the CCPT treatment group ($n = 18$) and waitlist control group ($n = 18$). Over the course of the treatment period, two children from the treatment group moved from the area, and one child from the waitlist control group dropped out of the study due to substantial absences, resulting in 16 children in the treatment group and 17 children in the waitlist control group. The 16 children in the treatment group participated in 16 sessions of CCPT within 10 weeks. All 33 children completed posttest data at the end of 10 weeks.

Step 11. Conduct Posttest and Follow-Up

RCTs are characterized by evaluating the dependent variable(s) over the course of the study. Pretests serve as baseline assessments from which to measure change on the target outcome. Follow-up assessment may occur during, directly following, and/or substantially later after treatment. At minimum, RCT researchers provide a posttest assessment using the same measures from pretest directly following the treatment period. However, repeated measures over time improve the credibility of results for interpretation, as well as improving power in data analysis. Although follow-up assessment after a lengthy period is rare in RCTs, Kendall et al. (2013) advocate for follow-up data collection as a "signpost of methodological rigor" (p. 44). However, follow-up assessments delay treatment for the control condition participants due to the inability to start treatment prior to the last data collection point, a particularly salient challenge for RCT researchers who use waitlist control groups. For the case study, parents and teachers were administered the CAS and the CBCL/TRF at the end of the 10-week treatment period. Although the original design called for treatment to occur over 8 weeks, the treatment period was extended to 10 weeks due to absences and school holidays. All participants were administered posttesting in the same week.

The administration of posttest assessments appears to be a straightforward step in the RCT design. Yet experience reveals that the posttesting step of RCT design can be challenging. When subjective raters are used such as parents and teachers, or other reporters who have a relationship with the participant, it is often difficult to motivate them to complete assessments. Some challenges include avoiding contact with the researcher, hastily filling out assessments without thoughtfulness, or passive refusal to complete assessments. The RCT researcher is likely more successful at this stage if planning for these challenges has occurred. Strategies such as offering incentives, visiting homes, and providing a quiet space for assessments (e.g., volunteering to substitute or babysit while assessments are being completed) may address these normal challenges. Additionally, use of objective raters and measures circumvents the need for subjective raters. In the case study, researchers offered a "pizza day" after school for parent reporters to complete assessments. During the pizza day, researchers provided pizza and babysitting while parents filled out instruments. For teacher assessments, researchers served as substitutes in the classroom for 30-minute time periods while teachers went to another room to complete assessments.

Step 12. Explore Statistical, Practical, and Clinical Significance

The answers to RCT research questions are developed through analysis of statistically, practically, and clinically significant outcomes (Thompson, 2002). Statistical significance refers to the probability estimate regarding the null hypothesis that the intervention group will not differ from the comparison/control group at a predetermined probability threshold (i.e., $\alpha = .05$). If the treatment group performs in the desired direction at a probability difference below the set alpha level ($p < .05$), the result is determined to be statistically significant and the intervention is interpreted as effective. Yet statistical significance is artificially impacted by sample size; there must be substantial difference in outcomes between experimental conditions to detect significance when the sample size is small, but large samples often yield statistically significant results with small differences between groups. Statistical significance is seen by many as the traditional indicator of effectiveness but is limited in its scope.

Practical significance refers to the importance of the findings and is generally reported through effect sizes. Effect sizes quantify the difference between groups or the relationship between variables. In RCTs, effect sizes allow the researcher to understand the magnitude of difference or relationship between the groups, as well as between intervention and group assignment (Ellis, 2010). Clinical significance refers to the realistic value of intervention when applied to everyday life of a client (Kazdin, 2017). Although statistical and practical significance may be reached through a 2-point mean decrease in assessed symptoms, clinical significance addresses whether this 2-point difference means that the participants in the treatment group have a better quality of life following intervention. Clinical significance is often determined through comparison of participant groups to normative samples, which can be assessed through statistical methods (Kendall et al., 2013).

RCT researchers seek to answer their research questions through address of the three types of significance. What is the probability that the treatment group would improve over another experimental condition group (statistical significance)? How much of the detected change can be attributed to intervention? or How different are the experimental groups from each other at posttesting (practical significance)? Did the intervention make a difference for the participants in real life (clinical significance)? All types of significance are addressed through analysis of collected data over the course of the RCT. Brown, Costigan, and Kendziora (2008) suggested three major approaches to data analysis for RCTs including analysis of variance (ANOVA) models, latent growth models, and hierarchical linear models. In these approaches, RCT researchers seek to explore the impact of intervention through analysis of patterns within subjects over time, between subjects, and within different contexts (Brown et al., 2008). A full description and investigation of these methods is beyond the scope of this chapter. Notably, RCT researchers necessarily are well-versed in complex statistical methods to understand how to determine the impact of intervention over time and between groups in the context of probability, magnitude, and realistic outcomes. If you find that you are unsure of your ability to perform some of these analyses, there are often individuals in your community who may be able to lend their expertise. Don't be afraid to ask for support!

In the case study, researchers conducted four factorial ANOVAs using the pre- and posttest CBCL Aggression scale score, TRF Aggression scale score, CAS-Parent, CAS-Teacher Total Scores as the dependent variables and experimental group as the independent variable. Statistically significant differences between the means across time were tested at the .05 alpha level for the dependent variable scores. Practical significance was calculated through Cohen's d (Cohen, 1988), a group difference effect size used to compare standard deviations between the two groups. Clinical significance was explored through the Reliable Change Index analysis calculating the number of participants moving from clinical range to normative sample range (Jacobson & Truax, 1991; Kendall et al., 2013).

All the Steps Together

The steps for implementation of RCTs emphasize the level of detail and planning required for findings to be considered credible. Conducting RCTs is not for the faint of heart. RCTs require that you have considerable knowledge regarding the intervention, experience with outcomes of interest and statistical analysis, resources to implement data collection and experimental conditions, and time dedicated to intense monitoring of procedures. However, RCTs can also be exciting endeavors into exploration of different interventions. Although practitioners may experience certain interventions to be effective, it is encouraging to show through rigorous methods that the intervention can be proven effective. Alternately, outcomes from RCTs may indicate that intervention is ineffective, which can be discouraging but also helps practitioners to understand conditions that may contribute to or limit treatment effectiveness. Researchers who employ RCT designs contribute directly to client services through production of outcomes related to intervention effectiveness.

Resources for More Information

Resources for Conducting RCTs

Nezu, A., & Nezu, C. (2008). *Evidence-based outcome research: A practical guide to conducting randomized controlled trials for psychosocial interventions.* New York, NY: Oxford University Press.

Solomon, P., Cavanaugh, M., & Draine, J. (2009). *Randomized controlled trials: Design and implementation for community-based psychosocial interventions.* New York, NY: Oxford University Press.

Resources for Reporting RCTs

Consolidated Standards of Reporting Trials (CONSORT). Retrieved from www.consort-statement.org/consort-2010

Cooper, H. (2011). *Reporting research in psychology: How to meet journal article reporting standards* (6th ed.). Washington, DC: American Psychological Association.

Hancock, G., & Mueller, R. (Eds.). (2010). *The reviewer's guide to quantitative methods in the social sciences*. New York, NY: Routledge.

Resources for Power Analysis and Random Assignment

G*power. Retrieved from www.gpower.hhu.de/

QuickCalcs. Retrieved from www.graphpad.com/quickcalcs/randomize1.cfm

Research Randomizer. Retrieved from Randomizer.org

Resources for Finding Assessment Instruments

Mental Measurements Yearbook/Tests in print via EBSCOhost

PsycTESTS via EBSCOhost

Questions for Further Review and Application

1. In reviewing chapters from this book, what features of RCT design distinguish it from other designs?

2. In one column, create a list of obstacles that you might encounter in planning and conducting an RCT. In a second column, list strategies to address those obstacles.

3. Think of an intervention to which you are favorable. Search the internet to explore if RCTs have been conducted on this intervention. If so, what outcomes have been explored in these RCTs?

4. For one of your favorite interventions, develop a theoretical model that links the components of that intervention with an outcome of interest. Evaluate the possibility of testing your model. Develop a research question addressed through an RCT.

5. You are interested in the effectiveness of ABC intervention. You have already conducted a power analysis and know that you need 46 participants to run statistical analysis to compare two experimental groups. Go to the website for Research Randomizer. Follow directions to randomly assign your 46 participants.

6. Think of an outcome of interest to you. Search for instruments that measure aspects of this outcome. Use internet and academic sources such as Mental Measurements Yearbook or PsycTESTS (see Resources section in this chapter) to locate assessments. Find the reliability and validity support for the instruments.

References

Achenbach, T. M., & Rescorla, L. A. (2001). *Manual for the ASEBA school-age forms and profiles; Child behavior checklist for ages 6–18, teacher's report form, youth self report: An integrated system of multi-informant assessment.* Burlington, VT: ASEBA.

American Psychological Association Presidential Task Force on Evidence-Based Practice. (2006). Evidence-based practice in psychology. *American Psychologist, 61,* 271–285.

APA Publications and Communications Board Working Group on Journal Article Reporting Standards. (2008). Reporting standards for research in psychology: Why do we need them? What might they be? *American Psychologist, 63,* 839–851.

Brown, C., Costigan, T., & Kendziora, K. (2008). Data analytic frameworks: Analysis of variance, latent growth, and hierarchical models. In A. Nezu & C. Nezu (Eds.), *Evidence-based outcome research: A practical guide to conducting randomized controlled trials for psychosocial interventions* (pp. 285–314). New York, NY: Oxford University Press.

California Evidence-Based Clearinghouse for Child Welfare. (2017). Retrieved from www.cebc4cw.org/ratings/scientific-rating-scale/

Carroll, K., & Rounsaville, B. (2008). Efficacy and effectiveness in developing treatment manuals. In A. Nezu & C. Nezu (Eds.), *Evidence-based outcome research: A practical guide to conducting randomized controlled trials for psychosocial interventions* (pp. 219–243). New York, NY: Oxford University Press.

Cohen, J. (1988). *Statistical power analysis for the behavioral sciences* (2nd ed.). Hillsdale, NJ: Erlbaum.

Cooper, H. (2011). *Reporting research in psychology: How to meet journal article reporting standards* (6th ed.). Washington, DC: American Psychological Association.

De Boer, M., Waterlander, W., Kuijper, L., Steenhuis, I., & Twisk, J. (2015). Testing for baseline differences in randomized controlled trials: An unhealthy research behavior that is hard to eradicate. *International Journal of Behavioral Nutrition and Physical Activity.* Online publication. Retrieved from http://dx.doi.org/10.1186/s12966-015-0162-z

Ellis, P. D. (2010). *The essential guide to effect sizes: Statistical power, meta-analysis, and the interpretation of research results.* New York, NY: Cambridge University Press.

Halperin, J. M., & McKay, K. E. (2008). *Manual for the children's aggression scale.* Odessa, FL: Psychological Assessment Resources, Inc.

Heppner, P., Wampold, B., Owen, J., Wang, K., & Thompson, M. (2016). *Research design in counseling* (4th ed.). Boston, MA: Cengage.

Hsu, L. (2008). Random assignment procedures. In A. Nezu & C. Nezu (Eds.), *Evidence-based outcome research: A practical guide to conducting randomized controlled trials for psychosocial interventions* (pp. 179–200). New York, NY: Oxford University Press.

Jacobson, N. S., & Truax, P. (1991). Clinical significance: A statistical approach to defining meaningful change in psychotherapy research. *Journal of Consulting and Clinical Psychology, 59,* 12–19.

Kazdin, A. (2017). *Research design in clinical psychology* (5th ed.). Boston, MA: Pearson.

Kendall, P., Comer, J., & Chow, C. (2013). The randomized controlled trial: Basics and beyond. In J. Comer & P. Kendall's (Eds.), *The Oxford handbook of research strategies for clinical psychology* (pp. 40–61). New York, NY: Oxford University Press.

Nathan, P., Stuart, S., & Dolan, S. (2003). Research on psychotherapy efficacy and effectiveness: Between Scylla and Charybdis? In A. Kazdin (Ed.), *Methodological issues and strategies in clinical research* (3rd ed., pp. 505–546). Washington, DC: APA.

Ray, D. (2011). *Advanced play therapy: Essential conditions, knowledge, and skills for child practice.* New York, NY: Routledge.

Solomon, P., Cavanaugh, M., & Draine, J. (2009). *Randomized controlled trials: Design and implementation for community-based psychosocial interventions.* New York, NY: Oxford University Press.

Substance abuse and mental health services administration. (2017). Retrieved from http://nrepp.samhsa.gov

Thompson, B. (2002). "Statistical," "practical," and "clinical": How many kinds of significance do counselors need to consider? *Journal of Counseling & Development, 80,* 64–71.

What Works Clearinghouse. (2017). *What works clearinghouse: Procedures and standards handbook 3.0.* Washington, DC: U.S. Department of Education, Institute of Education Sciences. Retrieved February 18, 2017, from https://ies.ed.gov/ncee/wwc/Docs/referenceresources/wwc_procedures_v3_0_standards_ handbook.pdf

10 Phenomenological Methodology

Merging Research and Practice

Maribeth F. Jorgensen & Kathleen Brown-Rice

Carl Rogers stated, "So I have learned to ask myself, can I hear the sounds and sense the shape of this person's inner world? Can I resonate to what he is saying so deeply that I sense the meanings?" (Rogers, 1980, p. 8). Perhaps the most fundamental characteristic of effective counselors is their ability to listen as a means to understand clients' lived experiences. The counseling process has been the most common platform for practitioners to use counseling skills and gain access to clients' view of the world. However, particular research methodologies may be a natural fit for counselors and provide another passageway in understanding clients. Previous literature has supported the idea that qualitative research may be especially suitable for counselors given the interpersonal connection with participants, and it uncovers and represents voices in richer ways than through numbers and statistics (Jorgensen & Duncan, 2015; Kline, 2008; Reisetter et al., 2004).

Qualitative research is a broad term for different research methodologies such as grounded theory, narrative, case study, ethnography, and phenomenological (Creswell, 2012; Flick, von Kardorff, & Steinke, 2004). We will focus on phenomenological methodology, as it seems to lend itself to practice more than some other qualitative approaches do. The goal of phenomenological methodology is to explore and describe the experiences of individuals related to a phenomenon (Creswell, 2012). You would aim to do this by collecting data from persons who experienced the phenomenon in order to extract and give meaning to the what and the how (Moustakas, 1994). Phenomenological methodology seeks essentially to describe rather than explain and to start from a perspective free from assumptions and the belief that there is one reality (Husserl, 1931).

Haase and Johnston (2012) suggested phenomenological qualitative research serves to be the most similar to counseling, as it allows people to share their stories and is most compatible with the process and practice of counseling. A phenomenological methodological approach encompasses philosophies and practices that align well with a counselor professional identity. For example, counselors are trained to acknowledge that there are no absolute truths and that each client is an expert on himself (American Counseling Association, 2014; Anderson & Goolishian, 1992; Bedi & Duff,

2014; Rogers, 1980). Phenomenological methodology also fits counseling ethics such as bracketing thoughts and biases (Kocet & Herlihy, 2014), being culturally competent, ensuring confidentiality, acquiring informed consent from participants, ethically storing documents, and having appropriate boundaries (American Counseling Association, 2014). Also, the information-gathering process is typically done through interviews with participants, which shares similarities with counseling sessions (e.g., get informed consent, utilize questions, seek to bracket biases during interview, ask follow-up questions for clarity). According to Jorgensen and Duncan (2015), introducing research methodologies that fit with the skill set of practitioners and goals of counseling best bridges the gap between research and practice. This gives promise to the idea that counseling and research can easily overlap, and counselors can come to know themselves as researchers (i.e., develop their researcher identity).

The goal of this chapter is to provide you with a user-friendly approach to phenomenological methodology that fits your skill set and is meaningful to your counselor identity *and* researcher identity. To accomplish this, an introduction to the methodology will be provided with discussion of when to use phenomenological methodology. We will also provide sample research questions that would drive this methodology. Importantly, a case study and a step-by-step application of the methodology will be included to enhance understanding of the phenomenological approach. Last, a reflection process will occur by taking the reader through review questions.

Introduction to the Methodology

The qualitative phenomenological approach can be traced back to early 1900s when a German philosopher, Edmund Husserl, suggested people's realities and experiences of a phenomenon were the most valuable source of data (Flick et al., 2004; Husserl, 1931). Since that time, many phenomenological research traditions have developed such as empirical/psychological, hermeneutic (i.e., interpretive), existential, social, reflection/transcendental, and dialogue (Creswell, 2012; Flick et al., 2004; Husserl, 1931; Merriam, 2009; Patton, 2015). The main difference between the listed approaches relates to the researchers view of reality, how information is acquired and accessed (i.e., interview, letter, in-vivo experiences), and how findings are conceptualized and shared (Heppner, Wampold, Owen, Thompson, & Wang, 2016). Giorgi (1994 indicated that regardless of the variations across the approaches, all are similar in that they are descriptive, use phenomenological reduction, examine interactions between people and events, and capture essences of human lives. In order to provide a concrete understanding of the phenomenological approach, we will discuss the key aspects such as the influence of your beliefs about reality (i.e., research philosophy) on the research process and questions, the ways to gather information (i.e., research methods), and the ways to conceptualize information (i.e., data analysis).

Beliefs About Reality

Phenomenological research aligns with constructivism research philosophy. The constructivism research viewpoint honors that there is no absolute truth, and each person *constructs* his own reality around an experience (Heppner et al., 2016). The research questions that come from a constructivism philosophy are open in nature and aimed at understanding the *how* and *what* in relation to the phenomenon. This particular philosophy suggests we are the experts on our own reality and, thus, the richest source of data to understand a specific phenomenon that we have experienced (i.e., our lived experiences).

Ways to Gather Information

Phenomenological research methods are a fit with counselors' inherent skill set to seek and then condense a lot of information in to concise statements about human experiences (Hays & Wood, 2011). The first step in gathering data is to establish participant criteria, sampling method, and number of participants needed. Phenomenological research questions are developed to understand the lived experiences of persons who have been involved in the phenomenon under investigation. Therefore, the participant criteria should be developed so they can speak to the studied phenomenon. According to Merriam (2009), "You not only spell out the criteria you will use, but also say why the criteria are important" (p. 78). Basically, you define the lived experience you want to investigate and develop research questions you want to answer.

After participant criteria are developed, you need to decide how participants are sampled (i.e., sampling method). Some of the most common sampling methods options are snowball sampling, typical sampling, and convenience sampling (Merriam, 2009). Snowball sampling is the most widely used and involves participants providing contact information for others who have experienced the studied phenomenon. Typical sampling involves selecting participants who are the average (i.e., no extreme characteristics) representation of the participant group. Convenience sampling involves selecting participants based on easy access (Merriam, 2009). In regard to the number of participants you will need, some individuals suggest between 5 and 25 participants (Polkinghorne, 1989). However, other individuals state the number of participants is determined when you no longer hear any new information about the phenomenon during data collection (Merriam, 2009).

The methods for gathering information (i.e., data) are somewhat up to you, but it is important to use more than one method to develop thoroughness (Kline, 2008). According to Creswell (2012), methods for investigation under phenomenological approach include individual interviews, focus groups, visual representations, and artifacts (e.g., poems, pictures). According to Denzin and Lincoln (2008), "each practice makes the world visible in different ways. Hence, there is frequently a commitment to using more than one interpretive practice in any study" (p. 5). Although there are many options for gathering information, the most common in phenomenological approaches is conducting individual interviews (Creswell, 2012).

The structure of interviews is important to consider, as it can impact the depth of information provided by participants. Considering phenomenological research aligns with a constructivism viewpoint (i.e., multiple realities), it is important you develop interview protocols in ways that facilitate an open environment for the participant to express their realities. There are three most common interview formats: (1) structured, (2) semistructured, and (3) unstructured (Creswell, 2012). A structured interview involves you asking a predetermined set of questions, exactly as worded, and without asking follow-up questions. A semistructured interview allows for more flexibility due to you having predetermined questions, but order can be changed, and you can ask follow-up questions during the interview. Last, an unstructured interview is conducted without predetermined questions and allows for follow-up questions. Creswell (2012) suggested that semistructured seems to be the most common, with the use of approximately five open-format questions. Ultimately, the questions in the interview should help you answer the research questions. Other things to consider during interviews include strategies for bracketing your biases, ways to record the interview, appropriate length of interview, and mode of interview (e.g., face to face or over phone; Creswell, 2012).

Additional information-gathering strategies can be used during interviews. For example, you might ask the participants to draw a picture to offer another way to describe their experiences of the phenomenon. Poldma and Stewart (2004) stated visual representations "allow for the creation of new insights using art either as the starting point for creative thought generation or as the means by which new meanings in the research can be expressed" (p. 146).

Ways to Conceptualize the Information

Another important step in the phenomenological approach is the information conceptualization (i.e., data analysis) process. The overall goal of the conceptualization process is to develop five to six main themes (i.e., research themes) that give a voice to the lived experiences. The research themes need to be linked to the purpose of the study and research question(s) (Creswell, 2012; Merriam, 2009). Creswell (2012) created a simplified, comprehensive data analysis method as modified from Stevick-Colaizzi-Keen (as cited in Moustakas, 1994), which includes the following steps:

- Revisit and expand on the experience you have with the phenomenon under investigation (i.e., researcher epoche). This will assist you in setting aside biases and thoughts related to the topic.
- Find and list important statements made by participants regarding how they experienced the phenomenon. You will need to examine your written notes on transcriptions and other research documents (i.e., margin notes and codes).

- Group statements into main themes (i.e., research themes) that collapse many of the important statements based on overlap (i.e., meaning units).
- Describe what happened in relation to the phenomenon (i.e., textural description).
- Describe how the phenomenon was experienced (i.e., structural description).
- Narrate the experience by combining the textural and structural descriptions.

It is important to note that during the processes of gathering and conceptualizing information, you need to be involved in procedures that hold you accountable to most accurately interpret the participants' words (i.e., trustworthiness procedures). Trustworthiness procedures are intended to make sure the findings are valid and credible (Giorgi, 1994; Kline, 2008; Moustakas, 1994; Polkinghorne, 1989). These steps might be compared to the strategies practitioners use to bracket their thoughts when seeking to understand the pure meaning from client stories. Some examples of trustworthiness procedures include first being transparent about your own experience in relation to the phenomenon being investigated (i.e., research epoche), writing notes about your thoughts during the research process (i.e., research memos, field journal), having another person review the research materials (i.e., expert check or peer check), and sending research materials to your participants to have them verify accuracy (i.e., member check) (Creswell, 2012; Giorgi, 1994).

When to Use Phenomenological Approach

Research questions drive the methodology; therefore, it is only appropriate to use a method if it answers the research question(s) (Heppner et al., 2016). The phenomenological approach answers *how* and *what* questions that are derived from curiosities and few assumptions about a topic, believe there is no absolute truth, and believe the best informants about a reality of a phenomenon are those who have experienced it (Creswell, 2012). Phenomenological approach has a lot of utility and can be used in various settings and within multiple disciplines (Patton, 2015). It has been used to explore research questions in educational, counseling, nursing, and medical fields with clients, athletes, patients, educators, parents, and multiple other persons (Merriam, 2009). It has also been used to conduct program evaluation by sampling program participants (Patton, 2015).

Research Questions That Drive Phenomenological Approach

One main research question with multiple subquestions geared toward the topics and issues found in the literature is what has been recommended (Creswell, 2012). This main research question should be in the most general form and should start with *what* or *how*, as that allows researchers to get at the essence of experiences. Some examples of main research questions that start with *what* include: "What helps clients cope with depression?" (phenomenon being depression) or "What does it mean to be a counseling client?" (phenomenon being a counseling client). Some examples of how questions might include: "How do children of alcoholics be resilient? (phenomenon being resilient)" or "How do counselors cope with grief in their own lives?" (phenomenon being grief). Again, the main questions would become more specific through associated subquestions. *How do addicts cope during w/ depression the COVID-19 pandemic? isolation anxiety*

Case Example: Where Did the Client Go?

In this section, we present a case study to take you through a user-friendly, step-by-step process of designing a phenomenological research study. This will allow you as a professional counselor to have the skills to conduct a qualitative study using a phenomenological approach in your current practice setting.

Carol graduated with a master's degree in clinical mental health counseling 2 years ago. She is employed as a licensed professional counselor (LPC) and works in a community counseling setting with five other LPCs. She schedules between 20 and 30 sessions per week. While having weekly case consultations with her colleagues, she notices a trend across therapists that there are clients who never return to counseling after the first session. This makes her become curious about understanding what contributes to clients quitting after their first session. She feels strongly that if she can learn more about the reasons, perhaps she can create different elements during the first session and keep clients coming back to get the services they need . . . and the research begins!!

Carol Designs Her Study

Based on previous information, we know that Carol will need to consider all of the following: her beliefs about reality (i.e., philosophical assumptions and phenomenological traditions), what she wants to know (i.e., research questions), how she will gather information (i.e., research methods), how she will conceptualize the information (i.e., data analysis), and how she will share the information (i.e., presentation of research findings).

Carol's Beliefs About Reality

Carol believes there is no absolute answer to the question she has about clients quitting counseling after one session. Although she has some existing biases, she believes there has to be multiple reasons, as many of the counselors she knows have had clients quit after the first session. Carol believes the best way to access answers to this question is to interview clients who have dropped out of therapy after one session. Carol's study will follow the transcendental phenomenological tradition because she believes philosophy should be based on lived experiences, she will seek to suspend her beliefs and biases, she acknowledges reality is based on awareness and believes the meaning of something can only exist if meaning is ascribed (Husserl, 1931).

Carol Wants to Know

In the process of talking with her colleagues and conducting a review of primary sources (e.g., peer-reviewed scholarly journal articles), Carol begins to figure out what she wants to know. The literature review process allows her to develop the need for her study and refine her phrasing of what she wants to know (i.e., research questions). It also helps her confirm she is not replicating research that has already been conducted (Merriam, 2009). During her literature review, she finds that all previous studies have utilized quantitative methodology, been done in inpatient treatment environments, and suggests related variables such as sex, age, employment status, marital status, family issues, and substance use (Kelly & Moos, 2003; Saxon, Ricketts, & Heywood, 2010; Claus & Kindleberger, 2002). That information helps Carol also think about what setting and participant variables she might want to consider when creating participant criteria.

Carol decides she mainly wants to know (i.e., research question): *What are the lived experiences of counseling clients who quit counseling after one session?* Other aspects she would like to know include (i.e., subquestions): *What does it mean to clients to have a counseling experience they don't want to continue? How did the client come to the decision to quit counseling after one session? What role, if any, did a client's personal characteristics play in the decision to quit counseling after one session? What role, if any, did a counselor's personal and professional characteristics play in the client's decision to quit counseling after one session?*

Ways Carol Will Gather Information

Another step Carol will take while designing her study is to select methods she will use to gather information (i.e., research methods). She will need to decide important aspects such as sample, participant criteria and recruitment, ethical considerations, procedures to collect information, and trustworthiness procedures.

Participants

Carol will be purposeful in her sampling in that she will sample participants who have exited counseling after one session. In the process of creating other specific participant criteria, Carol will need to consider previous literature to understand participant variables and settings that have not been studied before. She will also need to revisit the research question(s) to make sure her participants can inform what she wants to know. Carol develops brief criteria for participants that includes the following: (1) started a counseling experience in an outpatient counseling environment (private practice, community agency); (2) stopped seeing that same counselor after only one session; (3) that event occurred within the last one year (must have accurate recall of the event); (4) and over the age of 19 (must be able to consent for self). Given research is time intensive and finding participants can be difficult, Carol believes using a convenience sample will make the research process more doable because of easier access to participants.

Other participant considerations include recruitment and number of participants needed. Considering Carol is using a convenience sampling approach, she decides she will recruit participants in her community by posting fliers in the local grocery stores, local gyms, local counseling offices, local doctor offices, and on the university campus. She can even recruit friends and family if they meet the participant criteria; however, she would need to think about how her established relationship with those individuals may impact their openness to answer the questions in honest ways. Last, she decides to recruit participants until she no longer hears new information from her participants about her study topic (i.e., data saturation).

Procedures to Collect Information

Carol must next decide how she is going to collect information. Carol learns the hallmark of phenomenological research is to conduct interviews, with the most common format being semistructured. Carol will ask the following questions in her semistructured interviews:

1. *Tell me about the counseling experience you exited after one time.*
2. *What, if anything, did the counselor do that contributed to you wanting to exit that counseling experience after one session?*
3. *What, if anything, did you do that contributed to you wanting to exit that counseling experience after one session?*
4. *Draw a picture of the visual you get when thinking about that counseling experience (explain the picture to me).*
5. *What are your thoughts and feelings now as you reflect on your decision to leave that counseling experience after one session?*
6. *What, if anything, would you want to be different during the first session if you see a counselor in the future?*

Carol decides she will record the interviews via an electronic device as it will allow her to be more present during the interviewing process. After interviews are recorded, she will transcribe them on to a Word document, delete all identifiers and assign pseudonyms for the participants, number each line, use large text, and put a space between when she speaks and when the participant speaks. She will attach the picture the participant drew to the associated transcript. All of her research documents will be stored in a way that follows research ethics (see Ethical Considerations section that follows).

Trustworthiness

Trustworthiness strategies will help Carol control her biases and establish thoroughness within her qualitative work. She will write a researcher epoche, keep research memos, use member checks, a peer check, and an expert check of her audit trail. In the process of writing her researcher epoche, Carol will write a thorough description of her own meanings that will include her thoughts and feelings about the reasons clients exit after one session. Carol's researcher epoche is provided here:

> I have been a counselor in an outpatient counseling setting for 2 years. At first, I did not give much thought to clients no-showing sessions. I figured they had other things going on or did not want to commit to counseling. I then noticed a few clients here and there stopped coming after the first session and I never heard from them again. I heard my colleagues mention this in case staffing meetings, and it made me wonder about what causes clients to stop after the first session. I had actually started counseling before and decided after the first session that it was not a good fit and I could not travel to see her on a regular basis. I particularly did not like the approach of the counseling because it seemed more like a casual dialogue with little professionalism. I also noticed that she often asked me questions that related to what I had just previously said. I essentially felt that I was not heard, that she was not listening or attuned to what I was saying. Reflecting on my own experience in relation to exiting counseling after one session made me even more curious about this.
>
> When it happens with my own clients, I often think it might be because clients do not have time, financial resources, adequate transportation, family support, or a commitment to change. I also wonder if it related to something I did—perhaps a lack of personal fit in that they did not appreciate my approach to the counseling session, thought my use of humor was ineffective, or did not like the way I had my office decorated. I also wonder if my clients did not feel heard or understood.

Member checks will involve Carol sending participants their transcribed interviews to make sure there has been an accurate, word-for-word representation of what they said. Carol will also send main themes (i.e., research themes) and associated quotes from each transcript back to all participants once she has completed her conceptualization of the information she gathers. Carol will have one of her counseling colleagues serve as a peer reviewer of the research process. This will involve Carol asking her colleague to read a few of the transcripts and go through the same process she goes through to conceptualize the information (See Ways Carol Will Conceptualize the Information section). Carol will also have an expert check completed by a local university professor. This will involve Carol submitting her audit trail (i.e., research journal) and all other research materials (e.g., transcripts, member checks, research themes) to the professor so he can review the materials and check for biases and so forth. Carol will cross-check her research materials during the entire research process in order to capture variations of meanings.

Ethical Considerations

As in all research processes, there are ethical considerations Carol must follow. Carol must be ethical by thinking about how she will recruit in ways that respect the privacy of participants. Further, she will get documented consent from participants, conduct interviews in private locations to promote honest responses and confidentiality, securely store research materials, and remove participants' actual names (i.e., use pseudonyms) when reporting the findings. Carol will need to submit her research information to an institutional review board (IRB) to get official approval of the study prior to actually collecting data. Carol can get information about the IRB process by contacting a local university.

Given Carol is recruiting in her local community and counseling has associated stigmas, she has unique privacy aspects to consider so she is successful in getting participants. She decides she will post her fliers in private areas such as bathroom stalls in grocery stores, gyms, hospitals, local campus, and in doctor's offices. She will develop a consent form, which all participants will sign prior to starting the interview. She will let the participants choose their preferred interview style (i.e., face to face or over the phone) and location while emphasizing the location needs to be private. She will suggest areas such as library study rooms or a room in their home. She will also need to let participants know interviews will be around 60 to 90 minutes.

Last, Carol will store her research materials (e.g., transcripts, consents, recorder, researcher memos, data analysis documents) in a locked filing cabinet behind a locked door at her counseling office. She believes her counseling office is a secure location, and having research materials at her office will further accentuate the merging of her professional identities of counselor and researcher. She will have separate filing cabinets for her counseling documents and research documents.

Ways Carol Will Conceptualize the Information

In the process of conceptualizing information (i.e., data analysis), Carol will start by revisiting and further developing her researcher epoche, which will allow her to reflect again on her own meaning of the phenomenon (i.e., reduction of her own beliefs through researcher epoche). While reading the transcribed interviews, she will need to write notes on the transcriptions and other research documents (i.e., making margin notes) to put herself in a reflective state and capture her own thoughts about the process. She will also put a few keywords to the right of sentences to summarize what is being said every few lines to draw out significant statements. She will need to do this with each transcribed interview. These steps will help her find and list important statements made by participants and group those words to create units of meaning. Ultimately, the goal of the information conceptualization process is to create main themes (i.e., research themes) that are representative of the collective experiences of all participants.

Once Carol has the main themes, she will construct text to give meaning to each theme. This will involve Carol describing what happened (i.e., textural description) and how what happened was experienced (i.e., structural description). Let's consider Carol discovers a main theme of *financial stressors*. Textural descriptions would provide understanding about the types of financial stressors. For example, the furnace went out, a tire blew, or a vacation is planned. Structural descriptions would provide understanding about how the stressors were experienced by the participants. For example, financial stressors could cause participants to panic as they realize they do not have enough money to pay for counseling and unexpected costs. On the other hand, financial stressors could also prompt feelings of resolve, as it could help participants better understand their priorities (e.g., traveling being more important than counseling). These examples would highlight that participants share in common that financial stressors contributed to them quitting counseling after one session, but the types of financial stressors were different and also experienced in different ways.

Ways Carol Will Share the Information

Once Carol has collected and conceptualized the information, she will need to share the information in ways that connect to her research questions. The bulk of her findings will be a narrative about the main themes (i.e., research themes) to describe components of each theme. She will feature several quotes from interviews under each theme to give voice to her participants and accentuate how the participants' words informed the findings in her study. Carol could also feature a participant's visual representation to give meaning to main themes (see Figure 10.1).

Carol will also need to give a synthesis of the textural and structural descriptions to provide a holistic understanding of the lived experiences of clients who quit counseling after one session (e.g., similar to the process of integrating everything when creating a client summary report).

To provide a concrete explanation of how Carol could share her findings, we will give an example of a main theme, description, and quote. Let's say Carol discovers a main theme of *financial stressors*. These might include job changes, loss of insurance, unexpected costs, or lifestyle costs. Carol would want to describe the types of financial stressors and how those were experienced. Carol could feature a quote to highlight a type of financial stressor and how the participant experienced it:

I found myself feeling very stressed after I attended the first session and got the bill. I was surprised by the cost as that wasn't something discussed during the session. My insurance did not pay out and I was left with the entire bill of

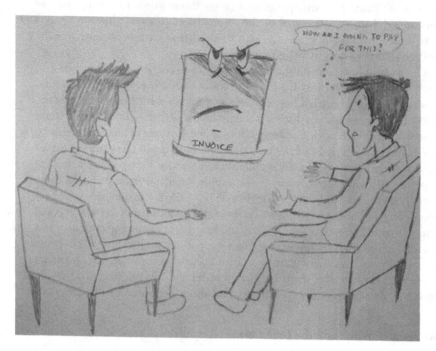

Figure 10.1 Client Drawing

Note: The participant drew a picture with a focal point of a "mean bill". He said, "I couldn't find a way to pay for counseling so I had to quit after the first session".

$180.00. I wasn't sure how I was going to afford to pay for counseling. Then, my furnace went out! I was so stressed and now facing the problem of not being able to afford all my bills. I was basically living paycheck to paycheck. Something had to give and I didn't know what to do. I ultimately decided that I had to quit counseling. I felt really sad about quitting because I needed counseling and I really liked the counselor, but I didn't know how else I could solve my money problems. I just wasn't prepared for how expensive counseling was.

Parting Message

Professional counselors in practice have unique insight regarding what will improve client care, and research is a mechanism that can push our profession forward for the betterment of our clients. Further, this methodology is the type of research that is applicable and manageable for you to accomplish in your current practice setting. It also provides an excellent opportunity for you to further develop your clinical expertise by understanding human experience in ways that cannot be captured through the counseling process. The phenomenological approach of exploring and telling the lived experiences of people related to a specific phenomenon (Creswell, 2012) is the perfect overlap between counseling and research. In that, what makes you a skilled counselor (e.g., understanding there are multiple realities, asking open questions, bracketing your thoughts and beliefs, desiring to be interactive with people to understand them) can help you become a skilled researcher.

Resources for More Information

Peer-Reviewed Journal Articles

Brown, T., & Kimball, T. (2013). Cutting to live: A phenomenology of self-harm. *Journal of Marital and Family Therapy, 39*(2), 195–208. doi:10:1111/j.1752–0606.2011.00270.x

Davidsen, A. *(2013)*. Phenomenological approaches in psychology and health sciences. *Qualitative Research in Psychology, 10*(3), 318–339. doi:10.1080/14780887.2011.608466

Hays, D., & Wood, C. (2011). Infusing qualitative traditions in counseling research designs. *Journal of Counseling and Development, 89,* 288–295. doi:10.1002/j.1556–6678.2011.tb00091.x

Sackett, C., & Lawson, G. (2016). A Phenomenological inquiry of clients' meaningful experiences in counseling with counselors-in-training. *Journal of Counseling and Development, 94*(1), 62–71. doi:10.1002/jcad.12062

Wertz, F. J. (2005). Phenomenological research methods for counseling psychology. *Journal of Counseling Psychology, 52*(2), 167–177. doi:10.1037/0022–0167.52.2.167

Books

Berg, B., & Lune, H. (2011). *Qualitative research methods: For the social sciences* (5th ed.). Boston, MA: Pearson.

Corbin, J., & Strauss, A. (2008). *Basics of qualitative research* (3rd ed.). Thousand Oaks, CA: Sage Publications.

Creswell, J. W. (2014). *Research design: Qualitative, quantitative, and mixed methods approaches* (4th ed.). Thousand Oaks, CA: Sage Publications.

Merriam, S., & Tisdell, E. (2015). *Qualitative research: A guide to design and implementation* (4th ed.). San Francisco, CA: Jossey-Bass.

Miles, M., Huberman, A., & Saldana, J. (2014). *Qualitative data analysis: A methods sourcebook* (3rd ed.). Thousand Oaks, CA: Sage Publications.

Moustakas, C. (1994). *Phenomenological research methods.* Thousand Oaks, CA: Sage Publications.

Patton, M. (2015). *Qualitative research and evaluation methods* (4th ed.). Thousand Oaks, CA: Sage Publications.

Seidman, I. E. (2013). *Interviewing as qualitative research: A guide for researchers in education and the social sciences* (4th ed.). New York, NY: Teachers College Press.

Questions for Further Review and Application

1. What is the aim of qualitative phenomenological methodology?
2. What are two reasons a phenomenological approach seems especially fitting for professional counselors to utilize?

3.   What are two ethical considerations counseling and phenomenological research have in common?
4.   Name and describe the three different formats of interviews that can be used in this research approach.
5.   Describe two reasons why it is important to utilize trustworthiness procedures when conducting phenomenological research.

References

American Counseling Association. (2014). ACA *code of ethics*. Alexandria, VA: Author.

Anderson, H., & Goolishian, H. A. (1992). The client is the expert: A not-knowing approach to therapy. In S. McNamee & K. J. Gergen (Eds.), *Therapy as social construction* (pp. 25–39). London: Sage Publications.

Bedi, R. P., & Duff, C. T. (2014). Client as expert: A Delphi poll of clients' subjective experience of therapeutic alliance formation variables. *Counselling Psychology Quarterly, 27*(1), 1–18. doi:10.1080/09515070.2013.857295

Claus, R., & Kindleberger, L. (2002). Engaging substance abusers after centralized assessment: Predictors of treatment entry and dropout. *Journal of Psychoactive Drugs, 34*, 25–31. doi:10.1080/02791072.2002.10399933

Creswell, J. (2012). *Qualitative inquiry and research design: Choosing among five approaches* (3rd ed.). Thousand Oaks, CA: Sage Publications.

Denzin, N., & Lincoln, Y. (2008). *Strategies of qualitative inquiry* (3rd ed.). Thousand Oaks, CA: Sage Publications.

Flick, U., von Kardorff, E., & Steinke, I. (2004). A companion to qualitative research: What is qualitative research? In U. Flick, E. von Kardorff, & I. Steinke (Eds.), *What is qualitative research: An introduction to the field* (pp. 3–13). Thousand Oaks, CA: Sage Publications.

Giorgi, A. (1994). A phenomenological perspective on certain qualitative research methods. *Journal of Phenomenological Psychology, 25*, 190–220. doi:10.1163/156916 294X00034

Haase, T., & Johnston, N. (2012). Making meaning out of loss: A story and study of young widowhood. *Journal of Creativity in Mental Health, 7*, 204–221. doi:10:1080/1 5401383.2012,710170

Hays, D., & Wood, C. (2011). Infusing qualitative traditions in counseling research designs. *Journal of Counseling & Development, 89*, 288–295. doi:10.1002/j.1556–6678.2011.tb00091.x

Heppner, P., Wampold, B., Owen, J., Thompson, M. N., & Wang, K. T. (2016). *Research design in counseling* (4th ed.). Boston, MA: Cengage Learning.

Husserl, E. (1931). *Ideas pertaining to a pure phenomenology and to a phenomenological philosophy: First book*. K. Kersten (Trans.). New York, NY: Springer.

Jorgensen, M., & Duncan, K. (2015). A grounded theory of master's-level counselor research identity. *Counselor Education and Supervision, 54*, 17–31. doi:10.100 2/j.1556–6978.2015.00067

Kelly, J., & Moos, R. (2003). Dropout from 12-step self-help groups: Prevalence, predictors, and counteracting treatment influences. *Journal of Substance Abuse Treatment, 24*, 241–250. doi:10.1016/S0740–5472(03)00021–7

Kline, B. (2008). Developing and submitting credible qualitative manuscripts. *Counselor Education and Supervision, 47*, 210–217. doi:10.1002/j.1556–6978.2008.tb00052.x

Kocet, M. M., & Herlihy, B. J. (2014). Addressing value-based conflicts within the counseling relationship: A decision-making model. *Journal of Counseling & Development, 92*(2), 180–186. doi:10.1002/j.1556–6676.2014.00146.x

Merriam, S. (2009). *Qualitative research: A guide to design and implementation* (3rd ed.). San Francisco, CA: Jossey-Bass.

Moustakas, C. (1994). *Phenomenological research methods.* Thousand Oaks, CA: Sage Publications.

Patton, M. (2015). *Qualitative research and evaluation methods* (4th ed.). Thousand Oaks, CA: Sage Publications.

Poldma, T., & Stewart, M. (2004). Understanding the value of artistic tools such as visual concept maps in design and education research. *Art Design & Communication in Higher Education, 3*, 141–148. doi:10.1386/adch.3.3.141/1

Polkinghorne, D. (1989). Phenomenological research methods. In R. S. Valle & S. Halling (Eds.), *Existential-phenomenological perspectives in psychology: Exploring the breadth of human experience* (pp. 41–60). New York, NY: Plenum Press.

Reisetter, M., Korcuska, J. S., Yexley, L., Bonds, D., Nikels, H., & McHenry, W. (2004). Counselor educators and qualitative research: Affirming a research identity. *Counselor Education and Supervision, 44*, 2–16.

Rogers, C. (1980). *A way of being.* Boston, MA: Houghton Mifflin Company.

Saxon, D., Ricketts, T., & Heywood, J. (2010). Who drops-out? Do measures of risk to self and to others predict unplanned endings in primary care counselling? *Counselling and Psychotherapy Research, 10*, 13–21. doi:10.1080/14733140902914604

11 Photovoice

Heather Trepal & Yuliya Cannon

Introduced originally by Wang and Burris (1994) as *photo novella* (meaning photo story), photovoice has emerged as an innovative qualitative research method. In this method, individuals take pictures of their experiences and use written reflections to express themselves with the goal of promoting insight, action, and change. In creating the term *photovoice*, Wang and Burris (1997) used the word "VOICE" intentionally to represent "Voicing Our Individual and Collective Experience" (p. 381). The goals of inspiring personal and community change and taking grassroots actions lie at the heart of photovoice research. Photovoice aims to achieve the following three goals: (a) capture concerns and strengths using pictures/photographs; (b) facilitate critical reflection and dialogue about individual and community concerns; and (c) reach and engage policy makers with a goal of making social change (Wang, 1999). Along with using photovoice as a research methodology, it can also be used as a clinical intervention with individual clients who are facing barriers to their growth (Sackett & Jenkins, 2015).

> Remember, photovoice is not research "on" or "about" something but rather research "with" your participants. They are involved in all steps of the process including designing what you will research, approaching the research, analyzing the data, and communicating the findings.

When you use photovoice with individuals or even with your clients as an intervention, the combination of narrative and visual data in photovoice research allows you to capture individuals' realities from their own perspectives (McIntire, 2003). We will talk a little about how you get both forms of data in photovoice and how you would combine them. Before we begin giving some more depth about the methodology itself, there are some other important points to know. First, in photovoice, people are viewed as the experts on their own lives, and they need to have a say in the creation of policies that impact their communities (Wang & Burris, 1997). Thus, an essential step in photovoice is connecting participants and policy makers, with the goal of raising policy makers' awareness about critical community issues. This awareness raising, in turn, could potentially lead to changes in policy that could positively impact the community. In this chapter, we provide some information about the theoretical underpinnings of photovoice methodology, walk the reader through the steps of conducting a photovoice study, illustrate the process through a case study, and discuss the limitations of this research design.

Theories That Influenced Photovoice

Three theoretical sources that influenced the development of photovoice include (a) key theoretical concepts of critical consciousness, (b) feminist theory, and (c) contemporary and documentary photography. All three sources aim to inspire community participation and action.

The Brazilian theorist Paulo Freire's approach to education for critical consciousness was an important lens in the creation of photovoice. The central idea of Freire's praxis lies in the premise that education cannot be viewed outside of the context within which it occurs. The theorist believed that education could liberate individuals and empower them to have a voice in their own lives. In his work, Freire engaged participatory strategies in designing and conducting adult literacy programs (Carlson, Engebretson, & Chamberlain, 2006). Embracing social knowledge is an important part of education that inspires people to gain control over their lives. In participatory strategies, a dialogue approach is used to empower individuals to critically evaluate the root causes of their concerns. Freire's ideas have been instrumental in informing the development of education, literacy, community development, and health education programs worldwide. Although Freire utilized drawings or photographs that captured individuals' realities, photovoice methodology extends his approach of using photographs and drawings by allowing people to create images themselves (Wang & Burris, 1997).

Photovoice is also rooted in feminist inquiry (Wang, 1999). Feminist scholars focus on giving voice to underserved and vulnerable populations by illuminating how the dominant forms of power act in tandem to silence and oppress these voices. Another important aspect in feminist methodology is the honoring of women's experiences. Wang (1999) maintained that photovoice challenges the traditional notions of positivistic research by honoring women's knowledge and experience and including them as coresearchers, advocates, and participants in the process of the scientific inquiry. Through photographs, women are empowered to express their unique experiences and challenges and engage in critical discussions about the nature of these issues.

The third theoretical root of photovoice is contemporary and documentary photography. Photography captures the lives and struggles of vulnerable populations, giving voice to those who otherwise may feel unheard (Rose, 1997). In photovoice, individuals "who may otherwise not have access to such a tool" use cameras to capture a range of experiences that may be difficult to express using words (Wang & Burris, 1997, p. 370). The creators of photovoice believed that pictures allow people to take a deeper look at experiences from a perspective of a person other than a professional photographer. The ~~main distinction between photovoice and traditional documentary photography is in its prominent focus on empowering individuals to become active participants in discussing the issues they face rather than the passive subjects of photographs captured by others.~~ For a more in-depth history on the development of photovoice, readers can refer to the original article by Wang and Burris (1997) referenced at the end of this chapter.

When to Use Photovoice

When you consider your clinical practice, you may be wondering when photovoice is most appropriate to use and what types of questions you might ask that photovoice would be particularly useful to answer. Photovoice is a flexible research method that has been used by researchers from various disciplines with a common goal of addressing the health and social needs of diverse populations and cultures.

Textbox 11.1 Goals and Uses of Photovoice

Photovoice can be used to:

- Teach, influence, highlight/provide voice, create action
- Identify, represent, and enhance a community through a specific photographic technique/process
- Understand (deeper participant awareness), transform (participants' social action), or both

There are three main goals:

1. Enable people to record or reflect something (e.g., community strengths, barriers, concerns, experiences)
2. Promote critical dialogue and knowledge about an issue
3. Reach policy makers and/or others

Essentially, photovoice can be used when you or your clients see a potential problem. That problem may be one for which the client may or may not have words to express or a problem they experience that others may not understand fully. As a mental health practitioner, you can't follow the client's day-to-day life and see all the things that your client is expressing. This is true for others in the community who may not understand the client's experience, either. Thus, photovoice can become a way to show others what the experience is, what barriers they may face, and what strengths and assets they possess. So there are many considerations about when to use photovoice as a methodology in your practice. Photovoice is something to consider using when you need more depth, a different perspective, or a framework that can allow your clients or other individuals with whom you are working to engage in social action.

A Discussion About Social Action

Due to the focus on social action, some assert that photovoice is a research method that has implications for social justice and advocacy (Sackett & Jenkins, 2015; Smith, Bratini, & Appio, 2012). Thus, this is a methodology that can fall within advocacy-based research (which you will read more about in Chapter 14). Sanon, Evans-Agnew, and Boutain (2014) examined photovoice studies and found that there were three categories of social justice: awareness, amelioration, and transformation. Some researchers are interested in raising social justice awareness at the individual or community level—or, more specifically, highlighting personal insights which can result in making people aware of an issue. Others are more interested in ameliorating a social condition, pointing out the factors or barriers leading to injustice, or actually promoting change with social transformation.

Of course, you could gain this same information about participants' perceptions of their concerns through needs assessments, surveys, or even interviews. Photovoice, however, offers the possibility of *perceiving* the world through the lens of the participant. In some ways, photovoice is the methodological representation of the saying "a picture is worth 1,000 words." The photovoice method values the knowledge put forth by individuals as the experts around an issue, but it does so in a way through which you can not only hear what individuals are saying but see how they perceive their world through pictures. Through this lens, participants' pictures can affirm the world of individuals who may be vulnerable, oppressed, or marginalized. In addition, photovoice goes beyond the typical needs assessment by inviting participants to become their own advocates, allowing them to engage with you and with others around them to create social action. Remember that social action is an important goal of this method, and that action may take the form of awareness, amelioration, or transformation (Sanon et al., 2014).

Photovoice has been utilized to examine social and health issues (McIntyre, 2003), issues related to youth (Wang, 1999), poverty (Willson et al., 2006), experiences of living with mental illness (Thompson et al., 2008), employment-seeking behaviors of individuals with various diseases (Rhodes, 2006), experiences of people with intellectual disabilities (Jurkowski & Paul-Ward, 2007), indigenous research (Castleden & Garvin, 2008; Harper, 2009), exploring barriers and supportive resources when considering revealing affectional orientation (Sackett & Jenkins, 2015), in after-school youth programs (Smith et al., 2012), and immigration (Schwartz, Sable, Dannerbeck, & Campbell, 2007). There have been reviews of photovoice studies specifically in mental health (Han & Oliffe, 2016), which can provide you examples of how photovoice has been adapted to meet the needs of different topics or contexts.

Other benefits of this research method in clinical practice include the way that photovoice can be used with participants who have limited proficiency in writing or speaking English, those who have physical limitations, or individuals who may not have access to other ways of expressing their needs due to a low socioeconomic status. It can also be used with clients who feel like others don't understand them or by clients who are having difficulty expressing their experience verbally. These examples suggest that photovoice is especially valuable in examining and affirming the experiences of individuals who may live on the margins of society. While we have been focusing primarily on the photographs of photovoice, it should be noted that the photovoice methodology is much more than that. It contains aspects of critical dialogue, which we will talk more about later in this chapter. But know that by using photovoice, you have a unique opportunity to encourage people to come together to share their concerns and discuss ways to generate change. In some situations, when clients come together with a similar concern and talk through their photographs, it can provide a normalizing experience. Ultimately, photovoice aims to empower individuals to advocate for their rights. Thus, an important part of a photovoice study is capturing individuals' strengths and assets (Wang & Burris, 1997). Knowing these qualities allows you to capitalize on the existing strengths of the community in reaching policy makers and generating change.

Outside of the impact that photovoice can have as a powerful research tool, there are many unique benefits for participants who become active collaborators in the research process. In photovoice, you intentionally offer individuals a safe place to reflect on their unique experiences and challenges. Through this process, participants may develop a greater sense of awareness and in-depth knowledge of sociopolitical issues that impact their communities. Participants may gain skills and confidence in self-advocacy, lobbying, and empowerment (Blackman & Fairey, 2007). In addition, by engaging in photovoice research, participants can gain immediate benefits by cultivating relationships with each other (Wang & Burris, 1997).

Photovoice Methodology

While photovoice investigations may differ from one another depending on the focus of a particular study, the overall design of photovoice research can be implemented in a sequential fashion. Although in some instances these process steps may overlap, the guide in Table 11.1 can help you design and implement a photovoice study.

Table 11.1 Photovoice Step Process Guide

Preparation Stage
    Planning the project
Implementation Stage
    Recruiting participants
    Data collection
Data Analysis
    Selection of photographs
    Contextualization of photographs
Action Stage
    Preparing and sharing photovoice project
    Reaching policy makers or others to create social change

Preparation Stage

Planning the Project

The planning of the project is a critical part in the execution of a successful photovoice study. It requires you to create a timeline for the study, organize necessary resources, and define ways to address potential challenges that may arise. This process will depend on who your participants are but also on what the topic of the photovoice project is. During the planning phase, you need to consider ways of accessing communities to recruit participants for the study. In this effort, it is advisable to target a group or community that can directly speak to the phenomenon under the investigation or one with which you directly work. For example, if you work in a school or run counseling groups, there may already be students/clients who work together as part of a community. Other populations or groups of individuals may be more difficult to access, and finding ways to access these groups is an important step in planning when considering your timeline, resources, and challenges.

Developing trust is an essential aspect of photovoice research because many communities may be hesitant to speak with researchers, viewing them as outsiders unable to understand their unique needs and challenges. Establishing relationships requires researchers to connect with communities and gain their trust. Building relationships with stakeholders in the community establishes the foundation for a lasting collaborative coinvestigation and community involvement during the research process (Palibroda, Krieg, Murdock, & Havelock, 2009). Building genuine relationships often takes time, commitment, and effort on behalf of the investigator. Therefore, you may be required to spend time observing communities, possibly attending their meetings, and, in general, learning about the community culture. Getting involved with the community is a good way to develop relationships, not only with individual members but also with the community as a whole (Palibroda et al., 2009). Furthermore, you should begin involving community members when clarifying the goals for their photovoice projects. Most photovoice projects begin with conversation about the issue in the community that will be the focus of the team's collaborative work.

A photovoice investigation may require additional resources to cover the cost associated with the execution of the study. You should anticipate allocating resources to purchasing cameras (or making sure those without access to cameras on cellular phones have them), covering participant traveling expenses associated with the study, and securing a place for group discussions. Depending on the focus of a study, additional expenses may be necessary; therefore, you should address any financial or resource matters during the planning phase of a photovoice project.

Another important part of the planning phase is to begin identifying the target audience for this research. Who do you want to reach as a result of the project? People who have power to make decisions and implement change should ideally represent a target audience. You should consider ways to approach and to engage the target audience (Wang, 1999). Who represents the target audience? How will you and participants be able to meet the decision makers? Making concrete steps to reach the target audience should be a collaborative process that involves community members and leaders. Palibroda and colleagues (2009) suggest seeking the target audience within city or town councils, human service agencies, schools, and/or various government and community agencies and departments.

Last, an ethical researcher tries to anticipate how any barriers and issues may be addressed if they should arise during a photovoice investigation. Although various challenges may come up in the process of a photovoice study, some may be associated with (a) the cost of materials, (b) securing of the space for group meetings, (c) facilitation of the group process, (d) potential conflicts that may emerge within group members, and (e) participants losing interest in the group process and the study (Palibroda et al., 2009).

Implementation Stage

Participant Recruitment

As stated earlier, an important consideration in the recruitment phase of the project is to ensure that the potential participants have a firsthand experience with the phenomenon under investigation. Depending on the focus of their study, participants can be recruited using formal or informal ways. Sending emails, brochures, or posting flyers may be a more formal way of recruiting participants, while personally inviting participants to take part in the study can be viewed as informal recruitment (Palibroda et al., 2009). Participants can be recruited in the community or even from your clinical practice or school setting. Make sure to abide by all ethical principles when you recruit participants (see Chapter 3 for more on ethics in research).

Wang (1999) believes that an ideal size in a photovoice study is 7 to 10 people. In a group of that size, you can facilitate a more personal and in-depth discussion among participants. In addition, participants may feel more comfortable and safe discussing their concerns and issues in a group of a smaller size. Since photovoice empowers community members to advocate for themselves, participants may play multiple roles in the research process (Wang, 1999). Specifically, participants in the photovoice investigation assume the responsibility of becoming coresearchers who discuss research goals and engage in the data collection and data analysis processes (Wang, 1999). You should keep that information in mind during the recruitment process and be able to discuss the importance of their coinvestigation roles with potential participants. In addition, you need to discuss any ethical issues that may be associated with this type of research and obtain a written consent from participants that clearly explains the significance of the study and all potential risks and benefits associated with it, as well as the voluntary nature of research (Wang, 1999).

Data Collection

The data collection process starts with organizing a meeting with research participants. During the initial meeting, you can introduce the contributors to the study and present the topic under investigation with the goal of initiating a group dialogue. Carlson and colleagues (2006) suggested that the expected participation may not occur without active facilitation from the researcher. Therefore, you should be intentional in creating a safe environment for participants to engage in a reflective discourse. To facilitate a thoughtful dialogue with participants, a variety of communication methods can be utilized. For instance, you may show a movie clip or PowerPoint or read an article on the issue to explore with participants. The material used in the presentation should be relevant for participants and their community. Following the presentation, you can invite participants to share their reflections about the presented issue. Participants are also encouraged to explore ways to use the research findings to advocate for their communities through reaching various policy makers (Wang & Burris, 1997). Once the goal of the investigation is clarified and the participants' commitment is gained, you introduce participants to the concept of photovoice (Wang, 1999). You also discuss with participants the importance of recording their meetings, noting that the information from these meetings will serve as additional forms of data in the following analysis process.

Depending on a technology that is used to capture images, participants may need to be trained in the use of a particular tool. Some photovoice experts recommend inviting a professional photographer to teach participants about the principle techniques in photography. Using photographic techniques may allow participants to capture images that more vividly and creatively represent what they want to express. Once participants are trained in the use of cameras, you may want to discuss the type of images they are able to take. Photographs have the unique power to leave an indelible impression on people. Considering that, you should discuss the importance of an ethical photo practice and explain ethical concerns associated with taking and using certain images (e.g., confidentiality, safety of participants and people around them, emotional reactions evoked by certain images). You should instruct participants not to take images that may potentially embarrass or stigmatize subjects. Last, you need to establish a timeframe for participants to turn in their photographs for the analysis (e.g., a few days; within 2 or 3 weeks). Keep in mind that during this time frame, when you ask participants to go back into the community and take photographs about the problem or experience they are representing, you can often ask participants to take as many pictures as they would like. You will find in the data analysis phase that not all pictures will be used, but opening the possibility of taking an infinite number of pictures can provide participants with freedom and not make them feel constrained to represent their experience within just one or two monumental photographs.

Data Analysis

The data analysis stage involves selecting images that can be contextualized to represent a story and then codifying these images (Wang, 1999). This process requires a great deal of the participants' collaboration with you and can be done either individually or during the group discussion. The group context may be particularly beneficial for establishing relationships between group members (Palibroda et al., 2009). There are multiple steps within data analysis in terms of receiving, contextualizing, and discussing photographs, which results in selecting and coding themes.

Selection of Photographs

Once the images are returned from participants to you, a follow-up meeting with participants is scheduled. The goal of that meeting is to invite participants to discuss the images they produced. You can ask participants to select one or two images they believe best represent the issues under investigation (Wang, 1999). As mentioned earlier, this can be done between you and the participant or between participants as more of a critical dialogue within a group setting. The ultimate goal of photovoice is to embolden participants to have a voice and feel empowered to advocate for their needs. A critical dialogue that inspires action is at the heart of photovoice research. In this critical dialogue, participants are invited to actively participate in the discussion about the way their images/stories should be presented to policy makers (Wang, 1999). This can be done through a slideshow or exhibit but has also been done in the way of books, websites, or pamphlets. Keep in mind that while social action is one of the goals for photovoice, this action of presenting the photographs and findings to others may also be viewed as political activism and evoke reactions that may lead participants to face various consequences, whereas you (the researcher) may not be directly impacted by the study. For this reason, Wang and Burris (1997) suggested allowing participants to choose the images they are willing to share. This means that while participants may have consented at the start of the photovoice study, another consent process occurs at the close of the photovoice process by allowing them to select which pictures they are comfortable with you sharing with others.

Contextualization of Photographs

During the critical dialogue process noted already, defining the image is a critical step in contextualizing the data (Wang, 1999). Rather than interpreting participants' images in isolation, your job is to encourage a critical dialogue on the meaning participants attribute to their images. How do these photos represent their world? Participants may be encouraged to reflect on and express their feelings associated with photographs. You must be sensitive to participants' feelings and create a safe environment for them to process various emotions that may arise (Palibroda et al., 2009). This requires you to utilize group facilitation skills.

In order to contextualize photographs, first—as noted—have participants select the photographs they are going to show to you or the larger group. These selected image(s) should be pictures that most descriptively capture their concerns. Once they have the few photographs, invite participants to reflect on them. The SHOWeD method can be used to engage participants in critical reflection on their realities. The questions in this method include: (a) What do you See here? (b) What is really Happening here? (c) How does this relate to Our lives? (d) Why does this situation, concern, or strength exist? (e) How can we become Empowered by new social understanding? and (f) What can we Do about it? Using the SHOWeD method allows participants to discuss concerns depicted in their photos and to seek action strategies to create change (Wang, 1999). While most photovoice studies use some version of the SHOWeD method, you can also be creative and use other means to promote reflection, such as having participants caption their pictures.

Coding Themes

The codification of themes involves identifying the topics or issues that emerge from the participants' photo stories and sorting them into categories of issues (Palibroda et al., 2009). Wang and Burris (1997) maintained that in photovoice research, participants play an active role in selecting and contextualizing images with stories they tell as well as identifying themes or key issues in these images that serve as a medium for their voices to be heard. Depending on the goal of the study, you and the participants may choose a specific way to organize the images that represents specific themes or issues. The investigation ensures that the team (which, remember, includes both you and the participants) focuses on selecting the issue or theme that can be realistically targeted and addressed (Wang & Burris, 1997).

During this phase of coding, the group can discuss their hopes and desires for the outcome of the project. We mentioned this earlier in selection of photographs, but this is a good time for participants to determine which pictures they would like to be used to represent the themes and potentially which pictures they would like to remain private—thus not displayed for others to see. Last, you and the participants discuss ways to organize the selected images that tell stories about their communities and their unique concerns. This can be done, as noted, in slideshow or exhibit or any other format that best matches the data that you would like to show, respects your participants, and reaches the target audience. Another consideration other than just exhibiting the photographs is to provide contextual data, which can include both themes and captions. One way to organize and tell these stories is through the SHOWeD method that was described earlier. However, you may select a less structured way to organize your data.

Action Stage

Taking action is the last step in a photovoice study, but it is a critical step. During the action stage, participants have a unique opportunity to provide input and bring forward their concerns about a policy they would like to address and change (Palibroda et al., 2009). As Wang (1999) stated, "using photovoice as a tool for action reflects the [participatory action research] PAR's commitment to meaningful social change" (p. 190). The data analysis process in photovoice produces rich knowledge. But how can this knowledge and the pictures that capture it influence policy and generate change? Without a concrete plan of how to reach the target audience and a way of accessing the decision makers, the photovoice research may not realize its goal of stimulating action. Thus, creating an individual and communal action plan is an important part of photovoice research. As noted earlier, starting this part of the process begins in the planning stage, but it can also be brought into conversations with participants in the critical dialogue phase once experiences have been discussed and themes have been generated.

Finding a way to present the findings of a photovoice study with people in power may be a challenging process. One way that participants can share their experiences with policy makers is through the organization of community forums. To prepare for the forum, participants need to prepare their photovoice exhibit in a way that will help them to discuss issues with the target audience. Palibroda et al. (2009) make some useful recommendations that you may want to keep in mind when preparing for a photovoice exhibit. For instance, they suggest that you ensure the images that are selected for the exhibit are vividly speaking to the issue that will be raised during the exhibit. Once selected, the organization of images should not be done haphazardly. Hanging pictures separately and making sure that captions are attached to the right photograph can ensure the target audience is engaged and not overwhelmed by the presented exhibit. Additional consideration should be given to the size of the photovoice exhibit, because it needs to be transportable to a location where the meeting with the target audience will take place (Palibroda et al., 2009). Last, you should have a discussion with the participants (who are your coresearchers) about their participation in the exhibit and their ability/desire to speak about the images they captured. You may find that some participants want to attend and be present in the exhibit, while others may not. After the presentation, a debriefing with all participants about their experiences during the presentation should be held.

The photovoice process we just described is further detailed in what follows using a case study from a project that we completed. In each section, we describe how the method was used in our project. We hope that having these concrete examples will help to clarify the steps.

Case Study: Body Image Resilience in College Women

Preparation Stage

Planning the Project

Planning for the Body Image Resilience Project began during a class discussion about women's struggles with body image in the face of media pressure. The students shared an idea that women were the best voices on their own experiences of body image resilience. We decided that we wanted to create a project in which women could express their ideas about body image resilience. The goal of the project was to raise awareness about this important issue. We (a group of four researchers) met and planned the project. We developed a media presentation to get participants talking about the issue. We also prepared instructions for completing the photovoice projects.

Implementation Stage

Recruitment of Participants

Our team developed a flyer advertising the photovoice project and spread copies all over campus. The flyer instructed women over the age of 18 to call or email one of us if they were interested in learning more about the project. When someone contacted us, we gave them the information about the project including the time involved. The project involved two groups of women (8–10 in each group). We met for a 2-hour meeting on campus in which the women listened to a PowerPoint presentation about media and body image and were engaged in a lively discussion about the topic.

Data Collection

Afterward, photovoice was introduced and the women were given oral and written instructions on how to complete their projects. We asked them to take a series of three pictures and develop the accompanying written reflections in a modified version of the SHOWeD method mentioned earlier. See Figure 11.1 for a sample photovoice picture and reflection.

Participant Caption

My stomach does not have "abs of steel," it is more like a flabby pit. However, I am not ashamed of this. In fact, I love my stomach because one day it will hold inside

Figure 11.1 Example Photovoice Picture and Reflection

it another life. It will be the home and shelter of another human being. It will guard and protect and grow another person. One day, I will have a precious baby growing inside my stomach, and the extra flab will help to protect the innocence of my baby. I love my stomach because it will be the place I rest my baby when he/she is born. I love my stomach because when he/she grows up and needs some comfort they will wrap their arms around me and feel a sense of peace. I love my stomach because it gives me the ability to love unconditionally a child who has not yet been conceived, but that will one day need me. I love my stomach because it is a part of my past and will be a part of my future.

Data Analysis Stage

Selection of Photographs

Both groups of women met a second time, separately, to discuss their photovoice projects. Each woman in the group was asked to select her favorite picture, which was the one photograph that was projected in the group on a large screen. When their picture was displayed, each participant was able to read their reflection (from the modified SHOWeD reflection that they were instructed to complete in the data collection phase) out loud and add anything else that they wanted to share. Other women in the group were able to ask questions and comment on each person's photo and reflections.

Contextualization of Photographs

During this meeting of selecting and displaying photographs, the women were also asked to talk about commonalities (themes) that they saw between and among their photovoice projects. The research team was present at the group discussions, so they participated in the discussions and guided the participants to facilitate sharing. The group decided that the photovoice projects and our group discussion resulted in two distinct themes: (1) Beauty Ideals (created and reinforced by the media) and (2) Self (self-awareness and self-criticism). Note Figure 11.1 to see if you can observe how the themes were represented in this photovoice picture and reflection.

Once the groups were over, the team met separately and reviewed the themes the participants created. We (the four members of the research team) created a visual model of the themes and emailed all of the participants to get their feedback and input, ensuring that they continued to be active with the research team as well.

Action Stage

Preparing and Sharing the Photovoice Project

We decided to partner with a student organization that was holding events for Eating Disorders Awareness Week on campus. Our overarching social justice goal and the focus of the exhibit was to raise awareness about body image resilience in the face of pressure and messages from the mainstream media. The intended target audience was other students on campus. The participants' photovoice projects and their reflections were printed out and displayed on poster board in the main lobby of our classroom building. The participants purposely chose pictures that represented the themes (Beauty Ideals and Self). The student organization had several speakers about the media, eating disorders, and body image.

Ethical Considerations in Photovoice Research

Like any research method, a photovoice study must be conducted within ethical guidelines that govern the process of designing and executing a study. Thus, a solid understanding about how to adhere to ethical research guidelines is critical. As stated previously, it is important for you to have clear steps to address any potential barriers that may emerge in a photovoice study. These steps must be created during the planning phase of the project and be clearly outlined in the project proposal, which will then be evaluated by the institutional review board or another ethical entity.

The Informed Consent

You should provide complete information about the study to participants and discuss potential risks and benefits of engaging in this type of research. Keep in mind that providing photographs of one's experience and life can be identifying in ways that responding to a needs assessment may not be. Thus, participants should be able to consent to the study understanding what to expect and how to voluntarily withdraw from the study (Palibroda et al., 2009). Participants should also be aware of potential emotional distress that may occur during the photovoice study, as powerful pictures and images can sometimes cause difficult emotions to arise. Thus, it is important to prepare your participants for this potential result, as well as to have a plan in place for when or if this does occur (e.g., having more than one research team member in the group discussion or offering information about counseling resources in the community). Additionally, a negative outcome of the study may be associated with an inability to reach the target audience. Thus, participants should be made aware about this important limitation (Wang, 1999). Finally, if your participants are minors, the parents/guardians need to be involved in the informed consent process.

Privacy and Safety Issues

Anonymity, safety, and confidentiality are the critical aspects of photovoice. You need to educate participants about the importance of respecting individual privacy when taking images during the data collection phase (Wang & Redwood-Jones, 2001). During that process, it is important to educate participants on the risks of taking pictures that may identify individuals. Depending on a particular project, you may instruct participants to avoid taking photos that may link an individual to the image. Yet in some studies, pictures of human subjects will be permitted. Gaining informed consent from these subjects is critical; therefore, participants need to be trained on the proper way to facilitate this process. The use of personal devices (e.g., cell phones, personal cameras) also needs to be addressed as a special ethical issue.

The safety of participants and their subjects is an important part of an ethical photovoice research study. You need to instruct participants about the importance of maintaining safety throughout the research process and teach them skills to safely take pictures (Palibroda et al., 2009). Wang and Redwood-Jones (2001) maintain that the use of cameras allows participants to hold a certain level of power. Participants need to be aware of their environment and any potential risks at all times. Thus, the discussion about the responsibility, as well as the ethics and power of using cameras, should precede the training on the use of cameras (Wang & Redwood-Jones, 2001).

Photo Selection

During the training phase, participants are encouraged to take images that represent their communities authentically and respectfully. Depending on the number of participants, a photovoice study may produce a large volume of visual images. Selecting the most representative images that can expressively communicate with the target audience is an essential step in the photo selection phase (Wang & Redwood-Jones, 2001). You need to determine the number of images that will be selected for the exhibition. However, this should be a consent process with each participant. Specifically, each participant needs to consent to each image they would like to bring into the group discussion and photo selection phase. While this may seem like it is under their control, as participants may bring their images to the group, some researchers have participants email or send photographs prior to the group so that they are ready to be viewed or projected on a larger screen. Thus, it is important to ensure the specific photo(s) that are presented in the larger group are the ones that the participant consented to be used and displayed.

Photo Storage

You also need to have a clear plan for how you will safely and securely store the data collected during the study. Maintaining a clear organizational framework for tagging, organizing, and storing participants' images and meeting notes are an essential step in conducting an ethical photovoice research project.

Limitations of Photovoice

Every research methodology presents limitations that need to be taken into consideration when constructing a study. In what follows, we list some of the challenges that you need to take into consideration when designing a photovoice study.

Challenges for Participants

Time Commitment

Engaging in photovoice may require participants to dedicate a significant amount of their time to the project. Therefore, you need to discuss time commitment during the recruitment phase of the process.

Taking Photos

Participants may not be able to find images that represent their unique experiences. For this reason, educating participants on the symbolism of photography may be helpful in addressing this particular challenge.

Contextualizing Images

Reflecting on the content of the photos can evoke strong emotions from participants, who may also struggle to contextualize the images they select. You should rely on your group facilitation skills to allow participants to safely process their emotions.

Potential Challenges for You as a Photovoice Researcher

Time Commitment

Constructing and executing a photovoice study can take a significant amount of time. Therefore, you need to factor this in when thinking about a potential photovoice project.

Finding Participants

You may not be familiar with communities you would like to investigate and could find yourself needing to take a significant amount of time to establish relationships with individuals prior to conducting a study.

Resources

Another challenge may be associated with the cost of organizing a photovoice study. The cost may be associated with buying cameras, printing out photovoice projects, or securing space to invite participants into for group discussions.

Putting It All Together

Photovoice can be a powerful tool for researchers who want to bring their participants' voices to life. This method involves participants documenting their reflections on their own perspectives with photographs and then contextualizing them with written reflections. The participants work together to interpret the photographs and decide what perspectives and information to present. Further, photovoice can be an effective tool for reaching stakeholders in the community with participants' ideas about change. Now that you have learned about the photovoice method, what communities or clients do you think this method may work best with? The resources that follow can help you design your photovoice project.

Resources for More Information

Books and Manuals

Blackman, A., & Fairey, T. (2007). *The photovoice manual: A guide to designing and running participatory photography projects*. London: PhotoVoice.

Palibroda, B., Krieg, B., Murdock, L., & Havelock, J. (2009). *A practical guide to photovoice: Sharing pictures, telling stories and changing communities*. Winnipeg, MB: Prairie Women's Health Network.

Peer-Reviewed Journal Articles

Becker, K., Reiser, M., Lambert, S., & Covello, C. (2014) Photovoice: Conducting community-based participatory research and advocacy in mental health. *Journal of Creativity in Mental Health, 9*(2), 188–209. doi:10.1080/15401383.2014.890088

Smith, L., Bratini, L., & Appio, L. M. (2012). "Everybody's teaching and everybody's learning": Photovoice and youth counseling. *Journal of Counseling and Development, 90*, 3–12. doi:10.1111/j.1556-6676.2012.00001.x

Wang, C. C. (1999). Photovoice: A participatory action research strategy applied to women's health. *Journal of Women's Health, 8*(2), 185–192. doi:10.1089/jwh.1999.8.185

Wang, C. C., & Burris, M. (1997). Photovoice: Concept, methodology, and use for participatory needs assessment. *Health Education & Behavior, 24*, 369–387. doi:10.1177/109019819702400309

Questions for Further Review and Application

1. What types of research questions or concerns are best addressed by photovoice? How can you see this methodology being used in your work setting?
2. Note the photovoice picture in Figure 11.1. Can you see how important the reflections and group discussion/identification of themes are in a photovoice study? What do you think might happen if you just collected the participants' photos without the contextualization or group sharing aspects of this method? What opportunities might be lost for group/community participation, connection, and action?
3. What are some potential ethical concerns related to the use of photographs? How would you plan early to cover these potential pitfalls with participants?
4. What strategies would you use to engage stakeholders?

References

Blackman, A., & Fairey, T. (2007). *The photovoice manual: A guide to designing and running participatory photography projects.* London: PhotoVoice.

Carlson, E. D., Engebretson, J., & Chamberlain, R. M. (2006). Photovoice as a social process of critical consciousness. *Qualitative Health Research, 16*(6), 836–852. doi:10.1177/1049732306287525

Castleden, H., & Garvin, T. (2008). Modifying photovoice for community-based participatory indigenous research. *Social Science and Medicine, 66*(6), 1393–1405. doi:10.1016/j.socscimed.2007.11.030

Han, C. S., & Oliffe, J. L. (2016). Photovoice in mental illness research: A review and recommendations. *Health, 20*(2), 110–126. doi:10.1177/1363459314567790

Harper, K. (2009). Using photovoice to investigate environment and health in a Hungarian Romani (Gypsy) community. *Practicing Anthropology, 31*(4), 10–14. doi:10.17730/praa.31.4.2g576u570054w030

Jurkowski, J. M., & Paul-Ward, A. (2007). Photovoice with vulnerable populations: Addressing disparities in health promotion among people with intellectual disabilities. *Health Promotion Practice, 8*(4), 358–365. doi:10.1177/1524839906292181

McIntyre, A. (2003). Through the eyes of women: Photovoice and participatory research as tools for re-imagining place. *Gender, Place & Culture*, 10, 47–66. doi:10.1080/0966369032000052658

Palibroda, B., Krieg, B., Murdock, L., & Havelock, J. (2009). *A practical guide to photovoice: Sharing pictures, telling stories and changing communities*. Winnipeg, MB: Prairie Women's Health Network.

Rose, G. (1997). Engendering the slum: Photography in East London in the 1930s. *Gender, Place & Culture*, 4(3), 277–301. doi:10.1080/09663699725350

Rhodes, S. D. (2006). Visions and voices: HIV in the 21st century. Indigent persons living with HIV/AIDS in the southern USA use photovoice to communicate meaning. *Journal of Epidemiology and Community Health*, 60(10), 886.

Sackett, C., & Jenkins, A. (2015). Photovoice: Fulfilling the call for advocacy in the counseling field. *Journal of Creativity in Mental Health*, 10, 376–385. doi:10.1080/15401383.2015.1025173

Sanon, M. A., Evans-Agnew, R. A., & Boutain, D. M. (2014). An exploration of social justice intent in photovoice research studies from 2008 to 2013. *Nursing Inquiry*, 21(3), 212–226. doi:10.1111/nin.12064

Schwartz, L. R., Sable, M. R., Dannerbeck, A., & Campbell, J. D. (2007). Using photovoice to improve family planning services for immigrant Hispanics. *Journal of Health Care for the Poor and Underserved*, 18(5), 757–766. doi:10.1353/hpu.2007.0107

Smith, L., Bratini, L., & Appio, L. M. (2012). "Everybody's teaching and everybody's learning": Photovoice and youth counseling. *Journal of Counseling and Development*, 90, 3–12. doi:10.1111/j.1556–6676.2012.00001.x

Thompson, N. C., Hunter, E. E., Murray, L., Ninci, L., Rolfs, E. M., & Pallikkathayil, L. (2008). The experience of living with chronic mental illness: A photovoice study. *Perspectives in Psychiatric Care*, 44(1), 14–24. doi:10.1111/j.1744–6163.2008.00143.x

Wang, C. C. (1999). Photovoice: A participatory action research strategy applied to women's health. *Journal of Women's Health*, 8(2), 185–192. doi:10.1089/jwh.1999.8.185

Wang, C. C., & Burris, M. A. (1994). Empowerment through photo novella: Portraits of participation. *Health Education Quarterly*, 21(2), 170–186. doi:10.1177/109019819402100204

Wang, C. C., & Burris, M. A. (1997). Photovoice: Concept, methodology, and use for participatory needs assessment. *Health Education & Behavior*, 24(3), 369–387. doi:10.1177/109019819702400309

Wang, C. C., & Redwood-Jones, Y. A. (2001). Photovoice ethics: Perspectives from Flint photovoice. *Health Education & Behavior*, 28(5), 560–572. doi:10.1177/109019810102800504

Willson, K., Green, K., Haworth-Brockman, M., & Rachel, R. B. (2006). Looking out: Prairie women use photovoice methods to fight poverty. *Canadian Woman Studies*, 25(3), 160–166. ISSN: 07133235

12 Mixed-Methods Research

Ye He

Up to this point, you have learned about various quantitative and qualitative methodologies that, for the most part, are used in isolation. This means that you would be conducting solely a quantitative study or solely qualitative study. In this chapter, you will learn about the design of mixed-methods (MM) research, through which quantitative and qualitative data collection and analysis methods can be combined. This chapter introduces commonly used MM terms and approaches and illustrates how to apply MM research design. The use of the four leading MM design typologies is elaborated through a case example. Additional resources are provided for further exploration of specific application of MM in your research.

Overview of Mixed-Methods Research

MM emerged from the movement against the dominant use of quantitative research in the 1980s (Gage, 1989; Hammersley, 1992). Researchers such as Guba (1990) promoted the use of qualitative research methods. However, qualitative researchers also argued that there was a systematic set of beliefs guiding the use of research methods (Lincoln & Guba, 1985) and suggested that the use of both quantitative and qualitative methods in one research study is not appropriate (Guba, 1990; Howe, 1988). MM researchers challenged this perspective and proposed the compatible use of both quantitative and qualitative methods and established MM as "a distinct third methodological movement" (Teddlie & Tashakkori, 2003, p. 24).

A variety of MM definitions have been crafted and used by researchers and methodologists in the field. Two most commonly used definitions were proposed by Johnson, Onwuegbuzie and Turner (2007) and through the *Journal of Mixed Methods Research* (JMMR), the official journal including studies using MM and discussions regarding the use of MM at the methodological level.

Johnson et al. (2007) proposed a general MM definition based on the review of MM definitions used by 21 highly published MM researchers:

> Mixed methods research is the type of research in which a researcher or team of researchers combines elements of qualitative and quantitative

research approaches (e.g., use of qualitative and quantitative viewpoints, data collection, analysis, inference techniques) for the broad purposes of breadth and depth of understanding and corroboration.

(p. 123)

JMMR shared an even more general MM definition with its authors and readers:

mixed methods research is defined as research in which the investigator collects and analyzes data, integrates the findings, and draws inferences using both qualitative and quantitative approaches or methods in a single study or a program of inquiry.

(Tashakkori & Creswell, 2007, p. 4)

While these general definitions are commonly used by MM practitioners, it is important to note that the tradition of MM varies across different disciplines and geographic regions. Instead of adopting a single definition, some MM methodologists suggested detailing the characteristics of MM research instead (Teddlie & Tashakkori, 2010).

In their second edition of *Designing and Conducting Mixed Methods Research*, Creswell and Plano Clark (2017) detailed six core characteristics of MM including:

- collects and analyzes persuasively and rigorously both qualitative and quantitative data (based on research questions);
- mixes (or integrates or links) the two forms of data concurrently by combining them (or merging them), sequentially by having one build on the other, or embedding one within the other;
- gives priority to one or to both forms of data (in terms of what the research emphasizes);
- uses these procedures in a single study or in multiple phases of a program of study;
- frames these procedures within philosophical worldviews and theoretical lenses; and
- combines the procedures into specific research designs that direct the plan for conducting the study (p. 5).

Similarly, in a recent report presented by the Mixed Methods International Research Association (MMIRA), Mertens et al. (2016) highlighted two core criteria for MM including (1) "the use of more than one method, methodology, approach, theoretical or paradigmatic framework"; and (2) "integration of results from those different components" (p. 4).

Appropriate Use of Mixed-Methods Research Design

Combining the strengths of quantitative and qualitative methods you have learned, MM research presents many benefits. The major purposes of MM research include corroboration, elaboration, and development (Arnault &

Fetters, 2011; Creswell & Plano Clark, 2017; Tashakkori & Teddlie, 2010). *Corroboration* refers to the use of multiple methods (e.g., quantitative survey and focus group discussion) to triangulate and test the consistency of findings. *Elaboration* refers to the use of one method (e.g., follow-up interview) to substantiate the interpretation of data collected using another method (e.g., test scores). *Development* refers to the use of results from one method to inform the data collection and/or analysis of the other method (e.g., quantitative instrument development based on qualitative data; Arnault & Fetters, 2011).

Utilizing both quantitative and qualitative theoretical orientations, methodological designs, data collection, and data analysis tools, MM design offsets the weaknesses of studies using only quantitative or qualitative methods and can address research questions that may not be answered by one method alone. In addition, the mixing of quantitative and qualitative data, analysis procedures, display, and interpretation also offers new insights that may not be attainable using quantitative or qualitative research alone. As Creswell and Plano Clark (2017) summarized, you may think about using MM design if you think one type of data source (either quantitative or qualitative) may not be sufficient to address your research questions; the results you report based on quantitative data may need to be further explained and substantiated; you may want to further generalize findings from your qualitative data; or you may need to consider conducting your research in multiple phases to address your overall research objective.

Writing MM Research Questions

If you were to use an MM approach, you would typically take one of two general positions in terms of the role of research questions: (1) the dictatorship model; and (2) the reciprocal approach (Mertens et al., 2016). The dictatorship model states that the research questions drive the selection of MM design, sample procedures, data collection, and analysis processes. This position would also designate MM as only appropriate when the research questions call for the use of both quantitative and qualitative methods. The reciprocal approach, on the other hand, positions research questions in the center as the "hub of the research process" (Plano Clark & Badiee, 2010, p. 280). This position assumes an interactive and reciprocal relationship between research questions and other components of the research study including its purposes, theories, methods, and validity considerations. Based on this position, the research questions may shift and evolve as you carry out the literature review, data collection, analysis, and interpretation throughout the study. In other words, if you adopt the dictatorship model, you will typically specify an MM design once you identify the research questions. If you choose to apply the reciprocal approach, you may be more open to the modifications of the research questions and allow MM design to emerge during the research process.

MM research questions may take on different formats and rhetorical styles depending on the field of the study, the theoretical orientation used, and the specific MM design selected. In general, it is important to ensure that (1) your MM questions, design, and results are clearly aligned; and (2) the

Table 12.1 Sample Mixed-Methods Research Questions With Various Levels of Integration

Separate Questions—quantitative, qualitative, and MM questions are separate	• Is there a statistically significant difference between the pre/post RSEI scores? (quantitative) • How do participants describe the impact of the research methods course? (qualitative) • What is the relationship between participants' RSEI scores and their description of the impact of the research methods course? (MM)
Integrated Questions—MM questions implies the use of both quantitative and qualitative approaches	• How do participants with significant increase of RSEI scores describe the impact of the research methods course?

need for integration of quantitative and qualitative approaches is conveyed (Plano Clark & Badiee, 2010).

You may include separate quantitative, qualitative, and MM questions; or you can write all MM research questions for your study. For example, if you are interested in exploring the impact of a research methods course on graduate students' research self-efficacy based on a quantitative survey such as the Research Self-Efficacy Inventory (RSEI) (Chesnut, Siwatu, Young, & Tong, 2015) and focus group data, you may ask different sets of research questions that indicate the various levels of MM integration. Table 12.1 includes some sample MM research questions.

The sample integrated MM question in Table 12.1 also predetermines a specific sequential MM design of the study, in which the researchers would implement the RSEI instrument during the first phase of the research and select participants who illustrated a significant increase of pre/post scores for focus group discussions in the second phase in order to address the overarching MM research question. We will elaborate on the research design typologies in the next section through a case study.

Case Study

MM research may be designed in a variety of ways. In this chapter, we will focus our discussion on four most commonly used MM designs, including (1) convergent parallel design, (2) explanatory sequential design, (3) exploratory sequential design, and (4) embedded design (Creswell & Plano Clark, 2017). To further illustrate the design considerations, we use a research example examining the acculturative stress of international students in the United States. For each design type, we introduce the design prototype, sampling considerations, data collection, analysis, display options, and validity concerns that may need to be addressed.

Mixed-Methods Research Design

Convergent Parallel Design

Design Prototype

The convergent parallel design is set up so that you can implement quantitative and qualitative methods during the same phase of the research study in a concurrent manner. You can collect and analyze the quantitative and qualitative data separately and then mix your interpretation of the results. The purpose of this type of design typically is to elaborate or corroborate results using one method with another to reach a more comprehensive understanding of the topic.

For the case study, you may use one quantitative measure, the Acculturative Stress Scale for International Students (ASSIS) (Sandhu & Asrabadi, 1994, 1998), to collect quantitative data, and you may also conduct individual interviews to collect more information regarding students' acculturation experiences. Figure 12.1 illustrates the overall design.

Sampling Considerations

You may include either one or two sample frames in a convergent parallel design. If you use one sample frame, you will collect both quantitative and qualitative data from the same sample. For example, you may want to draw a stratified sample of international students at five local universities and colleges that represent various higher education institution types for the purpose of this study. You need to take the feasibility of both quantitative and qualitative data collection and analysis into consideration when determining your sample size. While 500 students may be a reasonable number for quantitative data collection, it may not be practical to conduct 500 interviews within the time frame of the study. Similarly, while 15 students can be a manageable sample of interview participants, the small number will likely limit the type of analysis you can use when analyzing your quantitative data.

To optimize the sample size for quantitative and qualitative data collection and analysis methods, you can identify two different sample sizes. You will

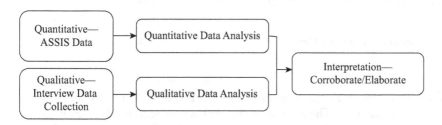

Figure 12.1 Convergent Parallel Design

then need to decide whether the two samples include the same set of participants (i.e., the qualitative sample is a subset of the quantitative sample) or include two independent samples of participants. If your goal is to corroborate the findings across quantitative and qualitative methods and your quantitative and qualitative share the same purpose, identifying a subset of the sample for qualitative data collection may be more appropriate.

Data Collection, Analysis, and Display

The convergent parallel design assumes separate data collection and analysis processes for quantitative and qualitative data, so you can use various quantitative and qualitative methods appropriate for the purpose of the study. The MM interpretation of the data occurs after the completion of independent quantitative and qualitative analysis. Depending on your research questions and initial findings, you need to specify what aspects you want to compare and represent the findings and interpretation of the comparison.

In our case example, you may find that *Homesickness* is the major source of international students' acculturative stress based on ASSIS results. Based on your interview data, you noted that students from a home country where the time difference presents challenges for them to connect with families and friends in real time expressed their experience of homesickness differently than others. The comparison of the quantitative and qualitative data in this case may allow you to elaborate on quantitative findings and draw further interpretation of your data.

Validity Concerns

The data collection and analysis procedure in the convergent parallel design may introduce some validity concerns that need to be addressed. During data collection, the potential use of unequal sample size may introduce validity threat. Strategic subset sampling for the qualitative data collection can be a strategy to address this concern. During data analysis, it is important to make logical comparisons of the results of quantitative and qualitative data analysis and focus on the research purposes and research questions. When interpreting the results, it is critical that you address any divergent findings and be mindful of the weight you give to quantitative and qualitative results.

Explanatory Sequential Design

Design Prototype

The MM sequential design assumes at least two phases of data collection and analysis in one study. The purpose of the explanatory sequential design is to use the qualitative method to explain the initial quantitative results from the first phase of the study (Creswell & Plano Clark, 2017). Quantitative results can also be used to guide the sampling, data collection, and analysis procedures for the second qualitative phase.

For the case example, ASSIS measure may be used during the first phase, and the sampling procedure and interview protocol during the second phase of the research may be determined based on the first-phase results. Figure 12.2 illustrates the explanatory sequential design.

Sampling Considerations

One of the key features of the sequential design is that the results of the first-phase analysis impact the research questions, sampling, data collection and analysis in the second phase. In the explanatory sequential design, the quantitative findings may identify specific subsets of participants for the follow-up qualitative data collection; may result in statistically significant findings that may become the focus for qualitative data collection, and may inform the data analysis procedures and framework in the qualitative phase.

In the case example, the ASSIS data analysis may result in the identification of the group of international students who expressed the highest level of acculturative stress and be identified as the subset of the participants for the second qualitative interview data collection. The use of extreme case sampling in this case helps explain the responses from this specific subgroup of participants. Major factors that lead to acculturative stress reported by the participants based on ASSIS can also inform the design of the interview protocol in the qualitative phase.

Just as in the convergent parallel design, you can use different samples for each phase of the study. The quantitative results in the first phase may not impact the sampling decision for data collection in the second phase.

Data Collection, Analysis, and Display

The quantitative and qualitative data collection and analysis are conducted in phases. Appropriate quantitative data collection and analysis methods can be used in the first phase, and relevant qualitative design can be used in the second phase. It is important to articulate the connection between the quantitative results and the second qualitative phase. The qualitative results are interpreted to explain and offer additional insights to the quantitative results.

Figure 12.2 Explanatory Sequential Design

Because the design of the second qualitative phase is dependent on the results of the first quantitative phase, you may not have a finalized qualitative research question, sampling procedure, qualitative instrument, or analysis method identified as you start the research study. The qualitative design emerges as you have a better understanding of the quantitative results. You may need to modify your overall research proposal and documentation for the institutional review board (IRB) as the study progresses.

In the case example, you may draft an interview protocol and determine a cut score that identifies a high level of acculturative stress based on the literature review. The quantitative results may alter your predetermined design. For example, according to the literature, a mean score above 109 on ASSIS indicates evidence of acculturative stress (Sandhu & Asrabadi, 1998). You may adjust the mean and standard deviation used as the cut score for your study depending on the overall group mean and standard deviation. In addition, your interview protocol may also be altered to highlight areas of significant findings based on your quantitative analysis.

Validity Concerns

The sequential design introduces unequal sample size that may be a validity concern. You need to be cautious when interpreting the qualitative results in explaining any significant quantitative findings, especially if sampling during the second qualitative phase is restricted by study context. It is important to keep in mind that even though qualitative results help explain the quantitative findings, causations may not be established through this type of design.

Potential bias may be introduced by overemphasizing the results of the quantitative data. In other words, it is possible that you may focus on the existing quantitative results when conducting the qualitative phase and find it hard to keep an open mind for potential divergent findings. On the other hand, there might be a tendency to keep the second qualitative phase too exploratory in nature and overlook the necessary connection to the quantitative results from the first phase.

Exploratory Sequential Design

Design Prototype

The exploratory sequential design is similar to the explanatory sequential design in terms of the assumption of two sequential phases in the research design. Different from explanatory design, the exploratory design starts with the qualitative exploratory phase. The purpose of the design is to generalize qualitative findings from the first phase to a larger sample with data collected and analyzed in the second quantitative phase. The initial qualitative phase is typically needed for three reasons: (1) lack of measures or instruments on the topic; (2) unknown variables for the purpose of study; and (3) lack of a comprehensive theoretical framework to guide data collection and analysis (Creswell, Plano Clark, Gutmann, & Hanson, 2003).

In the case example, you may observe that even though there is a literature base for the study of international students' acculturative stress, the ASSIS instrument is dated. In addition, the demographic backgrounds of international students studying in the United States have changed significantly in the last decade. There may be a need to explore various social, cultural, and academic variables revealed in recent literature and develop a new instrument. Figure 12.3 illustrates the exploratory sequential design.

Sampling Considerations

The exploratory sequential design typically involves two different sample sizes at the two phases. The qualitative phase typically involves a purposeful sampling procedure with a relatively small sample size, while the quantitative phase typically requires a much larger representative sample to achieve the generalizability of the study. Depending on the purpose of the study, the two samples may or may not involve the same subset of participants.

In the case example, you may purposefully select international students from different regions of the world, with different educational backgrounds and working experiences and seeking different degrees and majors in the United States as samples for your qualitative interview data collection during the first phase. During the second phase, you may draw a convenient sample from all international students in the United States who may respond to an online survey distributed through a listserv. The sample size in the first phase of the study is much smaller than the second phase.

Data Collection, Analysis, and Display

Appropriate qualitative data collection and analysis are conducted during the first phase. The qualitative analysis results inform the research questions, sampling, instrument, and data analysis framework in the second quantitative phase. During the second phase, appropriate quantitative data collection and

Figure 12.3 Exploratory Sequential Design

analysis are conducted and the results are interpreted, considering both quantitative and qualitative results. Similar to explanatory sequential design, the exploratory sequential design also involves emergent research design. Sampling procedures, instruments, and data analysis procedure may not be predetermined at the beginning of the study.

In the case example, you may uncover through your interviews that the major themes of acculturative stress include *Homesickness, Cultural Shock, Perceived Discrimination*, and *Academic Shock*. *Fear* and *Guilt* as defined in the original ASSIS may not emerge as major themes among the selected international students. *Academic Shock*, on the other hand, emerged as a major theme where participants commented on the specific challenges resulted from the different academic expectations and career readiness preparations (e.g., internships). The interview results can lead to the development of new items for the instrument, and modifications for the IRB may need to be submitted to reflect the change of study protocol.

Validity Concerns

Unequal sample size is typically introduced with the exploratory sequential design. The goal of the first qualitative phase is to explore theories and variables. However, due to the relatively small sample size typically involved in qualitative studies, themes drawn from the qualitative analysis may not be representative for the larger sample you intend to address during the second phase. Overall findings of the study may be restricted by the nature and size of the sample in the qualitative phase.

In the case example, it is also important to note that instrument development is a comprehensive and iterative process. Studies involving instrument development may be designed as multiphase MM studies involving iterative process of quantitative and qualitative data collection, analysis, and validation beyond a simple two-phase exploratory sequential design.

Embedded Design

Design Prototype

Embedded design entails the use of one method other than the overall study design to supplement results from the overarching design. The embedded element may be introduced before, during, or after the primary quantitative or qualitative design (Sandelowski, 1996). The purpose of the embedded design is to offer supplementary data to enrich findings from the primary design. Embedded design is most often applied with qualitative methods embedded in primary quantitative designs.

In the case example, you may be curious whether and how living on campus may impact international students' acculturative stress over time during their first year in the United States. To set up such a study, you can employ a quasi-experimental design to collect ASSIS data in a pre and post manner over one year from two groups of participants, one group residing on campus and the other off campus. In addition, you may want to collect supplementary qualitative data during the year of this study to explore experiences that may reflect or impact their acculturative stress through participant interviews and written journals. Figure 12.4 illustrates the embedded design.

In embedded design, the qualitative sample is either the same as the quantitative sample or a purposefully selected subset. In the case example, where the qualitative method is embedded in the overarching quantitative design, the qualitative sample may be identified based on initial analysis of the pre ASSIS data. While all participants may be instructed to maintain a journal, interviews may only be conducted with selected group of participants for the purpose of the study.

In embedded designs where qualitative design is the overall design and quantitative methods are used to collect supplementary data, using the same sample may assist you in building a more comprehensive participant profile to support data analysis and interpretation in general.

Data Collection, Analysis, and Display

Depending on the specific setup of the study, in embedded design, quantitative and qualitative data may be collected in a concurrent manner or a sequential manner. In the case example, the design specifies a sequence of data collection. The pre ASSIS survey data is collected at the beginning of the academic year. During the year, qualitative data including interviews and participant journals are collected. Finally, at the end of the academic year, the post ASSIS data is collected.

Quantitative and qualitative data may be analyzed separately in embedded design and combined for interpretation as in convergent parallel design. In the case example, quantitative pre and post ASSIS data can be analyzed independently from the qualitative data. To further integrate both quantitative and qualitative data to address the research questions, you may consider data conversion. Data conversion occurs when you turn quantitative data into qualitative data or qualitative into quantitative data. In the case example, we

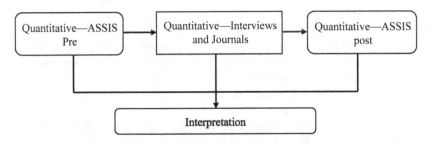

Figure 12.4 Embedded Design Sampling Considerations

may design a rubric based on the ASSIS instrument to record the occurrence of acculturative stress experiences. For example, any description in the journal or interview responses that is related to *Homesickness* receives a "1" on the rubric to tally for frequency by individual and then by group. You can then use this quantified qualitative data in quantitative analysis together with data collected using ASSIS to address MM research questions.

Validity Concerns

The selection of participants is a validity consideration in embedded design, especially if unequal sample size is used. When quantitative and qualitative data are collected and analyzed in a concurrent manner in an embedded design, it is especially challenging to identify specific rationale for sampling decisions.

In addition, you need to consider the meaningful use of supplementary data in an embedded design. In the case example, without a clear focus of the interview and instructions for the participant journal, you may not be able to successfully integrate your qualitative data in the integrated analysis to address the MM research questions.

Data conversion can be used in many MM designs beyond embedded design. However, the data conversion process may introduce validity concerns. When transforming quantitative data to qualitative data or qualitative data to quantitative data, it is critical that you specify the rationale and procedures for such transformation. You also need to be aware of the use of appropriate statistical analysis procedures (e.g., nonparametric statistics) when working with the quantitative data converted from qualitative findings.

Summary

You may consider MM research designs when using either quantitative or qualitative methods alone cannot sufficiently address your research questions. Before starting the MM research design, it is a good idea to review MM studies in your field. You can begin your search of these studies either using "mixed methods" as the key word in journals related to your field or using your disciplinary key word (e.g., counseling) to search in JMMR. As you read these MM studies, you want to pay attention to why the authors used MM and what MM definition they used. Whether you adopt the dictatorship model or reciprocal approach for your MM research questions, keep in mind that the congruence between your research questions and the MM design is critical. Throughout your research design and implementation, you also need to be aware of the validity considerations in the sampling, data collection, data analysis, display, and reporting decisions you make.

Effective design and implementation of the MM design rely on researchers' skills and having sufficient time and resources (Creswell & Plano Clark, 2017). If you are considering using MM design for your next project, make sure you take the time to assess your research strengths and readiness and establish a manageable research project plan to ensure the allocation of time and resources for your MM project. While more experienced researchers may use more complex MM designs, it is recommended that beginning researchers start with the basic MM designs such as those introduced in this chapter. You may also consider replicating the design from an MM study in your field. The growing MM literature research projects serve as great resources as you start to design MM studies in your area of study.

Resources for More Information

Online

Mertens, D. M., Bazeley, P., Bowleg, L., Fielding, N., Maxwell, J., Molina-Azorin, J. F., & Niglas, K. (2016). The future of mixed methods: A five year projection to 2020. *Mixed Methods International Research Association (MMIRA) Task Force Report*. Retrieved from www.mmira.wildapricot.org/resources/Documents/MMIRA%20 task%20force%20report%20Jan2016%20final.pdf

Onwuegbuzie, A. J. (2009, August 7). *Mixed methods research* [Video file]. Retrieved from http://videolectures.net/ssmt09_onwuegbuzie_mmr/

Books

Creswell, J. W., & Plano Clark, V. L. (2017). *Designing and conducting mixed methods research* (3rd ed.). Thousand Oaks, CA: Sage Publications.

Tashakkori, A., & Teddlie, C. (2010). *Handbook on mixed methods in the behavioral and social sciences* (2nd ed.). Thousand Oaks, CA: Sage Publications.

Peer-Reviewed Journal Articles

Archibald, M. M., Radil, A. I., Zhang, X., & Hanson, W. (2015). Current mixed methods practices in qualitative research: A content analysis of leading journals. *International Journal of Qualitative Methods, 14*(2), 5–33.

Collins, K., Onwuegbuzie, A., & Johnson, R. (2012). Securing a place at the table: A review and extension of legitimation criteria for the conduct of mixed research. *American Behavioral Scientist, 56*(6), 849–865. doi:10.1177/0002764211433799

Creswell, J. W. (2016). Reflections on the MMIRA the future of mixed methods task force report. *Journal of Mixed Methods Research, 10*(3), 215–219. doi:10.1177/ 1558689816650298

Dellinger, A. B., & Leech, N. L. (2007). Toward a unified validation framework in mixed methods research. *Journal of Mixed Methods Research, 1*(4), 309–332. doi:10.1177/ 1558689807306147

Heyvaert, M., Hannes, K., Meas, B., & Onghena, P. (2013). Critical appraisal of mixed methods studies. *Journal of Mixed Methods Research, 7*(4), 302–327. doi:10.1177/ 1558689813479449

Leech, N. L., & Onwuegbuzie, A. J. (2009). A typology of mixed methods research designs. *Quality & Quantity International Journal of Methodology, 43*(2), 265–275. doi:10.1007/s11135-007-9105-3

Mayoh, J., & Onwuegbuzie, A. J. (2013). Toward a conceptualization of mixed methods phenomenological research. *Journal of Mixed Methods Research, XX*(X), 1–17. doi:10.1177/1558689813505358

Mertens, D. M. (2012). Which comes first? The paradigm or the approach? *Journal of Mixed Methods Research, 6*(4), 255–257. doi:10.1177/1558689812461574

Mertens, D. M., Bazeley, P., Bowleg, L., Fielding, N., Maxwell, J., Molina-Azorin, J. F., & Niglas, K. (2016). Expanding thinking through a kaleidoscopic look into the future: Implications of the mixed methods international research association's task force report on the future of mixed methods. *Journal of Mixed Methods Research, 10*(3), 221–227. doi:10.1177/1558689816649719

Onwuegbuzie, A. J., Johnston, R. B., & Collins, K. M. (2011). Assessing legitimation in mixed research: A new framework. *Quality and Quantity, 45*, 1253–1271. doi:10.1007/s11135-009-9289-9

Plano Clark, V. L., Anderson, N., Wertz, J. A., Zhou, Y., Schumacher, K., & Miaskowski, C. (2014). Conceptualizing longitudinal mixed methods design: Methodological review of health science research. *Journal of Mixed Methods Research*, 1–23. doi:10.1177/1558689814543563

Teddlie, C., & Tashakkori, A. (2006). A general typology of research designs featuring mixed methods. *Research in the Schools, 13*(1), 12–28.

Teddlie, C., & Yu, F. (2007). Mixed methods sampling: A typology with examples. *Journal of Mixed Methods, 1*(1), 77–100. doi:10.1177/2345678906292430

Wisdom, J. P., Cavaleri, M. A., Onwuegbuzie, A. J., & Green, C. A. (2012). Methodological reporting in qualitative, quantitative, and mixed methods health services research articles. *Health Research and Educational Trust, 47*(2), 721–745. doi:10.1111/j.1475–6773.2011.01344.x

Review Questions

1. In your area of study, how do researchers define MM research? What are the key characteristics of MM research recognized in your field?
2. For your future work, what are some advantages of using MM? What are some challenges?
3. If you were to develop a study in your field using MM, would you adopt the dictatorship model or reciprocal approach to writing your research questions? Why?
4. What would be the specific validity considerations you need to be aware of when applying the four commonly used MM designs to your research?

References

Arnault, D. S., & Fetters, M. D. (2011). ROI funding for mixed methods research: Lesson learned from the "mixed method analysis of Japanese depression" project. *Journal of Mixed Methods Research, 5*(4), 309–329. doi:10.1177/1558689811416481

Chesnut, S. R., Siwatu, K. O., Young, H. A., & Tong, Y. (2015). Examining the relationship between the research training environment, course experiences, and graduate students' research self-efficacy beliefs. *International Journal of Doctoral Studies, 10*, 399–418. Retrieved from http://ijds.org/Volume10/IJDSv10p399-418Chesnut0914.pdf

Creswell, J. W., & Plano Clark, V. L. (2017). *Designing and conducting mixed methods research* (3rd ed.). Thousand Oaks, CA: Sage Publications.

Creswell, J. W., Plano Clark, V. L., Gutmann, M., & Hanson, W. (2003). Advanced mixed methods research designs. In A. Tashakkori & C. Teddlie (Eds.), *Handbook of mixed methods in social and behavioral research* (pp. 209–240). Thousand Oaks, CA: Sage Publications.

Gage, N. L. (1989). The paradigm wars and their aftermath: A "historical" sketch of research on teaching since 1989. *Educational Researcher, 18*(7), 4–10.

Guba, E. G. (1990). *The paradigm dialog.* Newbury Park, CA: Sage Publications.

Hammersley, M. (1992). The paradigm wars: Reports from the front. *British Journal of Sociology of Education, 13*(1), 131–143.

Howe, K. R. (1988). Against the quantitative-qualitative incompatibility thesis or dogmas die hard. *Educational Researcher, 17*(8), 10–16.

Johnson, R. B., Onwuegbuzie, A. J., & Turner, L. A. (2007). Toward a definition mixed methods research. *Journal of Mixed Methods Research, 1*(2), 112–133.

Lincoln, Y. S., & Guba, E. G. (1985). *Naturalistic Inquiry.* Beverly Hills, CA: Sage Publications.

Mertens, D. M., Bazeley, P., Bowleg, L., Fielding, N., Maxwell, J., Molina-Azorin, J. F., & Niglas, K. (2016). *The future of mixed methods: A five year projection to 2020.* Mixed Methods International Research Association (MMIRA) Task Force Report. Retrieved from www.mmira.wildapricot.org/resources/Documents/MMIRA%20task%20force%20report%20Jan2016%20final.pdf

Plano Clark, V. L., & Badiee, M. (2010). Research questions in mixed methods research. In A. Tashakkori & C. Teddlie (Eds.), *Handbook of mixed methods in social & behavioral science* (2nd ed., pp. 275–304). Thousand Oaks, CA: Sage Publications.

Sandelowski, M. (1996). Using qualitative methods in intervention studies. *Research in Nursing & Health, 19*(4), 359–364.

Sandhu, S., & Asrabadi, R. (1994). Development of an acculturative stress scale for international students: Preliminary findings. *Psychological Report, 75*, 135–448.

Sandhu, S., & Asrabadi, R. (1998). An acculturative stress scale for international students: A practical approach to stress management. In C. P. Zalaquett & R. J. Wood (Eds.), *Evaluating stress: A book of resources* (pp. 1–33). Lanham, MD: Scarecrow Press.

Tashakkori, A., & Creswell, J. W. (2007). The new era of mixed methods [Editorial]. *Journal of Mixed Methods Research, 1*(1), 3–7.

Tashakkori, A., & Teddlie, C. (2010). *Handbook on mixed methods in the behavioral and social sciences* (2nd ed.). Thousand Oaks, CA: Sage Publications.

Teddlie, C., & Tashakkori, A. (2003). Major issues and controversies in the use of mixed methods in the social and behavioral sciences. In A. Tashakkori & C. Teddlie (Eds.), *Handbook of mixed methods in social & behavioral research.* Thousand Oaks: Sage Publications.

13 Bringing It All Together
Effective Program Evaluation

Michael Walsh & Amy Allison

Introduction of Methodology

Program evaluation. The very words can strike fear and dread into the hearts of program staff and administrators alike. Visions of audits and reviewers, forms to fill out, onerous processes to follow . . . dogs and cats living together . . . Ahhh!!! Stop the madness!!!

Relax! We have some good news for you: program evaluation doesn't have to be scary or a big hassle. Program evaluation can actually become one of a clinician's best tools. The secret is to design a program evaluation process that is both efficient and effective.

While there are a number of different definitions of program evaluation floating around in the professional literature, the streamlined definition is often the most useful. For our purposes, program evaluation can be defined as *a systematic collection of information about a program, or aspects of a program, in order to make decisions about that program* (Walsh & Balkin, 2017). At its heart, program evaluation can be used to improve services and service delivery (Loesch, 2001). Throughout this chapter, we'll look at some basics in program evaluation, such as sources of program evaluation information and the basic types of program evaluation. We'll also look at some best practices and basic steps in program evaluation, then we'll practice applying some of those best practices and basic steps to actual program examples. Finally, we'll take a look at two program evaluation models that lend themselves well to practitioners.

Down on the Farm: a Quick Look at Information Sources in Program Evaluation

Program evaluation is an essential tool for practitioners. Three types of feedback contribute to good program evaluation: external evaluation, internal evaluation, and stakeholder feedback. External evaluation means gathering feedback from an outside source. Internal evaluation comes from within (employees, program staff, etc.) and is often not obvious to outsiders. Stakeholder feedback is a more inclusive term. This type of feedback comes from anyone who may be benefiting from the program—clients, donors, staff, and so on. It is important to note that stakeholders may also be community members who benefit from the overall impact of your program. Good program evaluation is constant and contributes to everyday operations while helping to produce change based on the interests and input of multiple parties. In the following three sections, we'll use a story to examine the different sources of information in program evaluation: external evaluation, internal evaluation, and stakeholder feedback.

The Power of the External Evaluation

Let's say, for example, it is 1772 and you were working on your farm. Your task is to get water from the stream that runs through the valley to the carrot fields on the plateau. You, being a good farmer and the innovative type, might design a state-of-the-art bucket-carrying system that carries four buckets on a pole. You hump it down to the water, fill up your buckets, and start the long climb uphill. The hill is steep, and you are focused on the work of moving up the hill smoothly so that you keep spills to a minimum. Your eyes are constantly scanning the ground in front of you for rocks and slippery points so you can stay on track. All in all, the system works fairly well, and you find that you reach the top with most of the water. You're rocking right along!

One day, you run into your neighbor at the post office. (Post office? In 1772? I know, I know, work with me here, OK?) Your neighbor fills you in on what she sees when she watches you work. Your neighbor, watching you from across the valley as you work each day, notices that when you fill up the buckets on one side, you have to lean the pole down to fill the other side, causing some spillage. The buckets also jostle a bit as the pole bounces when you walk, causing slightly more spillage. You suspected this but have been so busy getting this vital job done that you haven't been able to take the time to think about fixing it. Your neighbor notes that, if you attached ropes to your buckets, then the buckets to the pole, it might solve this problem. You do, and it works! You have improved your process as a result of the external feedback! This is the power of an **external evaluation**.

The Power of the Internal Evaluation

OK. You've gotten pretty good at this water-transporting business, and your farm has grown. You've hired some folks to carry some of the water and passed along your newly developed technology. Things are going fairly well.

One day, you notice that some workers are having more success than others. You gather your employees to discuss the differences. "I'm pretty short," one worker says, "and the ropes on the buckets are a bit too long. It slows me down." Another worker says, "I could carry more using a different setup. My legs are stronger than my shoulders."

You now have two new ideas that can improve your business, neither of which would have been obvious to an outsider. This is the power of an **internal evaluation**.

The Power of Stakeholder Feedback

OK! Now you've got a thriving business, and you have incorporated some excellent feedback into the process of delivering your service. Life is good, right?

One day, after buying a batch of carrots from your field, a local merchant approaches you. "Your carrots are OK," he mentions, "but I've got to tell you, Lisa's carrots from the next valley over are just incredible. My local chefs have asked about switching over to her carrots in my market."

You are gobsmacked! You've just figured out a great way to do business, you've improved your overall program, crops are growing better than ever, and now the consumers want to buy different carrots!

"Wait," you say, "what do the chefs want in a carrot?"

The market owner thinks for a minute. "Ah, I think that I heard them say they want a softer flesh when cooked, but I'm not sure. I'm not a chef."

You think back to how your business has developed from other feedback.

"I've got an idea," you say. "Let's get all of the local chefs together and explore what they want and need in terms of produce. Maybe Lisa can produce the carrots and I can produce the leaf lettuce. That will play to both farms' strengths."

The chefs agree, the meeting takes place, and each farm makes the requested changes.

Bam! You've improved both the process of your business and its long-term prospects using feedback from stakeholders. That is the power of **stakeholder feedback**.

Terms Used in Program Evaluation: When Do We Use What?

Good program evaluation is a constant process of internal and external evaluation, along with client and stakeholder feedback. This process informs the everyday operation of the program, "feeds back" into the program design (why the farm exists), and changes are made based on what is in the best interests of all of the stakeholders.

In the helping professions, this can happen with a program that serves clients with depression or a program that serves people with severe mental illnesses, or it can happen in a counselor education program that trains counselors. Good program evaluation is at home in any business.

There are as many potential program evaluation designs as there are types of programs. **The design and type of program evaluation depends on the questions we want to answer.** In our previous section, we explored different sources of program evaluation data. In the following section, we'll explore different types of program evaluation based on what we need to know about the outcomes of our program and/or the process of our program. Each type of program evaluation has its own format and its own goals.

Let's say we want to know about the impact of our program (outcomes)—specifically, whether our program is effective at helping clients with depression. This type of program evaluation is looking at **outcomes or the product** that we deliver. **Outcome-based** program evaluation is called **summative**

evaluation. We're looking at the sum total, or the bottom line. Does the program help people feel less depressed? (outcome/product). Other examples of summative evaluations may include program cost, program impact in the community, and program impact on clients.

Let's look at a graphic example of the summative evaluation design in Figure 13.1. We're wondering about whether our counseling program is effective in treating clients with depression. We'd look to our external feedback sources first: hospitalization rates or opinions of any external reviewers (e.g., such as accreditation bodies). We'd then look at internal feedback sources (e.g., employees, staff members, staff psychiatrists). Finally, we'd look at stakeholder feedback sources (e.g., clients, clients' family members, community members). We'd use these three sources of data to form impressions of our overall program effectiveness, as demonstrated in Figure 13.2.

While an outcome of the program is a common goal of program evaluation, other program evaluation designs help to answer different questions. Let's say that we want to know about our program's process. Maybe we have questions about how effectively staff personnel are communicating with each other within the program. Since this question has to do with the **process** of how our program runs, it is a **process-based** or **formative evaluation**. In this evaluation, we're looking at how well staff communicate within the program as it is running. Does our staff communicate effectively (process)?

Let's look at Figure 13.3, a graphic example of this formative evaluation design. We'd utilize the same data sources: external feedback (e.g., reviewer opinions, reviewer's comments after speaking with program staff), internal feedback (e.g., employee comments, staff opinions on communication and efficiency), and stakeholder feedback (e.g., client's comments, client's family members feedback on the way that staff work together). This data, represented in Figure 13.4, would inform our conclusions on how well our program is functioning.

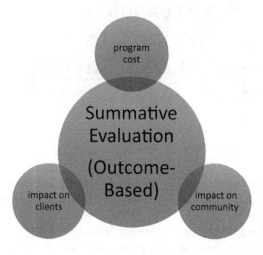

Figure 13.1 Summative (Outcome-Based) Evaluation

Program Effectiveness

Figure 13.2 Feedback Types Informing the Summative Program Evaluation

Figure 13.3 Formative (Process-Based) Evaluation

Other examples of formative evaluations include needs assessments, determining how clients define success, and examining how well a program operates in various phases.

While each of these designs can be used independently, in some settings, it may be important to understand both process and outcomes of a program. We'll look at mixed-method designs as we move along.

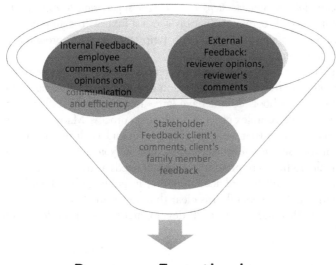

Program Functioning

Figure 13.4 Feedback Types Informing the Formative Program Evaluation

Do We Really Need Program Evaluation? Who Can Afford That?

The term "program evaluation" gets thrown around a good bit in the larger nonprofit world. Donors often want to know whether the money that they donate is doing the good deeds it is supposed to be doing. Funders want to know that the grants they make are well placed or that the dollars they send to a program are being well spent. As a result, much of the information related to program evaluation has been developed for the larger world of big money and big systems (Kellaghan & Madaus, 2000) or has such discipline-specific language that it is difficult to apply it outside of its intended field (Astromovitch & Coker, 2007).

As practitioners, we often need to scale these ideas down to fit our projects and programs. This involves financial as well as practical planning. As an example, the United States Office of Planning, Research and Evaluation (2010) suggests that the "rule of thumb" for planning program evaluation costs is 15% to 20% of the overall program budget. These are huge numbers, especially when considering a small operation.

Obviously, as a practitioner, you need to be able to scale these numbers to make them fit for the program in which you operate. When designing a program or budgeting for program needs, always remember to build in funding for program evaluation.

Further, as practitioners, we have an ethical obligation to make sure that the programs we deliver are effective. In the American Counseling Association's Code of Ethics (2014), Standard C.2.D states, "*Counselors continually monitor their effectiveness as professionals and take steps to improve when necessary. Counselors take reasonable steps to seek peer supervision to evaluate their efficacy as counselors."* Program evaluation is not a luxury, it is an obligation. Fortunately, good program evaluation can help to enhance a program. Just look what it did for our farm!

On another happy note, these ideas are very "scalable" to any size project. The secret is often in the program evaluation design. Specifically, many small programs, offices, or schools do not have large administrative staffs that can operate and monitor a complex program evaluation process. Many can be one- or two-person operations that work on a shoestring budget. If that is the case, it is important to *base your program evaluation in work you already do*. This will allow you the flexibility to respond to additional needs as they develop.

Finally, given the shift toward accountability in public policy, health care, and the helping fields in general, it is clear that a working knowledge of program evaluation (PE) and effective PE development is essential for helping professionals.

Sample Case Studies and Program Evaluation Questions

Program #1: Four-person private practice specializing in treating clients with anxiety disorders.

Problem: A funder wants program evaluation (outcomes) data, and the practice has no administrative staff available to compile data. The four partners in the practice also want to evaluate how successful they have been in treating clients for the past year. They also wonder if the practice is operating as efficiently as it could be (process).

Analysis: This program evaluation is looking for outcome (summative) data (are clients feeling less anxiety?) as well as process (formative) data, so this is likely to be a mixed-methods program evaluation.

Program #2: Mid-size counseling program in a university counseling center.

Problem: The trustees want a justification for spending the money on the counseling center. They simply want an answer to the question: Is this program helping our students?

Analysis: This program evaluation is looking solely for impact/outcome (summative) data.

Program # 3: Four-person private practice with a general caseload consisting of both adolescents and adults. These clients are mostly low income and utilize Medicaid to pay for services. The practice is enrolled as a Medicaid provider.

Problem: The state is now requiring the practice to be accredited. The practice must choose an accrediting body and begin the self-study process.

Analysis: This program evaluation will be driven, to a degree, by the standards called for by the accrediting body. The self-study and on-site reviews will examine both formative (process) data and summative (outcome/impact) data. Interestingly, most accrediting bodies deal more with process data than with outcomes. This makes sense when you think of the function of most accrediting bodies in the clinical world. They are primarily quality-improvement organizations designed to help organizations improve how they do things (process), which can lead to better outcomes. Their main focus is on helping organizations get better at doing what they do, which is mostly process.

Best Practices in Program Evaluation

As shown in Figure 13.5, The Centers for Disease Control (CDC, 2011) proposed six universal steps for effective program evaluation. In this section, we'll identify each of those six steps and apply each to our Program #3 as the case study.

Step One: Identify and Involve the Stakeholders

This means thinking about who benefits from the service. It also means thinking about program staff. Anyone who "has a horse in the race" is a stakeholder. That means clients, board members (if applicable), staff, and any interested vendors or third parties. It is very important to remember that while staff are also considered sources of internal evaluation data, staff are also stakeholders and, as such, can be an invaluable source of stakeholder data. Now, let's apply Step One to Case Study #3:

Case Study # 3

In this case, clients are clearly stakeholders. As a part of the informed consent process, it is helpful to remind clients that, just like they are doing in their own lives, the practice always tries to improve and to grow. Asking permission up front to involve the client in the quality-improvement process is a best practice. Not only does this process model the growth and development process for the client, it also allows the client to be at the heart of the program evaluation process. From an ethical standpoint, this makes sense, as we have a fiduciary duty to do what is in the best interests of those clients. Best of all, clients won't be surprised when you ask for feedback!

Staff are also stakeholders here. It is imperative that staff be involved in the program evaluation and quality-improvement process. This is a vital source of internal evaluation data!

The partners in the practice are also stakeholders in the process. It is their practice, after all! These folks are also great internal evaluation sources!

Third-party funders are stakeholders in this process. They have an interest, for example, in how well you are documenting your billing time and the services for which they are paying.

Interested third parties may be other organizations or agencies with whom you interact. Maybe you refer folks to the local vocational rehabilitation agency or the local mental health center. All of these "partner" agencies are stakeholders in how well your program functions. This feedback can be invaluable. Sometimes you get good ideas from these other organizations. Other times, they may provide a particularly valuable perspective. For example, they

1. Identify and Involve the Stakeholders

• **Food for Thought Questions:**
  • Who benefits from services?
  • Program Staff

2. Define the Problem

• **Food for Thought Questions:**
  • What the program does
  • What the program is designed to do

3. Focus on the Design of Your Evaluation

• **Food for Thought Questions:**
  • What we ought to measure
  • How we ought to measure it

4. Gather the Evidence

• **Food for Thought Questions:**
  • Ask clients
  • Interview staff
  • Gather numbers of people served

5. Analyze the Data and Draw Conclusions

• **Food for Thought Questions:**
  • Run the numbers
  • Are you meeting standards and accomplishing what you set to accomplish?

6. Present the Findings and Use Them

• **Food for Thought Questions:**
  • Provides an opportunity to plan interventions to improve areas of concern, strengthen areas, and call attention to successes

Figure 13.5 Best Practices in Program Evaluation According to the CDC may say, "We've noticed that when you refer folks, they are sometimes confused as to exactly what it is we do." This provides you the opportunity to improve your process of educating those folks and thereby likely improving their ability to be successful with this additional service.

Finally, and not to be forgotten, there is the accrediting body itself. Examples may be: The Commission on Accreditation of Rehabilitation Facilities (CARF), the Joint Commission on Accreditation of Healthcare Organizations (JCAHO), or another accrediting body. These accrediting bodies are also known by another name: **quality-improvement organizations (QIOs)**. They are designed to help organizations to improve and enhance their operations.

Now that we have identified the stakeholders, it is time to involve them. This may mean reaching out to clients and letting them know that, just like we discussed in our informed consent process, we need their input in our program evaluation process. A best practice here is never to burden a client with cumbersome tasks. Develop an estimate of how much time the feedback process will take and stick to it.

Step Two: Define the Program

This means thinking about exactly what the program does and what the program is designed to do. This allows you the opportunity to identify "program drift" or "mission creep." These are two things that commonly happen over time. A program that was designed to treat depression finds that it is dealing a good bit with anxiety, for example. The services then "drift" to cover the presented need. Soon, a program that was designed to treat just depression has "crept" into treating anxiety. No value judgment here. Again, this is very common. This step provides the program the opportunity to return to the mission statement of the organization and ask the questions: Are we still on target? Should the mission change? In short, you are asking the question: What is our program supposed to do?

Case Study # 3: This Is a Counseling Private Practice With a Broad Mission to Meet the Complex Needs of Its Clients

Now that we have defined the program, we have a better sense of exactly what to measure. We now know that we are striving to meet the complex needs of our clients. That gives us some latitude, but it also offers us a very specific target. In our case, we also have a driving need to begin the accreditation process. That helps us in many ways. In an accreditation process, much of the evaluation design is dictated by the standards of the accrediting body, the self-study, and the on-site review processes. If we didn't have those standards and procedures as a road map, we'd just have to design our own PE plan. Fortunately, we now have a very clear definition of the process we need to follow as well as a very clear definition of our program. Without this critical step of clearly defining your program, you can't know what to measure!

Step Three: Focus the Design of Your Evaluation

This means thinking about what we ought to measure and how we ought to measure it. Do we want to know about outcomes? Do we want to know about process? Both?

It is now far more feasible to develop an evaluation plan on the basis of a clearly defined program. In this case, we have defined that our mission is to meet the complex needs of our clients. Now we can focus our design on exactly the area(s) in which we are most interested. Are we meeting those complex needs (summative)? and/or How are we doing that (formative)?

Case Study #3: Let's assume that we want to begin the self-study process for the Commission of the Accreditation of Rehabilitation Facilities (CARF). This will involve both formative and summative data gathering. The specific areas that we'll evaluate will be proscribed for us by CARF. We'll examine the 2017 Standards Manual for our type of accreditation to each standard. For example, in our setting, we would be using the behavioral health program standards. The self-study process would form the basis of the internal evaluation process. Once that self-study is complete and sent to CARF, an on-site evaluation (external evaluation) will be scheduled. It is at this meeting that the evidence gathered in the next phase will be presented. Evaluators will also speak with clients and stakeholders (stakeholder feedback) when they arrive.

This gives us the chance to triangulate our data a bit. Remember, we already spoke with staff as part of our internal evaluation process. When our external reviewers (on-site folks) also speak with staff, it provides us an opportunity to compare the answers that our staff and clients gave to us with those answers given to the reviewers. In this way, we have the opportunity to ensure that we are getting a complete and honest picture of our functioning that is free of undue influence. This concept of data triangulation is a critical one in assessment circles and is considered a best practice in evaluation. In this way, accreditation bodies help organizations to hit the key points (internal, external, and stakeholder-based) of the program evaluation process, and they also help us to ensure that our gathered data is accurate and well balanced.

In our example, for a CARF self-study, we are asked to examine each of the specific areas called for in the behavioral health standards. So, during the self-study, we'd utilize a variety of program evaluation tools, such as internal and external evaluation, stakeholder feedback, and evidence gathering. These program evaluation tools help us look at the following: program structure and staffing, screening and access to services, individual treatment plans and progress notes, transition and recovery services, medication use policies and procedures, nonviolent practices (emergency procedures), and quality records review. We would look for evidence of how we are doing in each area and note any areas in which we come up short of the standards. We would then share the results of this self-study with the on-site reviewers (another example of a source of external evaluation data) and get their feedback on what they see as our strengths and areas for improvement.

That gives us an opportunity to leverage the experience and expertise of the on-site reviewers in the next step of the accreditation process. The important thing to remember here is that accrediting bodies are truly **QIOs**. The very best programs embrace this process and utilize it to enhance their programs.

Step Four: Gather the Evidence

This means actually gathering data. You may be asking questions of clients, gathering numbers of people served, or interviewing staff—whatever inquiries are appropriate for the information you need to gather.

Case Study #3: In this example, we would need the actual evidence that we have complied to a certain standard. While the self-study entails many different components as noted in Step 3, for the sake of an example, let's just look at standards related to transition and recovery services. In this evidence-gathering step, we'd be gathering examples of transition plans that our practice uses, whether that be the section of the treatment plan that addresses transition and discharge or whether we use a separate transition planning form. We would be gathering the actual examples that show the program meets that standard on an individual basis as well as on a systematic basis.

In other words, we will want to show evidence that we met the standard once and also show evidence that we have a system in place to meet that standard consistently. So we may go to a specific client chart, pull out the section that deals with transition planning for that client, and use that example to show actual evidence that our program actively addressed that transition planning standard in that case. Further evidence may also be gathered, such as a copy of our blank treatment plan that contains a section entitled "transition plan." The first is evidence that we addressed the standard in a specific case. The second is evidence that the program addresses the standard systematically with each and every client.

It is never enough, in program evaluation, to say "Yep, we do that. I'm sure we do that somehow . . ." We always have to show actual evidence that it is being done in the form of a working example. In this way, we retain the integrity of the program evaluation process and can be certain that we are getting an accurate look at what we do and don't do and thus where we may need to change or alter our program to meet our stated mission/definition and become more effective and efficient. During our CARF on-site review, we would be presenting this evidence to the reviewers and brainstorming ways to strengthen any areas in which we came up a bit short.

Step Five: Analyze the Data and Draw Conclusions

In this step, you run the numbers. Are you meeting the standards? Are you accomplishing what your program set out to accomplish?

Case Study #3: In our example, this is the step in which we look at five transition plan records that we collected in Step 4 and conclude: Yes! In five of five, we met the standard that insists we address transition and discharge in the treatment plan. That is 100% compliance with that particular standard. We'd do the same for other standards. Let's say that the standard calls for us to address the strengths, needs, abilities, and preferences (SNAP) for each client.

Let's also say that, as we examine the evidence, we find that two of our clinicians always talk about the SNAP profile of each client, but the other two do it only occasionally. That's less than 60% compliance with that standard. We may then make a decision to add a SNAP section to our treatment planning document, thereby ensuring that we examine, in each treatment planning session, the strengths, needs, abilities, and preferences of each and every one of our clients.

Step Six: Present Your Findings and Use Them

Program evaluation is a waste of time and resources if you don't use the results. Presenting the results of program evaluations to the board, partners, staff, and other stakeholders is a critical step to beginning to use those results. This provides an opportunity to plan interventions designed to improve areas of concern, strengthen areas that need strengthening, and call attention to your successes. Program evaluation can and should be an opportunity to celebrate the good work that you do. Don't let that opportunity pass you by!

Our best practice steps applied to our Case Study # 3 are shown in Figure 13.6.

Case Study # 3 Wrap Up

In our example, we'd present the findings of our self-study, as well as the results of our on-site review, and look for ways to improve where needed. We'd also have the opportunity (and this is vital!) to go back to our mission statement and program design and look for opportunities to improve our overall design, mission, or functioning. In this way, effective program evaluation becomes a self-sustaining loop that helps the program to continually grow and improve.

Textbox 13.1: Practice Exercise

Apply the CDC Best Practice Steps to Case Studies #1 and #2

Look at the best practices steps in Figure 13.5. See if you can apply those steps to thinking about how you might go about designing a program evaluation plan for these two programs. Remember, these are case studies, so you may have to add some details (like a program focus and mission statement) to inform your process. Do the best you can. The more you can get into the habit of thinking like a program evaluator, the more naturally the PE process will flow for you. Pay particular attention to the Food for Thought sentences next to each step. These are the questions that will help you to plan and design the most effective program evaluation for any given program.

Figure 13.6 Best-Practice CDC Model Applied to Case Study #3

Models of Program Evaluation

Models of program evaluation combine the best practices mentioned earlier into a series of steps that help us to ensure we have considered all that we can in developing and designing our program evaluation plan. These models help us to visualize and conceptualize our overall program evaluation approach, and they help us to consider the many different program evaluation data sources. In this way, we have the chance to combine all of what we have learned about program evaluation into a cohesive approach that seeks to maximize our effectiveness in getting our questions answered. This section will look at two models of program evaluation that may lend themselves to adaptation in the helping professions field.

Logic Model

Joseph Wholey (1979) developed a model that breaks the program evaluation process down into workable "chunks" and then presents them in a graphic model designed to help the user understand the flow of the organization while also posing basic questions about the program's effectiveness. Logic Models have been utilized in the counseling field, and, most recently, a logic model was developed in order to evaluate the ASCA national model in school counseling (Martin & Carey, 2014). Such work shows the applicability and adaptability of the logic model concept.

Wholey's logic model starts with a "situation statement" that is designed to sum up and present the need for the program, along with the circumstances surrounding it.

Taylor-Powell and Henert (2008) give us the basics of logic modeling:

- *baseline*—information about the situation or condition prior to intervention;
- *impact indicator*—evidence that an impact is being achieved;
- *inputs*—resources that go into programming such as staff time, materials, money, equipment, and so forth;
- *outputs*—the activities, products, and participation resulting from program activities;
- *outcomes*—results or changes from the program; the outcomes can range from immediate (short term) to intermediate (medium term) to final (long term).

Figure 13.7 shows an example of a basic logic model framework, which includes the components noted by Taylor-Powell and Henert (2008).

Logic Model in Action

Let's use Case Study # 1 to illustrate the logic model concept in action:

Case Study #1 Situation: Four-person private practice specializing in treating clients with anxiety disorders.

Situation: A funder wants program evaluation (outcomes) data and the practice has no administrative staff available to compile data. The

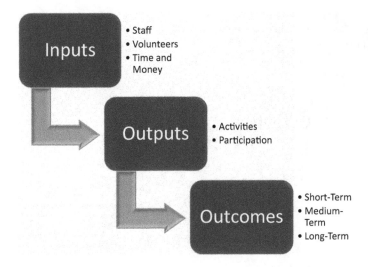

Figure 13.7 Generic Basic Steps of Logic Model

four partners in the practice also want to evaluate how successful they have been in treating clients for the past year. They also wonder if the practice is operating as efficiently as it could be.

Assumptions: Effective individual and group interventions can lead to better coping strategies. Better coping can lessen the symptoms of anxiety. Fewer anxiety symptoms may lead to better quality of life.

Inputs: Four counselors at $30/hour, rent at $1,000 per month, utilities at $10 per day, insurance and indirect costs at $85 per day.

Outputs: Client participation in one session per week, enrollment in a client support group for an additional hour per week, and client "homework" approximately a half hour each week. Client evaluation using Quality of Life Scale and Beck Anxiety Inventory (BAI).

Outcomes: Clients show a 22% reduction in week 2 of the BAI score (short term), clients report a 36% increase in the Quality of Life Scale by week 4 (medium term), followed by an overall 32% reduction in BAI score after week 6 (long term). This reduction stays stable for the measured timeframes.

First, we'll apply these basic steps and get a quick "down-and-dirty" look at inputs, outputs, and outcomes (see Figure 13.8). This is sometimes a helpful first step, as it allows us a quick peek at the "bottom line" features important to summative program evaluation designs.

The Logic Model's Fundamental Program Evaluation Question

The fundamental program evaluation question for Case Study #1: Is the program, given its situation and assumptions, worth the input cost (staff time and resources devoted to operations) and output costs (client effort and

Figure 13.8 Logic Model Inputs, Output, and Outcomes Steps Applied to Case Study #1

participation) for the short-, medium-, and long-term returns on the investment? Now that we've gotten a quick look at the bottom line, we'll next plug our Case Study #1 into a full logic model and see how the logic model process may be helpful in examining our program in a good deal more depth. But first. . .

Textbox 13.2: Pop Quiz Question

Is the example a summative evaluation or a formative evaluation?[1]

Keep in mind: Logic models can also be helpful in formative designs in that they help us to examine multiple facets of the program and present those facets in a graphic that is easy to follow. We are then better able to understand the ways in which different things connect and flow within our program, which helps us to better understand formative (process) questions. Let's take a look at Case Study # 1 using a full logic model.

Case Study # 1 Logic Model Discussion

As you can see in Figure 13.9, this logic model allows us to see, at a glance, the effectiveness of our program (summative data) in the form of the 22% decrease in the BAI score in week 2, the 36% increase in the Quality of Life scores by week 4, and the 32% overall reduction in BAI scores after week 6. This model also gives us a graphic look at how our program "fits together." We

Figure 13.9 Full Logic Model Applied to Case Study #1

*Note: Above graphic adapted from University of Wisconsin-Extension, Cooperative Extension, Program Development & Evaluation's Logic Model (Powell, Steele, & Douglah, 2013).

Credit line: adapted from University of Wisconsin-Extension, Cooperative Extension, Program Development & Evaluation's Logic Model

can also see the assumptions under which we choose to operate, and we can check those assumptions against the actual data (i.e., Do fewer anxiety symptoms lead to improved quality of life?). In our case, we can see that it seems that our assumptions are holding up against the actual data. If they were not, we would then have the opportunity to change our program, and we may be able to see exactly where the change would have the most impact.

As you may have noted, there is an external factors section that also influences our results. Let's say, for example, that we encountered a 40% reduction in service availability due to a funding source deciding to approve less of our services. We would then have the opportunity to see if that external factor made an impact. We could also use this same model to look for ways to offset that impact. We could, for example, note that we are only utilizing one half hour of "homework" per week. Given the service reduction, might we want to enhance our use of homework? Are there other opportunities to improve our outcomes or processes? What potential opportunities do you see?

Textbox 13.3: Practice Exercise 2

Apply the logic model to a program with which you are familiar

Ask yourself: Does this logic model help me to better understand this program and the way it works (formative assessment)? What does the logic model indicate about the way the program works? Are there areas for improvement that are apparent after examining the logical structure? Is the program worth the input and output costs (summative assessment)?

Accountability Bridge Model

As noted in Walsh and Balkin (2017), the accountability bridge model (Astramovich & Coker, 2007) combines the clinical evaluation steps typical in the counseling field with modern and very important business and accountability concepts popular in the corporate world (Ernst & Hiebert, 2002). The resulting accountability bridge takes into account the unique context and needs of a program while supporting the need for interactive and ongoing efficiency evaluation (Astramovich & Coker, 2007). It is this attention to the unique context of the program as well as to the process of gathering data that makes the accountability bridge unique. Though the accountability bridge is a model designed from counseling program evaluation, it can be applied to other fields and specialties within the helping professions.

As you can see in Figure 13.10, the central hubs of the accountability bridge are the counseling program evaluation cycle and the counseling context evaluation cycle. This represents, according to Astramovich and Coker (2007), *"an ongoing refinement of services based on outcomes, stakeholder feedback, and needs of the population served."* In other words, the feedback of all stakeholders, including clients, is constantly being fed back into the program design and evaluation process, allowing for the ongoing needs of the program to be accounted for, in addition to accounting for the ongoing environment and context of the program.

Consumer-driven service design is acknowledged as a best practice (Fenton, 2003; Fischer, 2006; Hamann et al., 2005). Using the accountability bridge, this consumer feedback is leveraged to its full potential while continuously being tested and refined, while the unique needs and context of the

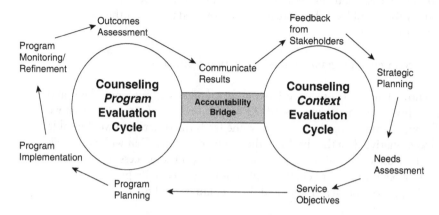

Figure 13.10 Accountability Bridge Model
Source: Astramovich & Coker, 2007, used with permission.

program are also considered. This allows for more culturally competent and community-driven program evaluation.

Accountability Bridge Applied

Let's apply Case Study # 2 to the accountability bridge and see if it can help.

Case Study #2: Mid-size counseling program in a university counseling center.

Problem: The trustees want a justification for spending the money on the counseling center. They simply want an answer to the question: Is this program helping our students?

Analysis: This program evaluation is looking solely for impact/outcome (summative) data.

The hubs around which we'll build our accountability bridge are:

1. The counseling center's program evaluation cycle.

The program's program evaluation cycle likely occurs periodically as accreditation visits happen, so we can start there. We can also assume that, because the trustees have asked questions, more program evaluation than normal is likely. That helps us to understand the type of data we'll be getting. We know, for example, since it is an accreditation-related process, we're likely to get lots of formative (process) data during the PE process. That's good, but it doesn't necessarily help us to answer the trustees' question, which seems to be much more summative (outcome-oriented) in nature. That's OK, though, because we know there will likely be more data than we need to answer the basic questions here.

2. The counseling program's unique evaluation context.

We know that the trustees are looking for summative (outcome) data, and that is driving this particular round of PE. We also know (see earlier) that we will have accreditation data—see how one feeds the other?—so we'll be able to find formative data that backs up the summative data. That will likely help with the trustees. In this case, as we move through the process, we can see a wealth of opportunities to connect different pieces of the PE process.

Let's apply our universal steps and the accountability bridge:

First, we identify the stakeholders. In this case, clients are clearly stakeholders, but so are our trustees! This gives us the chance to involve them from the beginning. What are their concerns? Fears? Hopes? We now have an opportunity to work that feedback directly into our program evaluation process. This helps to bring the trustees aboard as allies, as opposed to "judge and jury," thus, possibly enhancing buy in. It also allows a funder to have direct input into our evaluation process. That enhances both trust and the opportunity to design a program that is more efficient.

Second, we define the program. This is our second hub, so we can work to define exactly what the mission of the counseling center is. We involve our stakeholders and gain feedback from clients on this question (What would you want your counseling center to do?), trustees (What do you hope that we do?), and staff (What do you wish that we would do?) and feed the answers to all of these questions directly back into our program-design loop. In this way, we become a dynamic and growing organization that is responsive to stakeholder needs and desires as opposed to a static entity.

Third, we focus our design. Using the feedback loop, what should we be looking at? Are we doing what we want to be doing? Where should we look? How might that help, given all of our stakeholder concerns and questions?

Fourth, we gather the evidence. This is great, because we are gathering the exact evidence that we need. Best of all, having involved our staff and internal stakeholders, we aren't burdening them with new and unexpected tasks. They are more likely to buy in and are very likely to have given us invaluable ideas on efficient ways to gather this data. These may even be ways we would have never come up with ourselves!

Fifth, we crunch the numbers. This gives us an incredible chance to look at our program critically but in full context. It gives us a chance to celebrate our successes and plan for improvement, knowing we have complete buy-in from stakeholders and partners.

Sixth, we present the findings and use them. Again, we have advance buy-in here. Trustees are informed by outcome data that solidifies their commitment. Additionally, we are able to back up the summative data we present to them with valuable formative data that helps them to understand our unique needs and contexts.

In short, the accountability bridge helps all stakeholders, program staff, and administrators to have ownership of the program evaluation process. Ownership leads to buy-in, and buy-in leads to better data. Better data, you guessed it . . . leads to better program evaluation! In this way, a good program evaluation design is as important a tool as good program staff.

Textbox 13.4: Practice Exercise 3

Apply the accountability bridge model to a program with which you are familiar

Ask yourself: Does this model help me to better understand this program and the way it works? What stakeholders need to be involved? How could we make that happen? How might it help? What does this model indicate about the way the program works? Are there areas for improvement that are apparent after examining the context of this model? How about opportunities to improve the program evaluation process itself?

Chapter Summary

We first took a trip down to the old farm. I know . . . 1772, right? At the farm, we took a look at the vital sources of information for effective program evaluation: internal evaluation, external evaluation, and stakeholder feedback. Truly effective program evaluation involves all three of those sources.

We then examined the different types of program evaluation that are typically done: summative (outcome-based) evaluations or formative (process-based) evaluations. We agreed that both could be required (mixed methods), and we looked at a variety of different cases across a range of clinical settings.

We worked with the six universal steps for effective program evaluation design and applied those steps to a specific case study. We also utilized two additional case studies in different contexts. We examined a small private practice, a university counseling center, and a medium-sized private practice in the context of effective program evaluation design.

We also looked at two powerful tools in program evaluation, logic modeling and accountability bridge modeling, and applied case studies with both models. Throughout our exploration, we had practice sections with questions for reflection and review.

Resources for More Information

Program Evaluation

The program manager's guide to program evaluation (Office of planning research and evaluation). (2010). Retrieved from www.acf.hhs.gov/opre/resource/the-program-managers-guide-to-evaluation-second-edition

Logic Modeling

Accountability bridge model. (Astramovich & Coker, 2007). Retrieved from www.counseling.org/knowledge-center/vistas/by-subject2/vistas-assessment/docs/default-source/vistas/introducing-the-accountability-bridge-model-a-program-evaluation-framework-for-school-counselors

Program evaluation: Logic Modeling-University of Wisconsin-Extension. (2013). Retrieved from http://fyi.uwex.edu/programdevelopment/logic-models/

Questions for further review and application

(See Practice Exercises throughout the chapter)

A Word From the Authors

Our hope is that each of us now has a new program evaluation toolkit. Whether it is a fresh, new vocabulary surrounding program evaluation types, experience in using the six universal steps to program evaluation and design, new skill in developing logic models, or new skill in deploying the accountability bridge model of program evaluation, my invitation to each of you is to reach into that toolkit often. These conceptual tools (logic modeling, accountability bridges) only work efficiently when you become familiar enough with them that they become cognitive habits. Pull out these tools and practice exercises often, play with them, make them your own.

Having been active in the professional clinical world for almost 12 years, we can tell you that folks who are skilled in program evaluation are some of the most in-demand folks in the field. Perhaps this is because many are intimidated by program evaluation and all it entails; maybe they fear finding that a service isn't effective (Lusky & Hayes, 2001), or maybe they lack training in program evaluation (Whiston, 1996) or the skill to apply the results (Isaacs, 2003). Those that are not intimidated and those that have some skill with these concepts tend to thrive in the helping fields. They also tend to get their professional needs met more often because they have skills to make the case that their services are both vital and of value to organizations and communities. As Mike's grandfather used to say, the buffet is open. Feel free to make any of this your own. May your own buffet always be as full as you want it to be.

—Michael Walsh, PhD, LPC, CRC, and Amy Allison, MRC

Note

1. Answer: Summative! This is an outcome-based (summative) question—based on BAI and Quality of Life scores—and therefore a summative design. Did you get this one right?

References

Astramovich, R. L., & Coker, K. J. (2007). Program evaluation: The accountability bridge model for counselors. *Journal of Counseling & Development, 85*(2), 162–172.

Centers for Disease Control. (2011). *Evaluation steps.* Retrieved from www.cdc.gov/eval/steps/index.htm

Ernst, K., & Hiebert, B. (2002). Toward the development of a program evaluation business model: Promoting the longevity of counsel- ling in schools. *Canadian Journal of Counselling, 36,* 73–84.

Fenton, W. S. (2003). Shared decision making: A model for the physician-patient relationship in the 21st century? *Acta Psychiatrica Scandinavica, 107,* 401–402.

Fischer, E. P. (2006). Shared decision-making and evidence-based practice: A commentary. *Community Mental Health Journal, 42*(1), 107–111.

Hamann, J., Cohen, R., Leucht, S., Busch, R., & Kissling, W. (2005). Do patients with schizophrenia wish to be involved in decisions about their medical treatment? *American Journal of Psychiatry, 162,* 2382–2384.

Isaacs, M. L. (2003). Data-driven decision making: The engine of accountability. *Professional School Counseling, 6,* 288–295.

Kellaghan, T., and Madaus, G. F. (2000). Outcome evaluation. In D. L. Stufflebeam, G. F. Madaus, & T. Kellaghan (Eds.), *Evaluation models: Viewpoints on educational and human services evaluation* (2nd ed., pp. 97–112). Boston, MA: Kluwer Academic.

Loesch, L. C. (2001). Counseling program evaluation: Inside and outside the box. In D. C. Locke, J. E. Myers, & E. L. Herr (Eds.), *The handbook of counseling* (pp. 513–525). Thousand Oaks, CA: Sage Publications.

Lusky, M. B., & Hayes, R. L. (2001). Collaborative consultation and program evaluation. *Journal of Counseling & Development, 79,* 26–38.

Martin, I., & Carey, J. C. (2014). Development of a logic model to guide evaluations of the ASCA National Model for School Counseling Programs. *The Professional Counselor, 4,* 455–466.

Powell, E. T., Steele, S., & Douglah, M. (2013). *Planning a program evaluation.* Madison, WI: Division of Cooperative Extension of the University of Wisconsin-Extension.

Taylor-Powell, E., & Henert, E. (2008). *Developing a logic model: Teaching and training guide.* Madison, WI: University of Wisconsin-Extension, Cooperative Extension, Program Development and Evaluation. Retrieved from www.uwex.edu/ces/pdande

Walsh, M., Balkin, R. (2017). Program evaluation. In Balkin (Ed.), *Counseling research: A scholar-practitioner approach to research in the counseling profession.* American Counseling Association: Alexandria, Virginia.

Whiston, S. C. (1996). Accountability through action research: Research methods for practitioners. *Journal of Counseling & Development, 74,* 616–623.

Wholey, J. (1979). *Evaluation: Promise and performance.* Washington, DC: Urban Institute Press.

14 Advocacy-Based Research

Emily M. Janke, Laura M. Gonzalez,
Heidi Carlone, & Amy Vetter

We come from diverse fields (education, counseling, peace and conflict studies), study different social phenomena, and are comfortable with various research methodologies. As social scientists, however, our fields share common historical storylines that shape what counts as legitimate knowledge, what kinds of methods are considered rigorous, the kind of training needed to produce scholarly knowledge, and the desired audiences for the knowledge we produce. Often, these historical storylines encourage researchers to maintain emotional and cognitive distance between themselves and the populations they study. The advocacy-based research approach, however, blurs some of those traditional boundaries by asking questions grounded in the needs of the communities in which we work. The intention of the research is collaborative, including a wide array of academics and/or professionals *with* the individuals and communities connected to the individuals of focus, to make a direct and positive change to the situation or issue driving the research or inquiry. Issues of objectivity, the minimization of bias, and generalizability, which are important in other forms of research, are replaced with intentions to develop relational understanding. Perhaps a parallel example is the two ways you might think about a client—the cognitive process that goes through the back of your mind as you try to assess or diagnose concerns and the here-and-now efforts to build empathy and a good working alliance that are happening in the foreground.

Advocacy-based research allows you to gain a deep understanding of and appreciation for the interconnectedness of individuals through relationships and systems. Indeed, most time in this methodology is invested in the early phases, engaging with community members and building collaborations. An advocacy-based researcher values the knowledge that is gained through lived experiences and remembers to view the strengths and assets of the community, not just the challenges. Researchers try to support the development of relationships and the identification of new knowledge and resources. Many times, the knowledge needed to understand and solve a problem already exists within the community but has not been previously connected. For example, people who do not have health insurance may have identified some resources for their health concerns (e.g., speak to my pastor, take my children to free health clinics, work in the community garden so I can bring home fresh vegetables) that practitioners may not know about unless they honor community members' knowledge by asking.

This approach to research is grounded in tenants of participatory action research and community engaged research. Advocacy-based researchers are intentionally advocacy focused when they seek to support, advocate for, and empower the individuals and communities they serve through a process of investigation. The purpose is to advocate for that which makes individuals and communities healthy, vibrant, and socially just. This means that in this form of research, you work with advocates and may be an advocate yourself. Forms of advocacy-based research require an inclusive, reciprocal, and asset-based approach to engaging with individuals and the communities to which they are connected. We call this research "advocacy-based research," which aligns with a relatively new wave of other scholarship forms like scholar activism, participatory action research (Chevalier & Buckles, 2013), community-engaged scholarship (Barnes et al., 2016) or implementation science (LeMahieu, Grunow, Baker, Nordstrum, & Gomez, 2017).

Doing work as an advocacy scholar, scholar activist, participatory action researcher, or community-engaged scholar demands new tool sets, rules for how to conduct research, roles for researchers and participants, timelines to consider, and meanings of "impact." This kind of research brings two historically polar roles (advocate and scholar) and ways of knowing, *together*. Our chapter is not an exhaustive resource for approaches to advocacy-based research but is meant to provide some tools to create dialogue about the meanings and goals of research, breaking us out of historical dualisms of expert/nonexpert and researcher/participant that have unnecessarily limited the full scope of how research might foster healthy individuals and just communities. If you let yourself take on the role of "curious consultant," what might you learn by listening to your client with a sense of openness and respect?

Who Generates Knowledge?

If research is about generating knowledge for the purpose of understanding why and how, then it is critical to ask the question: Who generates knowledge? How is it created? Where is knowledge contained? In an advocacy-based research approach, you would take the view that knowledge is not held solely by counselors, researchers, and professionals who have formal training, certifications, and degrees, but that knowledge is also held by and generated in collaboration with those who are the focal point of the study. In this way, knowledge is gained not only through study of scholarly based literature and thought but also through engagement with individuals who have direct, lived experience.

Knowledge generated through reflection on and investigation of lived experiences is as legitimate and critical to creating informed understanding as knowledge that is gained through training and coursework. It is the *integration* of lived and scholarship-based knowledge that generates new insights and maximizes the potential to make a meaningful difference through inquiry. For example, imagine reading a textbook about substance abuse and then sitting in front of a client who is trying to break the cycle of addiction. Neither alone is sufficient; both are necessary. In what follows, we outline tenets of advocacy-based research. While these are not exhaustive, they provide a starting place for thinking about what counts as credible research while generating knowledge with this methodology.

Advocacy-based approaches to research require inclusion, reciprocity, and asset-based thinking and processes. The **inclusion** of more individuals with diverse viewpoints in developing understanding about a specific individual's (e.g., student, client) interests can generate richer understandings of the context that shapes the situation, as well as the tools, resources, and people who may contribute meaningfully. Indeed, *verstehen* (understanding and empathizing with participants' point of view) and multivocality (providing spaces for a variety of perspectives) are cornerstones of excellent qualitative research (Tracy, 2010), and advocacy-based research attends to these criteria particularly well. For example, a practitioner can learn about assets already present when she or he listens attentively to a client or conducts formal/informal assessments. Beyond the inclusion of the individual, however, is also the inclusion of the broader context of support and influence. Practitioners are typically trained to work directly with clients on their presenting concerns; we encourage them, however, to also consider including other key individuals and groups in the client's community. These individuals and groups can help us understand influences and solutions that engage others beyond the designated client to create systematic and lasting positive change. In this way, inclusive advocacy research is aligned with practice.

Reciprocity, a central tenet of advocacy-based approaches to inquiry, guides a practitioner or researcher's identification and selection of coresearchers. Reciprocity builds upon inclusion in that the client's key community members are not only identified and considered but viewed as experts in the dynamics of their context and consulted with respect and a genuine desire to learn. Knowledge is created jointly; it is not separate, and it requires ongoing collaboration among all relevant stakeholders. Reciprocity is the seeking, understanding, valuing, and inclusion of the diverse resources, including knowledge, that individuals bring as collaborators on a shared effort. For example, if a client says she has experienced relief by working with a shaman or spiritual leader in interpreting her dreams, then reciprocity suggests that the shaman be included in the counseling work or research if all parties agree. In advocacy-based research, practitioners and clients act as coinvestigators rather than as the lead or sole investigator. An important activity in advocacy-based research, therefore, is to engage with the full scope of coinvestigators. Enacting reciprocity requires you to actively identify all of those who are affected by the issue who have information that may benefit understanding and action or who could contribute to a solution. The focus on reciprocity in advocacy-based research brings to the forefront ethical issues of research, recognizing that mutual respect and dignity between you (as researcher) and your clients or clients' communities (as researched) is critical to producing valid knowledge (Tracy, 2010).

An **asset-based approach** to research and practice seeks out and draws on the talents and contributions of practitioners, students, family members, peers, cultural brokers, and other relevant service providers (e.g., educators, social workers, psychologists, clergy). Taking an asset-based approach is fully consistent with a counseling and positivistic worldview, which continually seeks to understand and build upon individual client strengths. A community-engaged advocacy approach extends this worldview to the assets that may exist at the group or systems level, in addition to the individual client level.

Purpose of Knowledge Generation: When and Why to Use an Advocacy-Based Approach

Advocacy-based research is a strategy to generate ideas about why things are the way they are for the purpose of then making recommendations that inform decisions and actions to improve the situation. An advocacy-based approach, then, is used when you seek to directly effect change in certain practices or experiences for the purpose of positive transformation, social justice, and empowerment. Practitioners and researchers involved in this research aim to make environments safer, healthier, and more vibrant for individuals, families, and communities through **empowerment**. The role of the practitioner and researcher is to emphasize the "responsibility of the people themselves who [are] making their own choices about how they [live] their lives" (Whitehead & McNiff, 2002, p. 136) and to act as a thought and action partner who is willing to commit their own talents in pursuit of that community-identified goal.

In clinical practice, we are often seeking to improve wellness and mental health outcomes for individual clients, but in this chapter, we also encourage practitioners to extend their focus beyond the individual to also consider the role of larger networks of people and to affect communities more broadly. If we consider an individual who experiences bias and discrimination in society, it is ethical behavior to both empower the individual *and* address the systemic oppression that contributes to his or her challenges. Advocacy-based research would also mean asking the "whys" about the systemic oppression and undertaking an exploration rather than just working with one client and then stopping.

As seen in the American Counseling Association Advocacy competencies (Lewis, Arnold, House & Toporek, 2003), counselors can build skills in understanding and responding to the individual, group, and systems levels. We have adapted their schema to illustrate how advocacy-based research work can include investigations undertaken with the client (e.g., offering support to ask critical questions so that clients are empowered to address an issue themselves) and on behalf of the client/student (e.g., practitioner can research the issue on behalf of the client and report back). These same activities that are enacted "with" as well as "for" clients can be undertaken at the school and community levels and in the public arena more broadly (Figure 14.1). Thus, an advocacy mindset encourages practitioners to consider both the micro level (individual client) and the macro level (systems with which client interacts). The figure highlights the significance that advocacy, empowerment, information, and collaboration can play in advocacy-based research with various partners. We will explore these styles and levels of advocacy further in the case study presented in this chapter.

Process Characteristics of an Advocacy-Based Research Approach

One goal of advocacy-based *research* that distinguishes it from practice is to help counselors and clients collaboratively understand the political, cultural, social, and economic context of clients' concerns. Such understandings can empower clients to engage in problem solving and to advocate effectively on their own behalf. A researcher mindset and approach is especially useful— asking good questions, collecting relevant data, and making informed conclusions based on findings—because the concerns that clients face often are influenced by many large, complicated, and interconnected systems. Engaging diverse individuals who affect and are affected by the concern requires a continuous, collaborative, inclusive, and iterative process.

Collaboration starts at the very beginning of the interaction when defining the purpose and focus and continues through design, implementation,

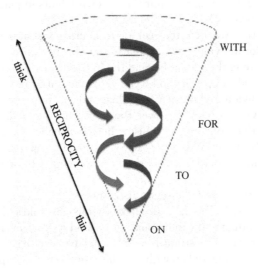

Figure 14.1 Cone of Activities Within Community-Engaged Partnerships

analysis, evaluation, and refinement. Each stage requires decisions about when, how, and with whom to collaborate as coinvestigators. Collaboration that is authentically reciprocal is challenging for many reasons, including different styles of communication, diverse experiences and perspectives, and the need for respect and trust among collaborators, as well as for logistical reasons such as time. In addition, when direct client care is involved, questions about what must remain confidential also come into consideration (for example, what can and cannot be disclosed to various collaborators). For this reason, it is helpful to consider when activities are jointly enacted or produced and when activities are done individually, or less reciprocally.

The cone of engagement (Janke, 2013) is an image that can be helpful to understand how different levels of reciprocity can be present within a single relationship or set of relationships. The image shows how individuals in collaborative partnerships may spend time doing certain activities, within the context of an activity or an ongoing relationship, in ways that can be described as being done *on*, *to*, or *for* others, as well as *with* others more jointly.

The cone of activities within community-engaged partnerships is useful for considering micro-actions within counselor-client relationships, such as what kinds of plans and decisions do we make together, and what kinds of plans and decisions are provided *to*, made *for*, made *on* behalf of the other? For example, client and counselor team may decide together (*with*) which stress-management strategies the client would like to implement, but the counselor would have to assume more authority in safety planning *for* the client if suicidal ideation were uncovered. Over time, the micro decisions made by the counselor and client that reflect various levels of shared knowledge and decision making, or the level of reciprocity, set up patterns and expectations for future levels of reciprocity. The level of reciprocity among partners may vary across activities within a community-engaged partnership. What kinds of things do we discuss and decide together, and what do we do and decide separately? Who is becoming empowered to engage with and make decisions as they relate to various questions and issues raised through the counseling process?

Advocacy-Based Research: A Practical Illustration

In this section, we present the steps of advocacy-based research, some sample research questions, and a case illustration. Similar to other forms of research and scholarship, advocacy-based research identifies a question to investigate, designs methods to answer the question, and examines the information gathered for the purpose of creating understanding. Key steps for advocacy-based research include:

- *Definition of purpose and focus*—What is the question or issue to address? What is our purpose?
- *Design of intervention or activity*—Who are key stakeholders? Who needs to be involved? What conversations or initiatives are needed? How will we collect information to know what we seek to know? Have we considered the individual, group, and system levels?

- *Implementation*—What roles will each of us play in carrying out the activities that have been jointly designed? Who has been empowered to engage with the issues?
- *Analysis and Interpretation*—What do we each make of what we saw? What more do we need to know? What works and why? How do we share what we know?
- *Evaluation of the collaborative process*—What could be done to improve our collaboration as coinvestigators? What might we do differently or keep the same in the future?

In the advocacy-based research case study we explore in what follows, the school counselor faces many choices. Among these are: she must decide how to define the scope of the problem she is observing, how to gather needed information and from whom, how to identify key collaborators, how to make sense of the additional perspectives she gathers, and who should be empowered to act. Throughout this work, she must keep in mind the needs of her identified client (student) and also consider who she needs to contact and what she needs to know and do more broadly at both the individual and systems levels.

Sample Research Questions

Advocacy-based research, applied to counseling, is useful for answering a number of questions. These questions to be investigated through inclusive and reciprocal collaborations include:

- What core competencies must a practitioner develop to work with underserved populations to ensure that they are serving individuals appropriately and meeting their needs effectively?
- What are the factors that influence the feelings of safety for a student or client working with a practitioner?
- How can practitioners enhance their ability to generate a strong working alliance with social identity groups different from their own?
- How do practitioners create a skills training workshop that effectively contributes to clients' understanding of and adoption of positive mental health strategies that are congruent for their worldview?
- What are the barriers and facilitators to students or clients from underserved groups seeking—or not seeking—services and mental health care?
- How do practitioners partner effectively with community-serving groups (e.g., churches, advocates, health care providers) or key cultural brokers (e.g., community leaders) that have expertise with specific populations of clients?

Case Study

We present a case study for the purpose of clarifying the choice points that can be made throughout the various components of advocacy-based research, from the beginning of inquiry through the later stages of analysis and interpretation.

The case is somewhat lengthy, but that is consistent with the advocacy-based research methodology, in which questions would unfold gradually and continue to be modified as more voices were included. We ask you to stand in the school counselor's shoes and see what questions and thoughts would emerge for you as we walk through her process of engaging with a student and the systems he lives in.

Crystal is a school counselor working with Jorge, a ninth-grade adolescent from an immigrant family. She is having a routine scheduling conversation with him about potential courses for the upcoming semester when he shares, potentially inadvertently, that someone in his family is not legally documented as residing in the United States (i.e., is "undocumented"). Crystal experiences a moment of doubt and panic as she realizes that she does not know how best to advise the student regarding his future goals. Learning of his family member's undocumented status causes her to wonder whether Jorge is himself documented. If not, is he eligible to attend college, if that is his goal? Would his family member be in danger of deportation if Jorge signed up for the PSAT with identifying information or completed a financial aid application with his parents' information? Crystal's head was full of potential scenarios, questions, and concerns. She was familiar with advocacy-based research and viewed the methodology as an opportunity to find possible solutions to her questions.

Definition of Purpose and Focus

Taking the time to reflect on one's intentions—what one hopes to be able to understand and to do as a result of her or his research—is a critical first step to crafting an effective process for investigation and action. In a more engaged approach, this question cannot be answered by you (or the professional) alone; discovery and definition of purpose is a jointly constructed activity.

After a few more conversations to clarify the issues and build some initial trust, Crystal and Jorge decide that they want to address the question: **What is the most effective way to support Jorge's educational and career development?** Their shared intent is to identify, together, the opportunities that Jorge seeks and any potential barriers or facilitators toward that goal. Beyond their shared goal of assisting Jorge, Crystal identifies a broader goal and research question: **What are the facilitators and barriers to supporting students of undocumented parents in pursuing their chosen educational and career ambitions?**

DESIGN OF INTERVENTION OR ACTIVITY

Design occurs when individuals plan the details of what needs to happen in order to address a question and create an informed decision or action. A design can be created individually (i.e., what I think should be done), or it can be approached in a way that invites all of those who are involved in the situation to inform plans for activities, collaborators, and timelines. When design is crafted collaboratively, it allows for diverse voices to be heard, encourages creative yet feasible ideas, and helps to gain buy-in from those who are most intimately involved and whose support may be needed in the future.

One possible avenue for action is to consult with school administrators, school counseling peers, or professional organizations as the "experts" who can illuminate these questions and help Crystal find answers. This set of information-seeking actions is an important part of a school counselor's approach. However, an advocacy-based research approach would also expand who Crystal consults to include Jorge, his family, and potentially even immigrant-serving agencies in their community.

Important questions to consider when choosing who to include as a core-searcher are: What would Crystal miss if she only consulted with her professional network and then translated that information into a solution for Jorge? Would she be acting "with" Jorge and students like him or acting in a less reciprocal manner, making recommendations about what he should or should not do, presumably on his behalf? If there were no immigrants or allies among the school administrators, school counseling peers, or professional networks, would Crystal be receiving a partially informed set of strategies that might or might not end up being helpful to Jorge? How can a service provider with some socially granted privileges (educated and working in a professional setting, US citizen) start to learn about a population with fewer social privileges in order to determine whether the clients are being served appropriately?

Starting collaboration in this very first step is important because it sets norms about working together through all phases of inquiry. Just as importantly, if not even more so, different people may have different ideas about what is happening, who is involved, and what should be done. In this way, the same issue is being viewed from very different perspectives. A practitioner, then, cannot assume that her/his ideas are exactly the same as those of people who are directly involved in the situation. It is critical, therefore, to find out who needs to be involved, and to uncover what they think is occurring and what needs to be addressed.

As Crystal and Jorge work together to define how they will go about answering their questions, they both realize that they would like to involve a broader set of stakeholders for this exploration. Crystal wonders, in addition to consulting with her professional peers, what would it look like to consult with the community most directly affected? She feels strongly that she is missing information about undocumented immigration status and how that influences daily realities and educational planning. She is also now acutely aware that she does not know Jorge's parents, as they did not attend the open house at the beginning of the year. Crystal begins to make a list of more community-based avenues to generate knowledge about the dilemmas that Jorge is facing.

Ana, the ESL teacher, also is a potential coinvestigator, someone who could help them to answer the question about how to best support Jorge's educational and professional development goals. Crystal learns from Ana about the many students at their school who have an undocumented parent and some of the challenges they face. Now, in addition to Jorge's face in her mind, she starts to see a group of students at their school with similar and very specific needs. She feels that she does not know enough to define the concerns these students might have or determine whether the school is meeting their needs and is certain that she needs to become better informed first. She searches for bilingual service providers in the community and finds a church with a Spanish-language service near the school, an immigration attorney, and a mental health agency with one Spanish-speaking social worker. She starts to write out the questions that she wants to ask each of those individuals, if they are willing to consult with her.

In her effort to address her two research questions, Crystal begins to meet with various service providers to immigrant communities. Crystal is humbled to realize that the service providers all know each other and are in regular contact around the needs of immigrant families. In fact, they have a monthly networking meeting that they invite her to attend in order to hear more directly about the emergent issues that they are working to address. Crystal chooses to attend meetings regularly, and in doing so, she learns a tremendous amount about the needs of the local immigrant community, including undocumented members. She starts to gain a greater appreciation for the resilience, optimism, and persistence of these families who gave up everything that was familiar in order to pursue a new life in the United States. She learns that the immigrants present in her community come from almost every part of the globe, not just from Mexico as the evening news might suggest. She feels that she is becoming a better-informed partner to Jorge and more capable of addressing their questions.

As a result of engaging directly with this community of practitioners, Crystal becomes comfortable enough to start asking questions in the monthly meetings and starts to see this group as her informal consultants around the complicated issues that she is uncovering at school. She wonders if the school leadership would be open to learning from these community members as she has or including some of them formally on the school's advisory board. She is not fully certain of what needs to happen to support Jorge and other students at school, but she is coming to a better understanding of the social and political context in which they live.

The next time Crystal sees Jorge, she feels that she has a better understanding of the dynamics of families with mixed documentation status. Because she is interested in how best to support his educational and professional development beyond high school and is new to advocacy-based research and practice, she asks Jorge to help her decide an appropriate balance of acting for and with him and his family. Although Jorge wants to advocate for himself and family, he realizes that he and his family are likely to suffer repercussions for speaking up. Jorge does start to share more about his home situation, his hopes, dreams, and fears, and thus adds to the picture that Crystal has been forming. Together they start to identify options and resources for Jorge's postgraduation pathway. With every step they take forward, more questions come up, but they start to utilize the community network to find more adequate information specific to families with mixed documentation status and keep making progress on Jorge's plan.

Implementation

Implementation is the process of translating ideas and plans into action. A collaborative approach to implementation means that many different parties are included in taking action, not just a single professional or person. A collaborative approach is especially helpful to create welcome spaces for people with diverse histories, experiences, and perspectives. Each person brings different relationships, networks, and abilities to communicate effectively with various individuals and groups. For example, consider how the style of the conversation (such as tone and openness), as well as the content, can be changed depending on who is involved—between friends, a parent and her or his student, a school counselor and a student, or a psychiatrist and a student.

Crystal feels better about her ability to create an educational plan together with Jorge and to connect him to some community resources that could help him. In addition to her networking outside of the school, Crystal schedules lunch once a week with Ana. Together they devise a system for Spanish-speaking parents to submit written questions anonymously to Ana, which Crystal then researches and answers in a newsletter that Ana translates and distributes to families. The initial implementation of the parent newsletter with Ana seems to be helpful to parents and students, so Crystal and Ana begin plans to organize a Spanish-language Parent Night at the end of the school year. Jorge has organized a new club for students with international connections, which he has used to encourage other students from mixed-status immigrant households to become aware of their resources and rights.

These are good implementation actions. However, Crystal becomes increasingly worried about what is happening at the systems level. She wonders what else she can do for her school so they can be more effective in addressing the concerns of the immigrant community. She starts to create a handbook to organize the information she is gathering (e.g., educational access, health care access, resources and services, legal implications, communication and outreach strategies) and researches ways that she can share it more broadly (e.g., in the newsletter, at community functions, on a website). She wants to invite the members of the community group to review it, as they have greater expertise and scope.

Analysis and Interpretation

Throughout a collaborative research process, counselors work with the range of coinvestigators, often including the student who is the focus of the effort, in the interpretation of information. Just as we mentioned with the issue of design, different people have different ways of seeing things. What did the various collaborators see, what feelings were associated with these observations, and what meaning did they make from them? Addressing these three questions, collaboratively, serves as an invaluable process for identifying decisions and next action steps. Again, interpretation activities that include key members help ensure buy in, but also promote creativity and effectiveness. In analysis, we must ask how each stakeholder in this story makes sense out of what happened.

Crystal and Jorge have been working collaboratively throughout the process to make sense of what they have learned, not just about Jorge's efforts to advance his own well-being and the legal issues associated with his undocumented parents and family members but also as it relates to facilitators and barriers to other students who are like him in their familial situations and ambitions to pursue higher education. For example, Crystal decides to ask a parent who has been very friendly with her to cofacilitate a conversation with some other parents who receive the newsletter about what works and does not work. Together with family members of immigrant students, they discuss why the newsletter is helpful and ways to improve the content and mode of delivery. They learn that some parents are willing to contribute their own stories and recommendations for how to navigate difficult conversations, situations, and decisions. They learn that parents prefer to receive the newsletter in print form and that students are reliable in their delivery of the newsletter.

Crystal and Jorge's work together and with fellow inquirers leads to new questions to explore, such as do we imagine that the school leadership is receptive to the initiatives Crystal has started and the ways she has been using her time? How much has Crystal's advocacy-based research pervaded the school culture or reached beyond her office walls? What other daily stressors and problems would be of concern to Jorge's parents or others like them? How have Crystal, Jorge, and Ana experienced their activities together? What have been the most effective strategies in this advocacy-based research project, and how do we know that? What else does the school community still need to learn and do better? How could they move to information sharing or solutions at the district level?

At a broader level, beyond her relationship with Jorge, Crystal wonders how the knowledge that she has gathered in her community conversations could be helpful to others in her school, in the whole district, or even in the school counseling profession. The school leadership has been aware of some of Crystal's initiatives, but they have not invested much time or other resources in supporting her. Crystal believes she has become more capable of assisting this one student but would like to have more feedback or input about that. She also feels a strong pull toward expanding her initiatives to make a difference to the school level or beyond. She wonders how the school system could do a better job of interacting with the immigrant community and if she could become an advocate for families at a larger level. At a minimum, she decides to submit a presentation proposal to the state-level school counseling conference and to make her handbook of resources available to all conference attendees.

Evaluation of the Collaborative Process

To enact an advocacy-based approach, Crystal and other key stakeholders would commit to evaluating their own process of collaboration. For example, if Crystal felt she had improved her competency, would Ana and Jorge agree with that assessment? What could she continue to improve? Did she act "for" or "with" Jorge? How could the school system become more open to the knowledge and experience of the community-based immigrant-serving entities? Could this become a formal collaboration, such as an advisory council? If there were immigrant parents who were comfortable serving in an advisory capacity, would the school system also make space for their voices to be heard? These questions will help illuminate the process of collaboration and the future steps for advocacy-based research.

At the same time that coinvestigators are analyzing the information they have jointly developed, it is important that they also discuss their own process of working together (e.g., What could be done to improve our collaboration as coinvestigators? What might we do differently or keep the same in the future?). This is important for helping everyone understand how best they can collaborate to address advocacy research questions in the future.

Crystal feels that she has as many questions now as when she started this project, but they are different questions. When Crystal asks Jorge what was most useful to him, he offers expressions of appreciation and acceptance but not many words of advice, guidance, or assessment. Crystal sometimes feels unsure as to whether there are additional contributions that he could share but is uncomfortable sharing with her. She is not sure whether this stems from her position as a counselor, their relative age or gender difference, her being of a different cultural tradition, or some other difference.

Similar to her relationship with Jorge, she wonders whether she is hearing all that she needs to hear from parents in order to serve them best. Again, she asks a parent to help facilitate a conversation about how best to communicate with school representatives, such as herself and teachers, so that they can best serve students of immigrant families.

Summary

Advocacy-based research is a methodology that is useful for instances in which you wish to address the needs and priorities of individuals and communities in ways that include them as collaborators. This is particularly important when working with individuals and communities who have experienced policies, practices, and structures that have marginalized and disempowered them in ways that diminish or limit their abilities to self-advocate. Key points to remember are: (1) advocacy may occur at the individual level, at the group level, or in the public domain, and (2) collaborating through reciprocal processes is a core tenet of advocacy-based research and requires that individuals and communities are included as collaborators in all phases of the research process. An authentically reciprocal process demonstrates respect for the lived knowledge, cultures, resources, preferences, and values of the individuals you are working with and the communities of which they are a part. The methods selected by the collaborative research team may draw from qualitative and quantitative traditions and strategies described elsewhere in this book. The difference in this approach is that decisions throughout the research process, including the questions to focus on, the methods to investigate the questions, and the strategies to analyze the findings and share results, are codeveloped from start to finish. Through the process of advocacy-based research, individuals and communities are strengthened to become their own best advocates.

In terms of the classroom that you may be sitting in right now, how could an advocacy-based research perspective be useful in improving your professional practice? Can faculty members help you formulate and start to answer questions that are relevant to your future work setting and the populations you intend to serve? These questions can be qualitative, as modeled here, but may also be quantitative or mixed methods. In the end, an advocacy-based research question is one that includes the researcher-practitioner and the clients/community members in a collaborative relationship. The emphasis is much more on democratic engagement with others to create shared understanding and ask the most inclusive questions (a methodology or approach to generating knowledge) and much less on a particular type of data collection or analysis (a research method).

Advocacy-based research is an important approach for counselors who seek to effect change not only at the individual level but also at a broader systems level that forms the environment in which individual students/clients live. As we saw in the case, Crystal acted as an advocacy-based researcher for and with Jorge (an individual), for and with similar students and parents (groups), and for and with her school system and her professional organizations (systems). She consulted not only with experts within her school (Jorge, Ana) but also with experts based in the affected community (immigrant-serving providers). This approach is unique from other ways of counseling in that it requires the practitioner to view her or his role and relationship differently from traditional notions that position a practitioner as "the helper" and the student/client as the "one with problems to be solved." Advocacy-based research intentionally seeks out the assets and strengths that already exist within individuals and communities. The role of the practitioner is to identify questions that, through the attempt to answer them, create understanding, as well as foster and support the development of relationships and activities that serve the larger goal of supporting healthy and vibrant individuals and communities.

Resources for More Information

Riemer, L., Schmitz, C., Janke, E., Askerov, A., Strahl, B., & Matyók, T. (2015). *Transformative Change.* Lanham, MD: Rowman & Littlefield.

Strand, K. J., Cutforth, N., Stoecker, R., Marullo, S., & Donohue, P. (2013). *Community-based research and higher education: principles and practices.* New York, NY: John Wiley & Sons.

Syed, M. A., & Palermo, A. S. (2010). Community engagement in research: Frameworks for education and peer review. *American Journal of Public Health, 100*(8), 1380–1387.

Questions for Further Review and Application

1. What are the benefits and challenges of doing advocacy-based research?
2. When would you choose to do advocacy-based research? When would you NOT choose to do advocacy-based research?
3. What are some potential ethical dilemmas involved in advocacy-based research? How could you work to minimize those dilemmas as you proceed with your research?

Table 14.1 Advocacy-Based Research

Micro Level: Advocacy with Individuals	Meso Level: Advocacy with Groups	Macro Level: Advocacy in the Public Domain
Acting "with" clients to empower them (e.g., helping someone decide and/or act on their own behalf)	Acting "with" groups collaboratively (e.g., facilitating dialogue between two groups)	Acting "with" clients to influence the public conversation (e.g., cowriting newspaper article)
Acting "for" clients to represent them as their advocate	Acting "for" groups as their spokesperson to advocate with other systems	Acting "for" clients at the public and political levels

Adapted from Lewis et al. (2003)

4. Think about a potential advocacy-based research approach in your field. What are some ways that you, the investigator, might build relationships with community members? What are some obstacles that you might face, and how can you work with partners to overcome those obstacles?

References

Barnes, S. L., Brinkley-Rubinstein, L., Doykos, B., Martin, N. C., & McGuire, A. (Eds.). (2016). *Academics in action! A model for community-engaged research, teaching, and service.* Oxford: Oxford University Press.

Chevalier, J. M., & Buckles, D. (2013). *Participatory action research: Theory and methods for engaged inquiry.* London: Routledge.

Janke, E. M. (2013). Community participation is not a proxy for reciprocity. *eJournal of Public Affairs*, (2), 2. Missouri State University.

LeMahieu, P. G., Grunow, A., Baker, L., Nordstrum, L. E., & Gomez, L. M. (2017). Networked improvement communities: The discipline of improvement science meets the power of networks. *Quality Assurance in Education*, 25(1), 5–25.

Lewis, J., Arnold, M. S., House, R., & Toporek, R. (2003). *Advocacy competencies.* Retrieved October 1, 2008, from https://www.counseling.org/Resources/Competencies/Advocacy_Competencies.pdf.

Tracy, S. J. (2010). Qualitative quality: Eight "big-tent" criteria for excellent qualitative research. *Qualitative Inquiry*, 16, 837–851.

Whitehead, J., & McNiff, J. (2002). *Action research: Principles and practice.* London: Routledge/Falmer.

Index